PUSHUPS IN THE PRAYER ROOM

Norm Schriever

AUTHORITY
PUBLISHING

Pushups in the Prayer Room: Reflections From a Year Backpacking Around the World

By Norm Schriever

1. Biography & Autobiography : Adventurers & Explorers 2. Travel : Special Interest - Adventure 3. Humor : General
ISBN: 978-1-935953-32-6

Cover design by Lewis Agrell, image provided by Bigstock.com
Typography by Stephanie Martindale

Printed in the United States of America

Authority Publishing
11230 Gold Express Dr. #310-413
Gold River, CA 95670
800-877-1097
www.AuthorityPublishing.com

Dedication

I would like to give a heartfelt thank you to the following people who have helped and supported me: my incredibly loving mother and hero, Angelika; my awesome sister Barbara, Sean, and my world: Colin, Ryan, and Madeline; my aunt Barbara; of course Phil Rigney — eternal thanks and blessings, bro — there is no one else I would want rebounding for me in the game of life; my best friend Mitch D, and Lisa and Jackson and Amelia; Mr. and Mrs. D; Nydia for your unwavering support and positivity; Sean Dolan, Caitlin and Cayla; the immortal Reilly, and Mel; Luis "El Toro" for being my first Tico friend and helping with the cover art, and Wendy; Jodi Martinez and fam; my agent (unpaid of course) Joey Famous; Uriel Carrazco and Bella; my buddy Adam Groth and fam; my Hamden posse, always keeping me grounded; the Goo Rasta tribe — all love; Monina Applebum; Sue Espo for helping us get to the airport 11 years ago; Stephen White and family; Dan Schuman; Steve Levine; Mike Mercurio and fam; Kristin Marshall for your friendship and helping to make this happen; all my peeps in Tamarindo; Pistol Pete — stay strong homie; Cynthia; Steve Rowland and the crew at Seasons, Jon Phillips; Trevor and Blade in SJDS; the Pueblo Del Mar crew; Bernard Agosta, "the paparazzi of Tama"; Sarita's Bakery; Sarah Long; the nice people at Rusty's Pizza; my friend Hector; Reese Fitzpatrick; Dirty Dieter; Bun Lai at Miya's Sushi;

May Chavez and fam. To my Sacramento family — a huge shout out to Tracey and Paul; Heath; Fidel and Steve; Gale and Joyce Flores; the amazing ML, and Pete; Sheila Garcia; JuCu making it rain; Dan Pearsen; Jasmine; Michelle B; Stephanie and Amberly at Authority Publishing; Jason Matthews; Jason Everett; Krysta Prater; Sherrie Larolo Matusz and Alison Fineman Seidenfrau for your help; Jason Sheftell; Judd, Patrick, and Mike from Tamarack; My brothers, and friends from UConn, Audra and Amy. To Marcus, Daryl, Aunt Lily, and Jobo, R.I.P. and love you all; Nancy and Jack Fuller for showing me how to live a life of honor; my kindergarten teacher Ms. Spillane for nurturing my creativity; all of my teachers who cared about me, even though I was a wise-ass punk; to my father, Ferdinand Johannes Schriever, R.I.P., who I will drink a beer with in heaven one day; and finally this book is dedicated to the richest street urchin in Cairo — may the world hear your voice now.

Contents

Foreword

You've thought of it. You know you have. We all have. What would it be like to walk away from it all? Not one piece at a time, but all of it. To change it all. To take the neatly shuffled 52 cards in the deck and throw them all into the air, all at once. That is what Norm and I decided to do: drop out, leave everything behind, and travel around the world for a year.

It started over drinks after playing basketball. Maybe it was the type of drunkenness you can only get after physical exertion, maybe it was the buzz of being in your mid 20s in San Francisco, or maybe it was that the conversation turned to shared heroes like Hemingway and Cassidy and Kerouac; likely it was a combination of all those things. But somewhere between the drinking, the daydreaming, and the dusk, it was planned. On the back of a bar napkin we sketched it out. Just walk away.

I had the "good on paper" life. Good, well-paying job. Law student girlfriend. Cheap rent in what I believed to be the coolest city in the world. But I couldn't help but feel like I needed to be doing something more. My girlfriend lived near the ocean, and I would lie awake at night and listen to the fog horns blow and the sound of them would haunt me. They were saying, "It's all out there. The journey, the experience, the unknown. And it is waiting there for you. But it won't wait for you forever. You will never be this young again." And if you scratched the surface a little further, there were cracks in the façade of the good-on-paper life. My job didn't stimulate me. I loved my girlfriend, but was self-aware enough to know that we were both better off with someone else. And my apartment, though cheap, was a dump. The fog horns became Sirens. And they were beckoning me toward something more.

It is a rare and great thing when you meet the right person at exactly the right time in your life. I have many good friends, but no one who could have ever been better to be on the road with than Norm. Too modest to sing his own praises, I will do it for him. Norm was naturally great with people and this transcended language. He lit up the room immediately. So it became easy to make friends in strange places. Because he was naturally athletic and adventurous, I could always count on him to take on physical challenges I set and for him to set challenges for me. Most importantly, he was good-humored enough to take the inevitable hardships of the road in stride and often turn them into some of the most entertaining events of my entire life.

I can never truly be 27 again, but the stories in this book are true, and because of them and my time on the road with Norm, a part of me will be 27 forever.

So what would it be like to walk away from it all? Here is the story of one guy who did.

—"Shane"

"The bigger the searchlight the larger the circumference of the unknown."

—Anonymous physicist

Introduction

I've been meaning to write this down. It's all been swirling inside my head, begging to get out for way too long, for more than ten years now. I've wanted to share with my friends and readers the year I traveled around the world, placing them right in the middle of all I've seen and experienced. Those 365 or so days felt more like 10,000 days and changed my life permanently and totally, shaping who I am and what purpose I have here on earth. But I was scared for so long to commit these words to paper because that would make them real and I was worried that my writing would fall short of the true thing; I was afraid my writing wouldn't measure up.

I started a few times but grew frustrated, or life got in the way. But then one day it came to me: I was right — my writing could never accurately portray everything I'd seen, nor do justice to the readers — but I could still give it a hell of a shot. I was doing more of a disservice to the people I've met all over the world by *not* telling their stories. So I got started.

In the spring of 1999, I left my old life behind and backpacked around the world for a year. I didn't return until the spring of 2000, a profoundly changed man coming back to an unfamiliar home in a new millennium. Along my journeys I touched down in Costa Rica, Venezuela, Brazil, Peru, Uruguay, Chile, Argentina, Bolivia, Ecuador,

New Zealand, Australia, the Philippines, Thailand, China, Japan, Israel, Palestine, Sinai, Egypt, Jordan, Germany, and the Netherlands. I stepped foot on the continents of North America, South America, Africa, Australia, Asia, and Europe, with only Antarctica left out.

I purchased a round-the-world ticket through United and the Star Alliance, which was ridiculously cheap — only $2,500 for 35,000 miles. That was good enough to drop me in the theaters of the world that I wanted to explore, and from there I took trains, motorcycles, commercial airlines, little puddle-jumper planes, buses, taxis, ferry boats, high-speed hydrofoils, bamboo rafts, horses, camels, and elephants to get to my outlying destinations.

I read somewhere that the circumference of the globe at the equator is about 24,000 miles. I sat down once to track all the legs of my travels that year, not only the big intercontinental flights but every jaunt to remote locales, and I estimated that I traveled around 70,000 miles total, or almost three times around the globe.

I had company, departing with my buddy Shane, a newfound friend whom I met playing basketball in my home city at the time, San Francisco. We conceived of the whole trip in a bar one sunny afternoon after playing hoops. Shane and I both longed to travel and had similar tastes in writers and pursuing unconventional adventures, so right there we scrawled out our future on bar napkins, changing our destinies in ways I never could have imagined. I couldn't have asked for a better travel companion. Sure, we sometimes got on each other's nerves because we grew at odds about what we wanted out of the trip, or our personalities sometimes clashed. Shane had a black-and-white view of the world that was non-negotiable, which served him well in overcoming a tough childhood and achieving great confidence and success, but sometimes it was difficult to soften his world view. I, too, had a strong ego and way too many faults of my own, so we were often in a tug of war about what we wanted out of the trip, but it was more like brothers who fought because they spent so much time together, and when it came down to it he had my back, and I, his. There is no one else I would even consider having in that foxhole with me.

We traveled about eight months together and then parted company so we could be free to roam unencumbered wherever our curiosities called us; he had never been to Europe and loved big cities, while I desperately wanted to experience the Middle East and explore the beaches and small towns. I give Shane a lot more credit than I can claim because he had to sacrifice almost everything to take that trip: a relationship with a girl he loved, a fun, full life in San Francisco, and a lot of money by taking a leave of absence from his job as a pharmaceutical rep. To walk away from all of that takes some real courage.

I, on the other hand, felt lost anyway so figured I might as well go for it and embark on something epic that would put my stamp on this world. Sure, I had good friends and good times in San Francisco, but I always felt like I was on the outside looking in. I watched people go to jobs they hated, stress about money and bills, go home to a lover they barely knew, laugh with superficial friends and get wasted on the weekends, only to start it all over again on Monday morning, and then add fifty years to that equation. There had to be more to it. I needed something that would separate me from that mindless monotony and challenge me every day. Ever since I was a kid I didn't want to be a medium-sized fish in a small pond, or even a big fish. I wanted to prove myself on the biggest stage possible, or fail with dirt and blood on my face, but at least I'd know I had fought the good fight. Like Bukowski said, "What matters most is how well you walk through the fire," and there was no bigger stage I could think of than the whole wide world.

And I had pragmatic motives as well for leaving the States. I was coming out of some serious legal trouble, getting cuffed and stuffed for possession of marijuana and mushrooms in Colorado. The judge gave me a couple weeks in jail, and suspended the rest of the four-year sentence, which meant that if I got in any trouble (even a ticket for jaywalking or drunk driving) for three more years, I would go to big boy prison immediately for four years — do not pass Go; do not collect $200. So I thought it would be best to flee the country to kill some of that time, where it was impossible to get in trouble with the U.S. police.

Traveling was not easy; I figured that on average I was on the road every two days, and believe me when I tell you that even a two-hour bus trip can be an excruciating, all-day affair in a Third World country. It was dirty and difficult and constantly uncomfortable. I got sick everywhere I went and had to fight off thieves, hustlers, and scam artists at every turn. I never had enough money and was constantly trying to keep my past life and relationships in the U.S. from unraveling. Most people in the States thought I was crazy and didn't understand what I was doing. Most people I met while traveling thought I was crazy and understood full well what I was doing. I was a pariah, an outcast, a citizen only of the world, blazing a trail that had very few footprints ahead of me. Was I scared? Hell yeah — every moment of every day, but it got to the point where I couldn't tell the difference between fear and feeling alive, and true happiness was having a front-row seat to watch the death match between the two.

In preparation for the trip I moved from San Francisco back home to Hamden, Connecticut, where I humbled myself by sleeping in my mom's basement on a futon and borrowing $800 to buy a car, a jet-black 1977 Chevy Nova. That wasn't exactly a glamorous existence for a 27-year-old whose friends were working responsible jobs and starting to get married and settling down in nice houses. But I had good friends around me, like Seanny Doles, who kept me well hydrated with pints of Guinness at the Irish pub, and my best friend, Mitch D, who helped pimp out my new car with black fuzzy seat covers, a stereo system rigged from a RadioShack intercom, and a disco ball hanging off the mirror.

The "Whip," as she was called, was a hell of a ride that looked like the Batmobile, and I didn't hold it against her that the brakes didn't really work so I had to stop a whole city block ahead of time to avoid screeching and smoking through red lights. Still, she served her purpose and even acted as my work truck for a small house-painting company I started that allowed me to stack some cash away. Before we departed the States, Shane even flew out to help me finish up my painting jobs so we worked 18-hour days for a week straight. We were so dead exhausted, our nerves fried from last-minute preparations to leave for a whole year, that it was comical. The Whip, too, was breaking down from the stress, and my last night the steering decided to join the brakes in noncooperation. She would only turn left, any right turn yielding metal-on-metal rubbing and smoke at a top speed of three miles an hour. We finished up our last painting job at 2 a.m. and had an hour's drive home so we could get a few hours' sleep before heading to the airport at 7 a.m. the next day. We did the best we could considering the Whip's handicap, but had to drive 30 mph on the highway and take three left turns every time we needed to actually take a right. It was time to get the hell out of there and hit the open road.

We departed from JFK airport in New York on May 3, 1999, eager to prove ourselves to the world and alter the course of our lives forever. They say that a mind stretched never returns, and looking back I truly believe that my psyche could only absorb so much before it suffered from sensory overload. Our normal day-to-day surroundings are so familiar to us that our minds hardly have to register any energy to navigate the details, but I was spinning on a dizzying carousel of sights and sounds and movement almost 24 hours a day for a year straight; every few days a new city, a new *country*, with new people and currency and language and customs. It took years for my mind to sort through and process all of the memories, like a box of dusty photographs that you take out to look at one by one on a rainy day.

In my idealistic youth I thought that I would conquer the world, when in fact the world changed me, giving me empathy for the millions of people whose existence I came to witness. That was both a blessing and a curse, for the more I grew conscious the more I had to carry with me, and the heavier my load became. More than anything else the journey was extremely humbling. It was quite a jarring revelation that in the eternal panorama of existence I was just floating here for less than a flash of a millisecond, no more important or immortal than any other, but until then I was alive, and I realized how amazing a gift that was.

The epiphany came to me one day on the road in an improbable setting: Every day while traveling I did pushups and situps — it was one of the few routines I could cling to, and the only way to guarantee a daily workout was to push out a few sets on the floor. I was staying in a hotel in Chang Mai, Thailand, and the room was so small that I couldn't even stretch out without bumping into the bed or without my head poking into the bathroom. So I walked down the hall to look for a place to do my daily exercises and came to a room at the end that was different from the others. It had a plaque over the door with writing in four languages. I didn't understand most of them, even though

I could recognize that they were Arabic, Thai, and French or Spanish, but the last words on the plaque were English and said, "Prayer Room."

I walked in and the room was empty and silent, chairs arranged neatly on the perimeter of a plush red carpet facing a gold-leafed altar with incense burning. It was a place where the hotel guests could come to pray. Muslims, Christians, Hindus, Buddhists, Sikhs, and Jews all make prayer and worship a regular part of their lives, and this room had subtle elements that would make a person of any religion feel welcome. I was in a Prayer Room.

I sat in the room for a while and collected my thoughts and felt a certain sense of peace. I still needed to do my pushups for the day and the red carpet in the Prayer Room looked spotless, so I sprawled out and started counting them off as my thoughts wandered.

I had seen so much during my journey, and yet no matter where I went, or how foreign and strange my surroundings seemed, people just basically wanted the same things: a roof over their heads, a safe place to sleep at night, a chance to earn a little money so they could feed their families, health, happiness, and to have a better life for their children. And they wanted to pray for these things, and sometimes that hope was the most essential of them all. It was no different anywhere in the world.

We were all on this wild ride together and sharing the same energy in the cosmos, but I realized also that there was so much that divided us and kept us from appreciating that connection. It was in our flawed human nature to feel the fear and the sense of self that bred anger, hatred, and jealousy, so we often chose to plant our flags in the false comfort of the citizenship of a nation, or being Muslim vs. Christian, Republican vs. Democrat, black vs. white, rich vs. poor, Biggie vs. Tupac, or even the Red Sox vs. the Yankees ... it went on and on. Those false separations kept us from sympathizing with our brothers and sisters and gave us an excuse to pretend they were somehow different or less than human. We all suffered from the same imperfections; there was good and bad in all of us, just like there were equal parts darkness and light in the world, but both were necessary and beautiful.

I jammed out a few more pushups — 34 ... 35 ... 467, and contemplated my role in it all. It was great to feel a kinship and love for all human beings, and I wanted to help make peoples' lives better, but I realized that was a hollow sentiment without conscious action. The world needed spiritual awareness *and* tangible action, no matter how small the steps; it needed pushups in the Prayer Room.

So what could I do to help? How could I possibly touch people's lives, not only giving them hope but breaking down some of the walls that separate us as human beings? How could one little person make a difference to the whole wide world? I didn't have the answers yet, but I was asking the right questions, pure questions, and that meant I was on the right path. What was I looking for on my odyssey around the world? I wasn't sure yet, but that really didn't matter because it was going to find me anyway.

Shooting at Superman

Costa Rica, May/June 1999

I t's as if the world was turned upside down, like we were characters in a novel by Gabriel García Márquez where the whole town retires in the noon heat with shutters drawn, and women are all beautiful and live to 139 years old. That's what I felt like when Shane and I touched down in San José, Costa Rica, the first stop on our trip around the world.

We found ourselves dropped in the vortex of the Third World without amnesty or orientation — the energy, the poverty, the gritty streets, the seduction of perpetual motion. We were two buddies from the United States with backpacks, round-the-world tickets, and a lot of starry-eyed dreams to burn; nothing was familiar, nothing easy, and as foreigners I realized that we would always be targets, like voodoo dolls of our past selves. And I loved it instantly.

Within a few days we found a little apartment in the sleepy suburb of San Pedro for our six-week stay in Costa Rica, next door to five Dominican girls who worked at the sleazy Hotel Del Rey at night. There wasn't much remarkable about San Pedro — a small college, a few bars, pizza shops, mom and pop grocery stores, and a small colonial church stained with centuries of bird crap overlooking a soccer field that was sloped at an improbable angle — except an enormous mall on its outskirts.

The San Pedro Mall couldn't have been more ill-planned, in typical Costa Rican fashion. It sits in the middle of a traffic circle where two highways spill out onto the city streets. They have no crosswalks, bridges, or even traffic lights to aid a walk to the mall, so thousands of patrons have to sprint across the traffic circle daily, dodging cars and yanking their children airborne by their arms but carefully protecting their new shopping bags. It's understood that your whole family might not make it back from a trip to the mall. Every man, woman, and child is on his or her own when it comes to crossing the six lanes of traffic, including the 100-year-old grandma scooting her walker across at record speed so she won't get clipped. Walking on a Costa Rican street is a full-contact sport. Stop signs and traffic lights are considered optional, and they have a saying that Ticos love to use their horns but hate to use their brakes. The scramble for safety on the roads around the San Pedro Mall even extends to the sidewalks, where it's customary for the woman to walk on the inside of the man when a couple strolls together, not only so people won't think she's a prostitute for sale, but so she'll be further away from traffic in case a car jumps the curb. It's so bad that the slang word for speed bumps is "*son muertos,*" or, literally translated, "the dead people."

The main form of entertainment for most of the local Ticos in San Pedro was to browse the mall, especially on rainy days. Other than the usual cell phone, video game, and teen fashion shops, it had a multiplex movie theater and a huge disco called Planet Mall that took up the entire top floor. The club was ultramodern and cavernous — the dance floor and bar area taking up a whole city block — so big that it was almost impossible to fill with people. The wall-length windows offered a view of the street far below and of the sun setting behind the green hills through the smog. Planet Mall was rumored to be owned by Sylvester Stallone, but supposedly it wasn't doing well because no Tico could afford to party there. Just the cover charge alone was an astronomical $20 USD. We didn't go to the mall often, preferring the dimly lit bars near the train tracks by the University of Costa Rica, or drinking beers in Escazu, where I tipped the waitresses with handfuls of weed, but I have to admit, the mall was a great place to people-watch. But every time I passed it, I had to keep reminding myself that one of the reasons

I left the United States was to get away from the consumerism of Bed Bath & Beyond and McDonalds on every corner.

Other than risking their lives getting to the mall to buy things they couldn't afford, the Costa Rican national pastime was hustling gringos for their money, which I learned the hard way. Shane and I — young, wild, and free — wanted to experience some of the indigenous wildlife, so we never turned down an opportunity to meet local chicks. We considered ourselves a couple palm-tree Casanovas, and the mall was a great place to meet women, but little did we know the hunters were actually the hunted.

On our first Saturday night in town we walked to a bar for pizza and beer to celebrate our new apartment. It was the typical dive bar where college kids could mass-murder their brain cells with pitchers of cheap beer, play a spirited game of foosball, and promote permanent hearing loss with Maná and Manu Chao rocking on the stereo. A middle-aged lady with enough makeup on to double as a rodeo clown sat across from us with her two daughters. The oldest daughter, Paola, was breathtaking, with coconut skin and icy blue eyes, natural blonde hair, perfect curves, and unusually blessed in the fun bag department. Her little sister, Tatiana, was even bustier, but her curves were squeezed into a 4'11" frame, making her look like someone was shooting a rap video in a fun-house mirror. For some unknown reason Tatiana was intent on packing her bodacious bod into clothing more suitable for an anorexic 13-year-old than a woman of her size, her jeans so tight they defied the laws of physics, swelling and straining the fabric. I considered putting on safety goggles in case her buttons started shooting around the room. We nicknamed the sisters the Titty Twins because, well, what the hell else were we going to call them?

When their mother invited us over for a beer, Shane and I both shot up and dove for the chair next to Paola, wrestling each other to the ground for the chance to sit next to the beautiful sister. I thought I'd won the seat with a good karate chop to Shane's larynx, but he managed to take control by threatening to stab me in the eye with a fork. I resigned to take my seat next to Tatiana and gave her a fake smile as Shane started to suavely chat up big sis. After a few beers, they invited us to another bar after pizza and got up to leave, assuming that we'd handle the bill. We weren't too cool with that move but agreed to hit the next spot, both of us still jockeying for the beautiful Paola. But unless Shane improbably fumbled the ball he was in with her, so I would have to employ an ancient Zen secret to accentuate the beauty in Tatiana: beer goggles.

The whole lot of us — including their mom — walked toward a rooftop bar in San José. The Twins and their mom wanted to stop in a little market for some things along the way. They ripped through the store and ended up with a pile of cigarettes, ice cream cones, gum, and even lottery tickets by the cash register, stepping back when it was time to pay, once again assuming Shane and I would pick up the tab. What the hell were the lottery tickets for? I asked. Tatiana told me that they were for her father's birthday next week. Oh, hell no! I threw them aside, but the girls did get all of their edible treats.

The bar was four floors up, but the elevator was broken, so we all hoofed it up the stairs. Tatiana didn't look like she was going to make it. She held a lit cigarette in one hand, a double-scoop ice cream cone in the other hand, and was chewing gum. By the third staircase she was bent over and wheezing, clutching the railing like she was going to have a heart attack. As we continued up, she kept stopping abruptly to rest, my face smacking right into her ass like an air bag was being deployed.

At the club, Tatiana and Paola led us to a table where their entire family was seated — not exactly what we had planned. The relatives introduced themselves one by one, and maybe I was a little buzzed but as far as I could understand, the girls had three moms. They ordered pitchers of beer and rum and Cokes to chug at the same time. I tried to keep up drinking with the three moms and the Twins, but after an hour I was shit-faced. After that, my memory gets a little hazy. I remember stumbling to the bathroom and Mom #2 grabbing my crotch under the table when I returned. Then I recall Mom #3 hitting Shane up for some money — "just a little loan until the bank opened on Monday." Instead, we threw some money on the table for our portion of the bill and promised to meet them at the mall at 3:30 p.m. the next day just so we could get the hell out of there. The moms tried to grab our shirts and hold us captive, probably so we could subsidize the entire family's drinking session for the rest of the night, but I executed a flawless jujitsu move on her wrist to get free and run for the stairs. I knew Tatiana wasn't chasing anyone.

Shane and I left the club drunk as skunks with empty pockets where our money used to be. The smart thing to do would have been to go home to lick our wounds and call it a night, but instead we jumped in a taxi to take us to Escazu, the upscale entertainment district in Santa Ana, to keep the dream alive. No sooner did we step out of the taxi than a gang of girls started whistling at us and calling out, "*Aye papi!*" and "*Rico carne.*" No matter how many times I hear those words — literally, "Hey, daddy" and "Rich meat" — it still cracks me up. The girls brought us to a disco called Coco Loco where I hung out with a cute girl named Hazel with pale skin and straight brown hair, and Shane with her friend Daisy, who looked half Chinese. They were Nicaraguans who had moved to Costa Rica for better work opportunities a couple of years prior. Hazel found work at a car dealership and Daisy as a kindergarten assistant. Hazel and I hit it off and it was great to finally meet good girls who weren't trying to hustle us. We boogied with our new friends to reggae, dance hall, and salsa tunes until we were all covered in sweat. Before heading home we exchanged phone numbers, exhausted but smiling because the night was an overwhelming success.

The next day, however, was an absolute freak show. We woke up with vicious hangovers and pockets full of phone numbers, feeling like big ballers. We'd made plans to meet the Titty Twins at the mall at 3:30 p.m., so we had all morning to lounge around and recover. A few minutes after we awoke, our phone rang. Shane answered it, talked in Spanish for a minute, and then hung up, looking confused. He reported that some girls had invited us to dinner that night at 6:00 p.m. at a place called Hollywood Burger in the mall. So what was the bad news? He had no idea who he had just talked to on the phone. His best guess was that it had been Daisy and Hazel calling with the invite, but he couldn't be sure. Oh well, we should be able to meet up with the Titty Twins and get rid of them and hit Hollywood Burger well before 6:00 p.m.

Shane and I waited for the Titty Twins to show up on the front staircase of the mall, making bets on which pedestrians would make it safely across the traffic circle like we were handicapping horses at the Kentucky Derby. I turned around and saw that the Dominican girls from next door had spotted us and were walking over. Much to our surprise, they were the ones who'd invited us to dinner. We tried our best to back out of it, promising them that we'd do it another time, but despite our best efforts they insisted, and one thing I had learned was that you never wanted to piss off a Latina. It was getting dangerously close to 3:30, so finally we acquiesced just to get them out of there before the Twins showed up.

We looked at our watches and breathed a sigh of relief — Paola and Tatiana hadn't shown up yet nor seen the Dominicans, but we weren't out of the woods yet. Shane tapped me on the shoulder and pointed out that Daisy and Hazel were at the mall doing a little Sunday window shopping, and they were coming over to say hi. They invited us into the mall for a beer and were in no hurry to leave our sides. We didn't want to be rude because they were sweet girls, so we agreed to meet them later on that day at the mall for a beer and they finally walked off, leaving us in the clear. It was now 3:45, so we decided to wait inside the mall and watch for the Twins' arrival so we wouldn't get caught again.

We were hanging out in the center plaza of the stores amidst benches and palm trees when I noticed a commotion. A dozen teenagers in matching football jerseys were getting jostled by two security guards. We found out later that a professional football club was appearing that night at Planet Mall. The unruly teenagers were supporters of the rival team from a nearby poor neighborhood and came to represent their barrio and stir up some trouble. I had seen kids like this hanging around on street corners and in the main plaza in San José, punks who worshipped the spirit of Che Guevara and hustled money so they could get wasted every day. In Latin American countries, unless you are rich you have very few opportunities in life, nor outlets to channel the frustrations and anger that all teenagers have. When you are poor and from the barrio, your only ways to escape are through drugs, gangs, soccer, or art. Unfortunately, most of the kids weren't footballers or fire dancers.

A middle-aged security guard wearing a white shirt with a black tie grabbed one of the kids and tried to hold onto him. The kid was having no part of being detained, and probably arrested, so he squirmed to get out of the security guard's grasp. The tension mounted as teenagers circled the two officers and pushed to free their friend. More security guards ran over with walkie-talkies squawking, armed with Mace and black metal nightsticks. The kid continued to pull and kick to get away from the officer's grasp, ripping his football jersey as the guard hung on for dear life. The other guards pushed into the fray and tried to grab the kid. Finally he wrestled free, leaving part of his ripped jersey in the security guard's hand. Another guard wound up and smacked him in the head, and all hell broke loose.

This unfolded in the span of a few seconds, only a few feet from where I was standing, and I took in every detail as if it were in slow motion. The football hoodlums swarmed in to defend their friend, unloading a fury of kicks and punches on the security guards. The guards, much bigger and well-armed, pulled out their nightsticks after absorbing the initial shock of being attacked and pushed the kids back with wild swings. Everyone started throwing their fists furiously. The fight spread through the lobby in a whirlwind of punches, kicks, and falling bodies. The kids instinctively made for the exits to get to daylight. People on both sides were getting clocked and falling to the ground, and I had to backpedal so I wouldn't be tripped by falling bodies and pulled into the fray. Mall patrons screamed and pushed to get out of there, causing an instant panic in the crowd and a stampede for safety.

The football ruffians were chased out of the mall lobby onto the staircase out front. Radios cackled panicked shouts as a phalanx of security personnel swarmed in from all parts of the mall, nightsticks drawn and Mace readied. The rag-tag and bloodied kids backed up and regrouped on the sidewalk at the bottom of the stairs, about 20 yards from a wall of security guards poised for violence. Shane and I had moved outside, too, though I don't remember walking there, and we found ourselves standing on the side of the staircase directly in between the two rival groups.

Everyone was pumped up with adrenaline and pissed off, shouting curses at each other, but no one dared to cross the no-man's land separating them. A few of the guards had pistols and shotguns because they worked at the bank or the jewelry store in the mall, so they came to the front. The kids picked up rocks and bottles and chunks of concrete — anything they could find on the street and the sidewalk — and threw them full blast at the officers. Debris whizzed through the air right in front of me and I ducked down a little so I wouldn't get hit by an errant bottle. Most of them fell short and clanked against the stairway in front of the guards, but a few found their mark. A rock smashed through the mall foyer's big plate glass window in an explosion of glass shards, eliciting screams from a woman somewhere. Then, the kid with the ripped jersey stepped forward and whipped a baseball-sized chunk of concrete toward his adversaries. I watched its trajectory and instantly knew it would be trouble. It collided with one of the guards squarely in the face, catching him completely unaware and sending him staggering backwards, a steady trickle of blood appearing down his cheek. His eyes filled with rage and he instinctively charged like a bull. He pulled out a black revolver and a collective moan of fear rose from the crowd. As he approached the kids he waved the gun around in anger, like it was an extension of his arm. The impoverished football thugs scampered onto the street to get away from him and out of range of his gun.

Everyone ran except one kid, a scrawny punk who was maybe 15 years old with a homemade Mohawk haircut. He actually stepped forward toward the guard. He was not tall, not big, not remarkable in any way except for his insane *cojones*. He walked right up to the guard, shaking like a leaf but not wavering in his resolve. The guard was still fuming mad and pointed the revolver in his direction. The kid was so charged with adrenaline that he could barely stand, and fell to one knee on the pavement, and then both knees, screaming at the guard. The guard moved forward until he was only an arm's length away and leveled the revolver at the boy's chest.

Possessed by some unearthly courage, the boy dared the guard to shoot. He pounded his own chest with his fists and yelled at the guard with his head thrown back, fully exposing himself to the gun. I didn't translate what he said, but I still knew what he was screaming: "Go ahead and shoot me! You don't have the balls! Shoot me then! I am only 15 and from the barrio but I have nothing to lose! I will die for my pride! Shoot me!"

Families with shopping bags, the whole line of guards, and all of the other kids looked on, awestruck and frozen. The guard pressed the gun against the kid's chest and got ready to shoot. The kid ripped open his shirt as if to give him a better shot. I had to blink to make sure it was real — the kid was wearing a Superman T-shirt underneath the shirt he had ripped away, but he wasn't Superman and this bullet wasn't going to bounce off of him. I thought for sure that the guard was going to shoot — everyone did. I was about to see a bullet rip through another human being's heart and end his life. This wasn't a movie or TV, and the gravity of the moment weighed me down so I couldn't move or yell out.

But the guard didn't shoot. He paused. When the kid ripped open his shirt and dared him to shoot, the guard lost his edge and became conscious and just like that, the millisecond when the universe crashed to a stop was over. The anger drained from the guard's face as he, too, was shocked by the kid's willingness to die to represent his barrio. He lowered his revolver. The Mohawked Superman got up and scampered away, no longer a superhero but just a scared punk again. The guard was suddenly aware of what he had almost done and the consequences, so he just yelled a half-hearted warning at the kids and walked back up the steps to the mall, holstering his gun. The guards milled about long enough to see the kids curse them out and give them the finger but walk away down the street, celebrating and slapping each other on the back.

I came back into my own existence. Oh my god, I couldn't believe I came that close to seeing someone murdered right in front of me. I wished I had my camera with me because a photo of what had just gone down would win some serious awards. The crowd breathed a sigh of relief and collected their possessions and children, unsure of what to do next, and either went back into the mall or made the sprint across the street to go home.

A minute later, the Titty Twins found us, sweating and grinding our teeth as we tried to explain what had just happened. For some unknown reason they'd brought two of their moms along again. They didn't even ask us how we were doing, but went right into a spiel about how they were hungry and wanted us to take them out to the American-style burger and milkshake joint in the mall and then treat them all to a movie. I looked up to see which burger joint they were talking about and was befuddled to see that it was Hollywood Burger — the exact place where the Dominican chicks wanted to meet. Shit! But it was too late — since everyone was packed in the front of the mall to see what the commotion was, we had been spotted by the Dominican girls and Daisy and Hazel. Shane and I took one look at each other and turned and walked away without speaking a word. I needed a drink.

We made a beeline for the stairs and ran all the way up to Planet Mall. We paid our steep cover charge to the burly bouncer and went in. The infamous football team had arrived and were autographing posters for the other disco patrons, completely oblivious to how much blood their presence had almost just spilled. My nerves were fried and I was still shaking with adrenaline from witnessing Superman almost get shot. The last thing I saw before I headed to the bar and got properly soused was the Titty Twins and their mom, the Dominican chicks, and a confused Daisy and Hazel outside the club entrance, clamoring to get in like wolves at the door, but being held back by the bouncer. They were all pointing at us to come get them and pay their cover charges. Forget that noise. I slapped every last dollar I had on the bar and told the bartender to line up shots of his cheapest tequila. Shane and I took deep breaths. We were safe, for now, but getting home to our apartment was going to be a bitch.

Pork Chop

Costa Rica, May/June 1999

I've learned that in this crazy world sometimes you're a pimp and sometimes you're a whore. And then there's Pork Chop.

The first stop on our trip around the world in 1999 was Costa Rica, where we rented an apartment in San Pedro, a sleepy suburb of the main city, San José. It was definitely a culture shock fitting into life outside of the U.S., but the subtle differences also held the most charm — people strolled to the little local market every day, run by a cantankerous old man Shane and I dubbed the "Grumpy Grocer," buying just enough small portions to fit in their small refrigerators. Every exterior wall around a house or a building had shards of broken beer bottles embedded in the cement, acting as a razor-sharp deterrent to any robbers who might otherwise climb over. People didn't have garbage cans out front of their homes but metal boxes sitting on a pole three feet off the ground, to keep the animals out. A soccer game could break out anywhere, at any time; the little school children in blue uniforms late for class or the construction workers on lunch break might strike up a game with a ball of rags, a coconut, or sometimes even a proper ball. They served beer in every movie theater and the banks got robbed so frequently that they had a team of very serious-looking guards with shotguns at the door requiring you to take your sunglasses off as you entered. The details are too many to recount, but they endeared me to life outside of the States instantly, for now navigating everyday existence was no longer monotony but a grand adventure.

For a couple of months Shane and I called the Apartmentos Williams home. It didn't have an address, but directions for cab drivers and mailmen alike: "*Tres cientos metres sur y cincuente oeste de iglesia San Pedro*," or "Three hundred meters south and fifty meters west of the church of San Pedro." Easy enough.

From the outside it looked more like a bunker than an apartment building — a square two-story structure with a halo of barbed wire, concrete block walls, and metal bars over the windows. Everyone had to be buzzed in by the attendant, Sergio. I can't be entirely sure but I think Sergio was a little bit touched in the head. He was a chubby Tico (the name for Costa Ricans) in his 20s with an overbite, who always wore a white sailor cap like Gilligan, and the zipper on his tight jeans was never closed. He was in charge of security and property management, though from what I could see he did nothing all day but whistle while simulating intercourse with his fingers for anyone who walked by. I washed my hands immediately after greeting Sergio.

The apartment was a fashion explosion, like Liberace had dropped acid at Ikea. The red velvet couches were hermetically sealed in plastic protective covers as was every chair, table, and lamp, all adorned with frilly lace doilies and crystal bead curtains. On the walls were framed photographs of fruit in a bowl — not paintings of fruit in a bowl, but photographs.

Shane and I had decided on posting up in an apartment so we could catch a glimpse of typical Costa Rican life. He had suggested Costa Rica as the first stop on our journey because it had a reputation for natural beauty and bustling nightlife, while still being safe enough for Americans. Before we moved in, I envisioned smiling families inviting us to their dinner tables every night, their kids high-fiving their new gringo friends on their way to school. We would help the old lady in 4B, Señorita Theresa, carry her groceries up the stairs, endearing us to the locals. "What amazing gentlemen and scholars," they would proclaim when they saw us play soccer with Little Jesús in his wheelchair in the courtyard. Of course, I wouldn't do it for the accolades but because it was the right thing to do. But I sure wouldn't object when they tried to marry me off to their smolderingly exotic daughter, who was being groomed to take over the family liquor store and was desperately in need of breast reduction surgery.

"No, we cannot stay — there's a whole world out there waiting for us," I'd explain halfheartedly as they begged me not to hit the road again. The daughter would throw herself in my arms, distraught that I was leaving. I would dry her tears with the back of my hand and promise to return for her. We could get married in the church in San Pedro with Little Jesús wheeling his trusty rig right up the aisle as the ring bearer. The Apartmento Williams would still be our happy home; she could work at the liquor store 14 hours a day while I supervised (a very important job), and with my encouragement she would realize that she didn't need the breast reduction surgery after all — I would accept her just the way she was. What a guy. For this, she would vow to wait for me in virginal anticipation, even if it took 99 years. In my opinion, I was well worth it.

As I'd turn to leave and look back one more time, Little Jesús would emerge from the crowd in his wheelchair (which, note to self, was rusting and needed a brake replaced) and present us with medals he hand-made from weaving Chiclet boxes together, hanging them around our necks like Olympic athletes. Everyone would burst into applause and start singing "Stairway to Heaven" in Spanish. As we'd hit the street and jump in a taxi, Perverted Sergio would stand at attention, zip up his fly, and salute.

But it didn't go down like that — not even close.

The first week as residents we didn't hear a peep out of our neighbors at the A.W. until one morning, Shane and I were chilling on the couch out front of our place when their door opened. Out walked girl after girl like a clown car unloading, most with coal-black skin, half asleep and with her hair wrapped in a bandana. They kept coming, five in all, and looked at us curiously and then smiled.

The girls were all in their late teens or early 20s and from the Dominican Republic, an extremely poor island nation that shared its land mass with Haiti. There was Helena, a cherubic light-skinned gal with a pretty face; two giggly sisters with cornrows in their hair; and Noelle, their ringleader. Noelle was tall and thin with perfect features and eyes that showed the intelligence of a wounded animal. She was the leader of the group because she had the sharpest business sense and was a tough cookie. Then there was Pork Chop.

The first time I met Ms. Chop I had to look up; she easily stood about 6'2" and was a Cadillac — built for comfort, not for speed. All of the other girls introduced themselves and we caught their names, but Pork Chop was too busy gnawing on a pork bone to say hi; hence, she earned her nickname. She was always eating — scraping last night's pot of rice and beans, deep-throating an ice cream bar, or attacking a roasted chicken with fury. She lounged around their apartment half-naked, her food stained undershirt pulled halfway up to get air flow to her gut, sucking her teeth but never speaking. She communicated with grunts in between picking beef kabob out of her grill. Although it was obvious that meat was her first love, she was a prostitute like the rest of them; every night she made a meal out of some freaky 5'4"-tall Japanese businessman who paid by the minute for Pork Chop to play sexual Godzilla to his downtown Tokyo.

Apartmento Williams was almost entirely occupied by prostitutes, home to a wolfpack of hos. We hadn't moved into a whorehouse, which would have made for a much more entertaining story, but it was the living quarters of choice for a lot of working girls. I guess it was a cheap, safe place where they all felt comfortable living together and could share taxis to work.

These girls had sex with guys in exchange for money. I don't say that to sensationalize but because that's exactly what it was: an exchange of a service commodity for currency — a career choice — but it wasn't *who they were* as people. They had to live in Costa Rica to gain access to the most foreigners with money. The cash they made from letting a drunken tourist climb on top of them would probably feed their whole family back home for a week. I imagine that's what they thought about every time they closed their eyes, clenched their teeth, and went numb.

It's easy for us in the U.S. to sit on our high horses and judge prostitution from a position of privilege, even though as a nation we're addicted to prescription drugs, material possessions, and an abdication of ethics that has us throwing around marital vows like hot potatoes. Even the word "prostitution" elicits visions of a woman dragging along the shadows of the street, disease-riddled and addicted to crack, trying to outrun her bad choices. But in the rest of the world, the *real world*, where people can't afford hypocrisy, prostitution is a social vice that's never going away. At its best, in places like the Netherlands and Costa Rica, prostitution has been legalized and women enjoy unions, membership cards, police protection, and health screenings and benefits. Sometimes, they are just "good girls" who have loving families and jobs as secretaries or school teachers, and even a college education, but want to make extra money on the weekends or during the off-season. They hang out at the local hotspots and are paid to "party" with tourists to supplement their income. Prostitution exists everywhere, but in Third World countries it's mostly driven by conscious choices and economics, not a lack of self-esteem because a woman's daddy didn't give her enough hugs or because she's strung out on crack.

The girls next door became our good friends. I have to be honest: At first I found it hard to trust them because of their vocation. I couldn't even shake Pork Chop's hand without thinking about where it had been the night before — probably donkey punching a Canadian tourist in a leather mask with a zipper for a mouth. But I came to find out that my shallow judgment couldn't have been further off the mark. The Dominicanas didn't drink, didn't smoke, and Noelle would chastise anyone within earshot who cursed or took the Lord's name in vain. The strongest language I heard out of her was when she barked, "*Esto ventana es animal!*" (this window is an animal!) when she couldn't open a stuck window, and even that sounded mysterious and bewitching, not crass. There was always a leather-bound Bible on the coffee table in their spotless apartment, opened to a new page every day.

They were young themselves but had families and their own children in the Dominican Republic that they had to support, so they sent every dollar home. I realized that Pork Chop and the girls were under incredible pressure — literally selling their bodies and risking their safety every night so their families could eat — but still they had smiling dispositions and never complained. They got a kick out of Shane and me because we were drinking and smoking almost every night, ripping up the bars and clubs of San José with wild abandon. Like a concerned mother, Noelle lectured us on which streets or clubs

15

were unsafe, but we never dared mention their nocturnal vocation and they certainly didn't volunteer the details.

All five of them crammed into their little two-bedroom apartment, sleeping on couches and doubling up in twin beds. During the day, they lounged around after a few hours' sleep until someone cooked a big pot of rice with fish and plantains. Noelle would eat first, and then Pork Chop would eat half of it by herself before spreading out on the couch and snoring like a lumberjack. Every night they emerged from the apartment dressed to the nines and caked with makeup, and jumped in a taxi van heading to the Hotel Del Rey. The Del Rey was infamous on the international sexual tourism scene, a hotel and casino in downtown San José that brought tourists and their money to partake in scores of prostitutes and mountains of boogie sugar nightly. That's where the girls, with an indefatigable work ethic, found customers, seven days a week. I couldn't really say how much money the girls made, but it was 5 a.m. by the time they rolled home every morning.

I didn't speak any Spanish but Shane conversed with them while I just smiled and nodded my head. I had no idea what they were talking about, but it seemed better to pretend to be in the conversation than just being straight-faced. It backfired terribly because they assumed I understood everything, and thereafter spoke to me in rapid-fire Español. The gals would come to me to talk about their problems and unburden their deepest hopes and dreams. To them I was the best listener on the planet; I tilted my head slightly like a puppy dog, smiled when they smiled, frowned when they frowned, and kept nodding my head like a bobble-head doll while they talked, never interrupting or making the conversation about me. I can only imagine what important life wisdom I dispensed with my silence, but they never seemed to catch on that I didn't understand a single damn word they were saying — or they didn't care — and that is how I became the personal therapist to a pack of Dominican prostitutes: the Ho Whisperer extraordinaire.

Every afternoon, just as the heat became unbearable, the clouds rolled in from the mountains and broke, dousing the city. When it rained that hard there was nothing for Shane and me to do but dash to take refuge in the nearest store and laugh as we got soaked to the bone. That's where we had to wait until the rains stopped and the sun reemerged, steam rising from the pavement. Sometimes it would rain for five minutes, sometimes for hours.

We tried to get home from playing basketball at the local park with our homie Luis "El Torro" Diego before the clouds broke, and spent the rainy afternoons in our apartment with Noelle, Helena, Pork Chop, and the girls playing cards and listening to the radio. We taught them gin rummy and had grand card tournaments, betting with M&M's, the radio on station Radio Dos playing American soft pop from the '70s, while we laughed and tried to cheat our way to victory.

The weeks flew by, and the girls were always respectful and appreciated our friendship. We didn't even lock our front door so they could come and go as they pleased, as if our apartment were the clubhouse for our gang. I could leave my wallet out in the open around them and not give it a second thought. I wondered how many people in the U.S. would be as honest as the Dominican girls, despite our opulence and blowhard morality. The girls cooked rice and beans for us and swept up our place with a horsehair broom. Helena showed me pictures of her daughter that she received in a rare letter from home, carefully pointing out the names of all of her family members and recounting the news from her town, before folding the letter away in its envelope like it was the original Magna Carta.

A couple of days before we were scheduled to leave Costa Rica, Noelle mentioned that it was going to be Pork Chop's 21st birthday. Shane and I brought home a birthday cake we found at the local grocery store chain, Mas Por Menos, where they spelled out "*Feliz Cumpleaños*" in blue icing. We invited the girls over for our last dinner, turned off the lights, and lit a handful of candles and stuck them in the cake. When the girls walked in, after prodding Pork Chop from her hybernative state on the couch, their jaws dropped. Five Dominican prostitutes, including a birthday girl named Pork Chop, stared in awe at a simple birthday cake.

The girls' faces glowed in the candlelight in our dark apartment, illuminating childlike smiles, as if the sky were filled with fireworks. We sang happy birthday in Spanish, mumbling through the part where we were supposed to say her real name, and turned the lights back on to cut pieces for everyone, serving them on the few mismatched plates, bowls, and saucers we had. But Pork Chop wasn't eating. I'd seen her brush her teeth with gravy before, so why the hell wasn't she hungry for the cake we bought for her? Was everything OK, we asked? Noelle whispered back and forth with her for a moment before reporting back to us: It was the first time in her life Pork Chop had ever gotten a real store-bought birthday cake and she didn't want to ruin it. Damn, that hit me. I realized that I had come to care about these women as sisters, as flesh-and-blood human beings, and I was genuinely concerned about the journey they were facing.

I wish I could tell you that we did something to help them, that there was some miraculous salvation that occurred to bring their lives from darkness to light, but that's not how it works in the real world. Maybe they weren't the ones who needed salvation; perhaps it was something in *me* that changed for knowing them, something that swept away my judgments and softened in my heart. Pretty soon, six weeks came and went and it was time for us crazy gringos to pack up our stuff and head to Venezuela. I hate goodbyes with those I care about because there's nothing you can say to make it better; that day, there was nothing but the empty crystal air, dancing with sunlight, and the smell of fresh rain on the streets of San José. In this dream we're all living no one lines up to applaud, and we don't get medals made out of Chiclets, but sometimes all we have is silence and an open Bible on a hooker's nightstand.

If nothing else, I'd like to think I helped them turn to the next page. In the real world, salvation isn't a birthday cake, but sometimes it can come pretty damn close. *Feliz cumpleaños*, Pork Chop.

The King's Inn

Venezuela, July 1999

Whenever I tell people that I spent a year traveling around the world their reaction is inevitably, "Oh, I'd love to be on vacation for that long." They envision me poolside working on my perfect tan with a postcard view of the ocean, a slim, brown-skinned waitress with a flower in her hair bringing me my fifth mai tai by 10 a.m. We laugh over some joke that only locals would understand, and my biggest stressor is whether to snorkel and then hit the seafood buffet or rent a moped for a tour of the island first. Even ten years later, when I tell friends about dropping out of polite society for a whole year to get the dust of far-off lands on my shoes, they tell me that it must have been so nice to "live in paradise."

Granted, I *thought* it was going to be like that; traveling around the world for a year brought to mind pristine beaches and a schedule completely free of anything but placid introspection and poolside drinks, and I fell victim to that dream. I mean, I could go anywhere I wanted and had nothing to do all day but enjoy it, right? But let me set the record straight right now: It was no vacation, and the best way I can plead my case is by telling you about my stay at the King's Inn, and how my life has never been the same since — and not for the better.

Shane and I landed in Caracas, Venezuela without knowing our asses from our elbows about where to go or what to do. We expected

Caracas to be a beautiful city with cheap, luxury hotels and warm-hearted people who loved us just because we were Americans. Instead, we found that the capital city of Venezuela is big, dirty, and unbelievably expensive. We hit a couple of hotels that were suggested in our outdated Lonely Planet guidebook, but the prices were still around $150 a night, an astronomic sum for two poor travelers in a Third World country back in 1999. Time and time again, we unloaded our heavy bags and schlepped into a hotel lobby, only to turn around dejected when we learned it was ridiculously overpriced. We'd flag down yet another taxi and move on to the next hotel.

We came to find out that Caracas is the epicenter of South America's production and distribution of oil, so everything caters to the ultra-rich and the international business community. The government also manufactures a false exchange rate for anyone exchanging American money, so it was über pricey. We'd hit five hotels already and were exhausted from the flight, so when the cab driver took a shortcut through a shitty neighborhood and we saw a neon vacancy sign we ordered him to stop. He strongly suggested that we keep trying to find a nicer hotel in a nicer neighborhood, but I assumed he just wanted to run up his fare, so we hopped out and walked up to the King's Inn, which boasted to be a certified two-star. Sweet.

A chubby lady in her mid-50s dozed behind the front desk. You could tell that twenty years earlier she had been attractive, if it was pitch-dark and you were really shit-faced drunk. But now she was resigned to pass the decades behind that desk, more interested in watching her novellas on a small black-and-white TV while she sucked on a greasy chicken bone than helping us check in. We asked her in broken Spanish if they had a vacancy and how much it would cost. She looked at us funny and puckered her lips, scratched herself in a few unmentionable places, and asked how long we wanted a room. When we answered that we wanted a room for at least a couple nights she looked like she was going to die of shock. The room would only cost us $14 a night while the next cheapest place we'd found anywhere else in town was $125 per night, so we eagerly signed on.

The elevator didn't work so we had to lug our bags up five flights of moldy stairs. The hallways, dimly lit with a lone light bulb, were lined with ancient wallpaper and smelled of bleach. One of the doors was half-open, revealing an old man in a wife beater but no pants, naked from the waist down and coughing up a lung. The carpet was so stained and frayed that I couldn't tell what color it originally had been, and was littered with newspapers, empty beer bottles, and a few abandoned car parts. Shane and I just looked at each other, shrugged, and said, "Fourteen dollars!" in agreement. Surely it must be nicer in our room.

We double-checked the number on our skeleton key and yup, we'd found good ole room #57. The door had been kicked in many times and rigged back up with cardboard and cheap plywood, and before we could even turn the key it nudged open with the slightest touch. The reveal of the room was even worse than I could have imagined. It was bare except for the first TV ever invented and two twin-sized beds, really just prison-style cots with flimsy mattresses and orange bedspreads from the 1970s. The bedspreads had "King's Inn" stenciled on them, as did the browning sheets, so no one would steal them — or the thieves would have to lay their heads on the evidence every night if they did. Our presence in the room must have upset the permanent residents, a squadron of bugs that took flight like a dust storm and roaches that scattered when we walked in and turned on the light. Wow, this place was a Grade A shit hole.

Shane and I threw our backpacks on our beds, which almost collapsed them, and jammed the door closed. It was about 120 degrees in there so Shane pried open the only window, which had been blacked out with paint. It gave us a lovely view of a cement wall about four feet away — an unfinished construction site with the sounds of jack-hammering at full volume that made our teeth rattle. Shane shut the window and told me to try the air conditioner. I walked over to the wall unit AC, which had no faceplate so it was all bare electronics and a filthy filter, and switched it on. It instantly shot 100 volts up my arm and sent me jumping back. That bastard just shocked me! We had to get the AC on before we died of heat exhaustion so I tried to creep up on it and turn it on again. It shocked me again, and this time I yelped in pain as I jumped back and gave it an angry kick. It came to life and we left it on full blast for the rest of our stay, scared as hell to go anywhere near it, even though it only dropped the temperature two degrees.

21

I noticed some curious water stains about three feet high on the walls, a mildewy line showing where there had been some long-ago flood. How the hell can a room on the fifth floor fill up with water three feet high? I pondered that one for a long time. Was it actually water? By the looks of this place, it could have been beer, human blood, semen, or elephant piss and I wouldn't have been surprised. I put it on my mental checklist to avoid the air conditioner and look out for flash flooding.

At least we had a semi-safe place to store our bags so we were free to wander the city. Surely we wouldn't stay in this roach motel for more than the one night, no matter how long we'd told Rosie Perez's mom we'd be guests. I was ready to clean up after a long, hot day of traveling and hit the town for some nightlife. No one wanted to take the first shower, as usual, so we utilized "rock, paper, scissors," to see who would go first, and I lost. Meanwhile Shane turned on the TV and flipped through the seven channels we got in, but they all showed football matches.

I hesitantly entered the bathroom and flipped on the light. The sink was half ripped out of the wall and the tile floor was filthy with what looked like dried mud. I jumped in the shower, not daring to take my flip-flops off, and turned the hot water all the way up. A tiny trickle of freezing cold water came out. It took me about twenty minutes just to get enough water over my body to have a serviceable wash. I grabbed one of the ratty towels with King's Inn stenciled on it, and tried to wrap it around myself, but it was stiff as a board. Someone had gone a little bit overboard with the starch. I positioned myself in front of the sink and spread shaving cream on my face. I turned on the sink to wash off my razor, and zap! — you guessed it — electricity ran through me, but this time from the floor up. It was a low current but still enough to make it damn unpleasant, especially since I was now standing in a puddle of water. After some repositioning, I found that if I stood way to the left of the sink and reached over I could avoid getting electrocuted again. My mental checklist was growing. I'm sure if you had plugged in a hair dryer the whole city block would have blown up. I came out and Shane grabbed his stuff and entered the bathroom. He asked me how the shower was and I told him it was fantastic and gave him no more warnings — let him figure it out for himself. What are friends for? A moment later, I heard him yell in surprise as he got shocked and then he good-naturedly cursed me out.

We walked downstairs feeling clean and looking snazzy for a night on the town. We hadn't really seen other victims — I mean, residents of the King's Inn yet, so we were pleased to spot a couple holding hands, a businessman and what looked like his niece passing on the stairway. We cheerily said hi to them and hoped to engage in a pleasant conversation about where the best places in town were to buy fresh fruit, and how the weather forecast was looking, but they just looked at the floor and rushed right past us. Wow, some people are just rude.

Rosie Perez's mom was pacing the lobby, fanning herself with a package of tortillas. I'm not sure if she had abandoned her shirt and was just wearing a bra or if she was in on the ground floor of a new Venezuelan fashion trend, but it appeared that she had only donned a brassiere. Her front butt threatened to pop out of her jean shorts, so she had the top button undone. She looked at us curiously as she sucked on a fresh chicken bone and told us that she was looking for rice. That's it? This bra-clad lady just wanders around looking for rice all night, like Moses in the desert? She asked if we were checking out. That was a damn funny thing to be asking someone — we had just checked in an hour ago.

The neighborhoods surrounding the King's Inn were completely empty — we didn't see another human being and only a few taxis sped through. Even the buildings were blacked out and looked vacant. Finally, we found a bar under a huge billboard promoting Polar, Venezuela's national beer. We walked in expecting beautiful women and a bunch of crazy college kids, but instead found ourselves face to face with twenty rough-looking cowboys, some with machetes hanging off their belts, playing pool and drinking warm suds to sad music. I swear the record skipped when we walked in as every squinting, inhospitable set of eyes fixed on us.

"*Hola! Cómo estás, amigos?*" was all I could muster, which even sounded ridiculously dorky to me, as we walked to the bar and ordered. I looked around — there wasn't one female in the whole place. Was this some sort of kinky Venezuelan gay machete bar? I'd heard about those kinds of places. If memory served, this was the exact spot where the Village

People got their start, so I kept my eye on the door in case the police officer, the Indian, and the Navy dude walked in — I wanted autographs.

The locals didn't warm up at all but mean-mugged us all night long. We managed to talk to the bartender, who spoke a little English. He asked us where we were staying and when he told him the King's Inn, he whistled and walked down to the other end of the bar. Pretty soon, we had all of the Polar we could stomach so we stumbled back to our new home.

Back up on the fifth floor we noticed that our door was slightly ajar. Had we been robbed? We investigated, but if we had been jacked they didn't take anything. Were our possessions undesirable even by Venezuelan slum standards? Damn, I needed an extreme wardrobe makeover. The flimsy door only took a butter knife to jam open, and by the looks of the worn and chipped-away frame, many had done just that. Whether we locked it or not our room was open game for the hookers, pimps, dealers, murderers, drunks, robbers, and cleaning ladies who might roam the halls of the King's Inn. (We saw most of them every night, except for the cleaning ladies.) From then on, every time we left our room we'd leave the lights on and the television blasting some football match in hopes that they'd think we were home, and this we labeled our "ghetto security system." That first night we were exhausted from all the traveling and too many Polars, so we both hit the sack after promising that it was going to be a one-and-done situation at the King's Inn; tomorrow we would check out and find a legitimate, nice hotel.

It was impossible to sleep. Once the lights went out the noise in the room was overwhelming. It had been pretty quiet during the day, but now, after midnight, there were sounds of people banging coming at us from five different directions. Believe me when I tell you that the sounds of people smashing guts is no fun if you're not involved somehow. Thankfully, most of the noisemakers were one-pump-chumps so it didn't last long, but just when one would end another two would start somewhere else. I was getting bitten by mosquitos mercilessly, but burying my head under the pillows only left me exposed to the armies of bed bugs and fleas and who knows what other prehistoric insects that savaged every part of my body. I itched like crazy until I was tossing and turning and tearing at my flesh like a lunatic. The only remedy was to cover up, so even though it was sweltering and airless in the room, I put on long pants, socks, and a long-sleeve shirt, and wrapped my head with a T-shirt. We spent a horrible night trying to get one little wink of sleep, and finally around six in the morning when we were able to close our puffy eyelids, the construction noise from outside our window started. A symphony of jackhammering and diesel engines roared to life and kept us wide awake.

Around midday we emerged from our tomb, backpacks in hand and ready to go, and muddled sleepily down to the front desk. Enough with this place! We slammed the key down in front of Rosie Perez's mom and told her that there was no way we were going to spend another night in that decrepit hellhole. We flagged down a taxi and asked our driver to take us to another hotel. He brought us to a decent-looking place and Shane ran in while I waited with our stuff. It was fully booked. We tried another hotel — it was $180 a night. Again and again we pulled up to hotels or rolled our luggage down the sidewalks of Caracas, but we couldn't find a damn thing. Eventually, we were so tired and discouraged that we just went back to … the King's Inn. Our friend behind the counter didn't say a word, in fact she acted like she'd never seen us before, but something behind her heavily painted eyes spoke volumes: "I knew you'd be back, you damn gringos — you're mine now!" She gave us our same room and we made the trek up the stairs again, sweating and cursing. It was three in the afternoon, the quiet time of the day, and maybe we could get a few hours' needed sleep before the symphony of banging started again.

That night was the same, but somehow we survived the oppressive heat, the rotting smells, the rats, the electric shocks, the high-volume lovemaking that knocked plaster off the walls, and the endless rashes and bites. The next day we tried again to find another hotel — and again we failed and returned to the King's Inn, completely defeated. Over the next week no matter how hard we tried to escape the King's Inn, we'd find ourselves back there with Rosie Perez's mom enjoying a smug sense of victory. It became a battle of wills, and we were losing badly. We made an executive decision to get the hell out of Caracas and take a bus to a neighboring smaller town, but two hours into the drive the bus broke down and everyone had to take another bus back to Caracas — and the King's Inn. We planned a flight to Brazil, but when we went to the airport, jubilant to board a plane to Rio and get the hell away from Venezuela, they informed us at the last minute that we needed visas to travel. Back to the King's Inn. At this point we didn't even check in; we just walked past the front desk with our eyes on the floor, walked right up to our old room, kicked in the door, and took our places on our rickety beds. It took a week to get our visas, but then we found out we had to get immunizations. Our one-night stay at the King's Inn turned into a three-and-a-half-week odyssey to escape the last place on earth we wanted to be. We were sleep-deprived and pocked with rashes and bug bites, and our tempers flared. I was so melancholy about our $14-a-night prison that I secretly hoped for the wobbly ceiling fan to come off its track and one of the blades to sever my head, so I could get merciful relief.

Sightings of the shadowy denizens of the King's Inn were few and far between. We noticed a few people coming and going during lunchtime, but the vast majority of activity was after midnight. Those were some strange hours for hotel patrons. People were always together — a man and a woman, and sometimes a man and two women, or a man and a midget, and once a leather-clad sado-masochist with a live goat on a leash. Who were these people? They came and went within the hour, and it seemed that the only other long-term resident (and by long-term I mean those of us who rented by the day, not the hour) was a 20-year-old hottie named Orlaney who I met by the soda machine. She was super friendly and I didn't mind at all that she was wearing clear heels and a miniskirt on a Sunday morning. We sat on the stairs by the soda machine and had a pleasant conversation. She confided in me that she was a stripper who worked at a club there in Caracas, but she was from a small town in the country and longed for a better life and a family of her own. We got along great; she really was a sweetheart, and — I'm not gonna lie — she was sizzling hot.

We talked for a while, she in broken English and I in bad Spanish, and eventually went up to her room on the top floor so she could show me pictures of her family. Wow, we were really vibing. Maybe there was a future here between us. Maybe, just maybe, I could look past the fact that she was a stripper and take her back to the U.S. and make a good, honest woman out of her. We could get married and buy a little white house and go to church every Sunday. I could join a bowling league and she would clip coupons and scrapbook and think of me in her spare time. We would be so happy, and I would never reveal the fact that I had been Captain Save-A-Ho and rescued her from the strip clubs of Caracas, even when I was obliterated on eggnog at the neighbor's Christmas party.

She led me into her room, which was surprisingly much nicer and neater than ours, and we sat down on the bed as she thumbed through her photo album. I remembered from high school that if a girl wanted you to sit on the bed and "look at pictures," it was really a code for hot monkey sex, and I was waiting for this to turn into a bad porn movie, complete with the cheesy "brown-chicken-brown-cow" soundtrack. She gave me a little kiss and then showed me some more pictures that I pretended to be interested in. "Oh look, it's a photo of your fat great-aunt on your dad's side at her cosmetology school graduation ... how fascinating!" Eventually, she would run out of photo albums and we'd be able to get to the good stuff and consummate our future marriage. But then she told me that she had to pack up for a business trip to Spain the next day.

Business? In Spain? What the hell kind of business could she be involved in where a poor stripper heads all the way overseas? Just as I was weighing that question, I saw her grab a huge plastic tube with a squeeze-tip bulb at one end — it looked like a two-foot-long turkey baster — and pack it in her luggage. What the hell was that? Was she a pastry chef working on a giant cake? An amateur beekeeper? Was she planning on taking well water samples for Greenpeace in Spain? Or was that the largest douche known to man? I'd never seen one, but I always assumed they came with white linens and horses galloping on the beach. I didn't know what that monstrosity was but I wanted no part of it, so I got up and ran out.

It finally hit me: The King's Inn was a sleazy motel for lovers, mostly adulterers and mistresses, where they could rendezvous for a few hours to get it on like Donkey Kong in a thong. And my sweet, precious Orlaney, my future scrapbooking, coupon clipping, subservient wife — the only long-term resident other than the roaches, rats, and bugs — was a hooker. Maybe she was heir apparent to Rosie Perez's mom, and old hookers don't die; they just retire behind the front desk of the King's Inn? Either way, there was no way I was marrying Ms. Turkey Baster. I ran down to the local pharmacy and grabbed two oversized bottles of rubbing alcohol off the shelves and doused myself, including my lips where I had kissed her. Yuck. This place was really getting to me, but then again the rubbing alcohol really seemed to help soothe the bug bites. I never saw Orlaney and her turkey baster again, but wherever she is I can only hope and pray that she's … ahh hell, actually, I don't give a shit.

It became clear to me that the only way to tolerate that Dantean level of hell was to get stinking drunk every night. Any time we left the hotel we headed immediately to the nearby dingy pool hall (still wearing our full body suits we slept in, even though it was over 100 degrees) to get smashed on lukewarm Polar beer and shots of firewater rum while the locals stared at us with hard looks. We didn't care. Not to be intimidated, we gave them hard looks right back and crushed our beer cans on the bar. They had machetes and outnumbered us twenty to two, but we were King's Inn survivors — a badge of toughness not even the surliest of them could claim. They backed off. No matter what time of day or night it was (it was all blending together at this point), we returned to the King's Inn semi-anesthetized to the tiger cage of discomfort and thankfully passed out for a few precious hours of sleep.

Eventually, we escaped the King's Inn, Caracas, and Venezuela, flying to Brazil with stenciled pillow case souvenirs stowed away in our luggage, but not before turning our miserable condition into a sport. Our last night there, exuberant that we were getting the hell out of that rat hole and three sheets to the wind, we decided in our ultimate wisdom that it would be a good life choice to surf our mattresses down the stairs. So we ripped the filthy foam off the bed, sending sheets and bugs flying, and positioned them at the top of the fifth-floor staircase. One, two, three! We took a running start and launched off the top step, surfing about ten feet before wiping out and tumbling down the rest of the way, head over heels, in a snowball of laughter and destruction. If we hadn't been so drunk I'm sure we would have broken our necks, but it turns out the only damage was to the walls, the staircase, and the other hotel patrons who had to leap out of the way to avoid being run over. Right then and there the Gringo Bobsled Team was born, and the score was getting closer: King's Inn - 147, Gringos - 1. After a couple of runs down our bobsled mountain, Rosie Perez's mom came hauling up the stairs, chastising us in breathless Spanish and waving her chicken bone at us. We ignored her, reloaded, and surfed again. After all, what was she going to do, kick us out?

Frisbee Head

Venezuela, July 1999

A cabbie warned us that our beach was the worst on the island. He was right.

It was littered with beer cans, food wrappers, and French people in banana hammocks. A sewage pipe intersected the south end of the beach, draining enough mystery sludge into the water that it stung your eyes when you swam. It was crowded with poor Venezuelan locals who guzzled back-to-back Polar beers from coolers, plastic bags with ice, and local vendors. You could barely find a spot of sand not covered with a cheap blanket and a drunken family inhabiting it. When they turned their heads left to see what was worth stealing on their neighbor's blanket, the neighbor on their right reached over and stole their beer. Naked toddlers ran around unattended, peeing all over the place as their parents made out shamelessly. On any given blanket you had a 17.5% chance of seeing a Venezuelan titty pop out, or worse. When they got up and brushed off the sand and stumbled to the bus stop, their only goal was to go home with some beer and approximately the same number of kids they came with.

Scrawny teenagers raced scrawnier horses up and down the beach at furious speeds. They rode bareback, hugging the horses with their bare feet and clinging to the mane with one hand, the other hand used to whip the poor beast mercilessly. Everyone cheered as they raced.

One kid got thrown from his horse when it stumbled in the sand and took a bad digger. I know Shane and I could have gone to the nicer beach and sat around with the pale tourists flopping around like sea otters, but what the hell was the fun in that? We wanted local. It was no postcard, but it wasn't terrible for the ass-end of paradise.

We took out the Frisbee and found some real estate to throw it back and forth. Everywhere we went the Frisbee came with us — it was the perfect way to amuse ourselves at any beach or public park, or even in the parking lot while waiting for the bus, and chasing after it and leaping into the air to catch it gave us a great workout. Throwing the Frisbee around also provided a perfect opportunity to meet people. Most places we went, people had never even seen a Frisbee before, and kids always loved it and grouped around us, wanting a turn. If we saw a group of hot girls we wanted to spit game at, we'd just throw the Frisbee in their direction. Either it landed near them, in which case we'd run up and collect it and chat a bit, or it would hit one of them squarely in the face and cause a nosebleed, in which case we'd get to spend more time with them manufacturing sincere apologies that it had been a complete accident, and offering to take them out to dinner to make amends. That was a win-win the way I saw it. Our Frisbee was yellow with a big smiley face on it, and we must have thrown that thing an hour or two every day. We always held it up in pictures to show where we were and yes, that we were still smiling, like a hostage holding up that day's newspaper.

And that is how we met our strange new amigo, a chatty guy around our age who walked by and asked if he could throw the Frisbee with us. After flopping it around unsuccessfully for five minutes he suggested that we have a drink with him and his friends instead and led us to a grove of trees. Several obviously unemployed fellows stood about, and a pregnant lady in a bikini sprawled out nearby on a tree stump. He introduced us to his brother, a sketchy bastard who was skinny and balding yet covered with thick body hair, like he was a little too far left on the evolutionary chart that showed man's progress to get his knuckles off the ground and walk upright. To make matters worse, he was sweating like a whore in church. I tried to push Shane toward him and stand closer to the pregnant chick.

They were drinking from a bottle of anise, a strong local firewater liquor, and filled little plastic cups and urged us to drink round after round, while yelling enthusiastically in Spanish about things I didn't understand and didn't care to. They refilled our cups and insisted we drink more with them since we were their new best friends. The stuff burned my esophagus on the way down and hit me between the eyes instantly. The hairy brother couldn't wait for the formalities of pouring it into cups, so he started drinking straight out of the bottle. He was a real kook, screaming because he was half deaf in one ear from the time a stick of dynamite misfired near him in a mining accident. I tried to stay on the side of his bad ear so he wouldn't want to converse with me, but he still badgered me with anecdotes about his days working on civil engineering projects while he was in the military. I made it very clear to the brothers that I didn't speak Spanish, but they ignored this fact and continued to catch me up on everything that had occurred in their lives over the last 25 years. The more I protested that I had no idea what they were saying, shamelessly pointing to Shane to divert their attention, the closer they got and the louder they yelled.

Someone didn't smell right. The hairy brother drank more and became animated, trying to headlock me. He waved his arms around like a gorilla, his eyes bloodshot and unable to focus, and tried to hug me with his dripping man-sweater. I stiff-armed him but did it subtly, trying not to be rude so he wouldn't turn on us and cut our heads off with a machete.

The only thing that seemed to calm these bad-breath bandits was Queen. Yes, Queen the band. A transistor radio sat on the beach next to them, antennae erect to pick up the only station on the island, and when a Queen song came on they went crazy. They loved rock and roll music, they said, and Queen was, of course, the best band ever. Really? I never got that memo. They wanted us to sing along and they wouldn't take no for an answer. It was either that or do more shots, so right there on the beach Shane and I belted out our best rendition of "Bohemian Rhapsody," "We Will Rock You," and "We Are the Champions." We had to make up most of the lyrics, repeat choruses, and switch songs mid-verse, but it seemed to soothe these savage beasts a little. The brother tried to clap along and stamp his feet to the beat, but the shrapnel in his head most have stricken him tone deaf as well. But as long as I kept singing, he relinquished his headlock on me. I didn't want it to end, so Shane and I went into repeat mode, mixing up the songs and singing chorus after chorus. They tried to keep up and sing along, to what I have no idea, and I didn't want to risk injury or a breach in my hygiene policy by stopping them.

"We swill, we swill, watch you!" they howled. Clap, clap.

"Key swill, key gill, wash you!" Drink, drink. Clap, clap. Everyone within earshot stared at them, embarrassed that these men had been appointed the drunken ambassadors of their country.

"Key argyle clampions my friend!" Dynamite Head soloed. I made eye contact with Shane to communicate our breakaway. We told them that we'd had a great time but it was getting late and we had to go. They protested. Sorry fellas, we have somewhere to be, we pleaded. They wanted to come with us. They wanted more drink, more Queen, more girls. More? Where the hell were the girls that we were supposedly enjoying now? We were finally excused after taking three more shots and promising to meet them in the same spot in an hour. An orgy of handshaking, hugs, missed high-fives, and vows that we were *hermanos* (brothers) ensued. We walked down the beach quickly, without looking back, and ran the second we couldn't hear Queen anymore. Shane thought that they were trying to take a crack at us, but I thought they were just blitzed out of their minds and overly friendly. When I got back to the hotel, I took a shower with extra soap and collapsed on the bed, passing put instantly from anise and sun.

When I woke up I was in a fog, confused about where I was and how I got there. That vertigo was becoming common, because on our trip so far we'd been in a different cheap hotel, or on a flight, bus, or train every third day. I got my bearings by looking at the hotel stationery. We were at the Blue Iguana in Isla Margarita in Venezuela.

That's right — how the hell could I forget? As I eased into wakefulness I thought about our journey so far. It had been a wild ride — only a few weeks ago I had been so innocent and carefree until everything went wrong. It had started with the rat-hole King's Inn, quite possibly the worst place on earth, ranking just ahead of several Turkish prisons, but after two hellish weeks there we had finally plotted our escape, booking flights to Brazil.

I had been so damn excited to get the hell out of Venezuela and leave the King's Inn behind forever. We got to the airport early and went to check in. The sleepy Varig airline worker asked for our tickets. Check. He asked us for our passports. Check. Our bags. Check. Our visas. Huh?

"Visa?" we asked. "No no, we already paid for our tickets on a different credit card."

But it wasn't a credit card Visa he required; we needed travel visas to enter Brazil. Ummmm … crap on a corn dog. Shane and I looked at each other blankly. We had booked the flights in December and the Brazilian embassy had started requiring a visa in July when we were already on the road. Could we get one when we landed? No. Could we try and get one quickly here in the airport? No. Did he care that he was subjecting me to a life of inhumane anguish by not letting me get on a plane to escape the King's Inn? No. We begged and pleaded with the guy, but he wouldn't budge. He gave us the address of the Brazilian embassy in Caracas and told us that we could probably get our visas in a few days. I felt like throwing myself on the luggage carousel and promising him my firstborn child if he would let us fly through, but instead we just dejectedly grabbed our bags and got a ride back into the city.

The next morning, we woke up early and grabbed a taxi to the embassy, determined to get the hell out of Caracas and the King's Inn as quickly as possible. The Varig guy had said it would take a couple of days, but maybe we could speed that up? That hope was dashed when it took our driver until noon just to find the embassy.

The Brazilian embassy was in a nice office building downtown. People lined up out the door to process paperwork with the disinterested worker who sat behind security glass. We found out quickly that the concept of an organized line hadn't really caught on yet in developing countries — I guess that was the part that was yet to develop. Service was based on who was the loudest and most aggressive, not who was actually next in line. People came in after us but walked right in front of the mob, waving their documents and screaming. We couldn't believe it when a slippery Brazilian guy tried to squeeze right in front of us. Well, if they wanted to play that game we could play, too.

Shane and I went agro, boxing out like we were going for a rebound on the basketball court, throwing elbows and bumping people off course with our big gringo asses if they tried to cut us. It took us an hour to get up to the counter, and just as we started to explain what we needed the lady put a "Will Return" sign up and walked away for her break. She did return in twenty minutes, with alcohol on her breath.

After telling her what was up, she gave us the appropriate forms to fill out and told us we had to pay a $10 fee at a certain bank and bring the deposit slip back to her. Shane ran out to find the bank and I went to the back of the line and started boxing out again. Poor Shane had to run to three banks to find the right one. He waited in line but then was told they only took American Express or Venezuelan money — not American cash or other credit cards. He waited in another line to change his money, but they wouldn't change big U.S. bills, so he ran out onto the street and found a Venezuelan bank machine that took his card and came back to the bank to start over. By the time he got back to the embassy, sweating and out of breath, I was near the front of the line. The lady took our deposit slips and told us that we needed photocopies of our driver's licenses. Son of a biscuit! It would have been nice if you told us that last time! We ran downstairs and asked around until we found an office supply store, copied the licenses, and returned to the embassy line. Forty-five minutes later we handed in our completed visa applications. She said that the visas would take a couple days to process. It was Friday, and over the weekend they didn't work, of course, and then there was a holiday on Monday, so we were looking at maybe next Wednesday if we paid extra for a rush. Lord save me. We also needed one more thing: medical certification that we had been immunized for yellow fever.

I had already had every immunization known to man before I left the United States; my shoulders were like pincushions over a three-week period at the Yale medical clinic. But Shane still needed his, so the next day we grabbed a taxi and headed out to try and find a medical clinic where he could get his shot quickly. Our driver took us all over the city, but every clinic or doctor's office was either closed or they couldn't fit him in for an appointment until the next week. Finally, the driver said he knew of a free medical clinic that would do it, but it was in a rough barrio and gonna be a crapshoot whether we got out safely or not. He took us deep into a shit-hole hood where young thugs hung out in the middle of the street blocking cars — he said the police wouldn't even go there. He pulled onto the curb in front of the medical clinic and told Shane that they had to run in together and get out quickly so they wouldn't be robbed or mugged or worse. He told me to stay in the back of the taxi with the doors locked and not to let anyone in, no matter what. He pulled something from under his seat and placed it on the back seat next to me with a newspaper over it, and then they sprinted into the building. I locked the doors from the inside and pulled back the newspaper; it was a huge butcher's knife he'd left me to fight off any carjackers. Damn, this was getting heavy.

They came running out twenty minutes later, just as the locals were starting to circle and discuss how to dispose of my body once they stole the car. We got back to the embassy, but even with his medical card it would take almost a week to process the visa paperwork. There was no way in hell I was staying at the King's Inn that long, so we hopped the first flight we could to Isla Margarita, a resort island off of Venezuela's northern coast where rich people from the mainland and poor island folks partied.

The island was a welcome break from dirty, polluted Caracas and the King's Inn. Our first night there we went downtown to check out a crowded strip of bars. Shane noticed several girls walking together up ahead of us. He was mesmerized by a tall, super-fly *chica* in their pack so we followed them for a while, trying not to be obvious by hiding behind trees and pretending to read newspapers when they turned around.

We were tailing them when they stopped abruptly for one of them to answer her cell phone. Shane and I couldn't hit the brakes in time, so we bumped into the back of them at full speed. Since it was obvious that we were going to follow them around all night like lost puppy dogs without introducing ourselves, one of the girls took pity on us and said hello. Shane talked to his tall girl and I chatted with her younger sister, who spoke surprisingly good English. It turned out that three of the girls were the president's nieces and their family was at Isla

Margarita for their summer vacation. Back in 1999 not many people had heard of the Venezuelan president, but pretty soon people started paying attention to the name Hugo Chavez in international news as he grew increasingly antagonistic toward the United States, positioning himself as the new Fidel Castro. I suspect that the girls were really in Isla Margarita for security reasons, because President Chavez was on shaky political ground in his own country when he illegally extended his term limits and quelled a political revolt by locking his congress out of the capitol. The girls were staying at the best hotel on the island and always had security officers hanging around. They were digging us, so we made a date to take them out to ice cream later, and then it was time for the Ciao Line.

What's the Ciao Line, you ask? In Latin American countries when you greet someone or say goodbye, no matter whether you've just met them or been exchanging bodily fluids with them for years, you kiss them on the cheek. Sounds painless, right? But the president's nieces and their friends traveled in packs, like over-populated coyotes. I should have applied Chapstick when I saw them coming. When they got up to leave, I stood still with my lips puckered, doing that fake little half-hug where you stick your butt out so your private parts have no chance of accidentally touching, and said ciao to each of them. One by one, they moved down the line and did the cheek kiss and said ciao, like a gringo conveyor belt.

We kicked it with them for a couple of days. They were beautiful but spoiled as shit. Who the hell did they think they were — the president's nieces or something? I would have loved to date the girl I was hanging out with, buddying up with "Uncle Hugo" and the presidential family and consummating my love for her with frequent relations, but that just wasn't going to happen because of the toothpaste all over my man-junk. I should probably explain.

Shane was our official trip doctor. Granted, there were only two of us, so the options were limited, but I couldn't even pass ninth grade biology, so the choice was obvious. Of course, he had no formal medical training but he was a pharmaceutical salesman, so that was good enough for me. Plus, he had a grab bag of pills in his toilet bag, so I could steal a random handful and wash them down with a beer whenever needed.

Frisbee Head

In Isla Margarita I developed a rash all over my man-junk region. Now, to be very clear, it turned out to be nothing — just a bad heat rash — but I'd never had something like that before, so I was freaking out. I pride myself on being as clean as the board of health, and I knew I definitely contracted it during my time at the King's Inn, but whether it was from the bed bugs or from sitting on Orlaney's toilet seat was the real question. I was rooting hard for the bed bugs. I bought a huge bottle of rubbing alcohol to wash myself down completely whenever I even touched a local, but it quickly broke in my backpack and doused all of my possessions, making me smell like a senior center on cleaning day.

I'd been trying to self-medicate for a few days, but the rash just wasn't going away. I remembered when I was a teenager and I got a pimple, people would tell me to put toothpaste on it at night before I went to bed and it would dry up by morning. I thought the same theory might apply here, so I slathered toothpaste all over my man-junk every morning and night. I had gone through three tubes of Aquafresh but it wasn't working so far — although I did enjoy the minty tingle. Finally, I started to panic and couldn't take it anymore. I booked an appointment with the trip doctor (Shane) to look at it and give me his professional opinion and hopefully some drugs to clear it up; nothing is sacred when you're traveling around the world with someone for a year.

We were crashing the breakfast buffet at the Marriot for the fourth morning in a row, our ritual of taking advantage of the hotel's amenities without actually staying there. No matter what country we were in there was always an ultra-modern and sparkling Marriot somewhere in town. They didn't seem to notice when we walked in like we were VIP guests and helped ourselves to some free coffee and breakfast, read the newspaper sprawled out in comfy chairs in their lobby, lounged by their pool, and even took our time using their majestic marbled bathrooms. After a few hours we'd leave the Marriot and retreat to our shit-hole hotel down the street, feeling refreshed. So Shane and I snuck into the Marriot bathroom for my doctor's appointment. It was embarrassing, but I reminded myself that he was a medical professional (sort of), so I dropped my trousers and he examined me right there in the Marriot bathroom stall. He looked for a second and then said, "Hmmm ... I'm not sure. It may be something."

Yeah thanks, I could have told you that. We waited until the coast was clear to come out of the bathroom stall so no one would get the wrong idea. But needless to say, I was excluded from having any relations with the president of Venezuela's niece because of my toothpaste. Ohhhh, if only Hugo knew.

After a long weekend on the island, we felt the calling to go back to Caracas to check on our visas. After more boxing out in line, we were told that it would be one more day. No problem. To pass the time, we hired an old taxi driver to drive us all around the city and show us the attractions — including a glimpse of the bad neighborhoods to see how the common person lived. He was hesitant, and we had to urge him again and again to drive us into these barrios. "This doesn't look so bad," we said to ourselves, as I snapped a couple photos of the scenery. When we turned up this one street the driver whipped the car around instantly and sped off in the other direction, tires screeching. When we questioned him why he abruptly drove off he only said, "*Ladrones*," which means "thieves." We thought he was crazy and just being paranoid, but found out otherwise pretty quickly.

We were waiting at a red light only a few blocks down, when all of a sudden a motorcycle rolled up with two skinny tattooed guys on it. They pulled up right next to my door and started yelling, and reached through the open back window, trying to grab at me. They were trying to rob us of our cameras, wallets, and watches, whatever a tourist might have on him. I was in shock, but in a split second it was obvious they were about to get violent, and there we were trapped in the back of this taxi. All of a sudden the old man slammed the gas and took off, speeding through a red light and dodging traffic. The thieves chased us for about ten blocks, trying to catch up and pull alongside the swerving taxi, but our cagey driver eluded them, and just as quickly they peeled off when we passed a police car. We were safe.

It took a minute for my heart to stop jumping. Our driver explained that they were gang members who controlled the barrio's drug trade with violence, robbery, and intimidation. He said that they had knives and guns and they weren't afraid to use them. So when they saw a taxi cab in their neighborhood (which never happens) and a white guy pulling out a nice camera (which also never happens), they decided to jack us.

Frisbee Head

We must have looked as conspicuous as if a helicopter landed in the middle of your street and Donald Trump got out. The driver turned his face around and showed us a big scar that led from his cheek to the side of his mouth. He told us that he'd been carjacked before in his taxi and the robbers pulled a pistol and shot him at close range. The bullet ripped through the side of his mouth and exited his cheek.

Our luck was changing, and indeed the next morning our shiny new visas were ready for us at the Brazilian embassy. We boarded a plane the following morning with our fingers crossed, hoping we were leaving behind the Dynamite-Head brother ad-libbing Queen songs, Hugo Chavez and his nieces, toothpaste on my man-junk, high-speed chases with *ladrones*, cab drivers with bullet scars, the Ciao Line, the Dantean hell of the King's Inn, and butcher knives in back seats forever. But we did remember to pack the Frisbee, just in case we wanted to hit someone else in the head, which was really just our way of saying hello.

Wolf Tickets

Man oh man, just when I think I've seen it all, someone runs game that blows my mind.

I was fortunate — or unfortunate — enough to travel all around the world for a year and witness an unbelievable array of scams. No matter where I went, someone was always selling wolf tickets. From Caracas to Cairo, Angeles City to Amsterdam, the objective was always the same: to graciously part this tourist from his money — but how they went about doing that was a completely different story. Everyone was on the take: drunks on the street, the maids in my hotel rooms, hookers and pimps, taxi drivers, common thugs, little kids, and even the police, and to let my guard down for one second amidst the vociferous chaos of the Third World guaranteed I'd be flying home early with slightly less luggage.

After traveling to almost 40 countries on six continents in my lifetime, I've learned to carry myself with the diligent eye of a paranoid gringo who understands that he's the prey and this is the jungle. I've won some and lost some, but lived to write another day. Here are a few of the most memorable scams I've seen.

The Fake-Drunk Pickpocket:

Pickpockets always operate with the aid of distraction, and one of the best ways to disarm a tourist's defenses, and lift his valuables, is to play the sloppy drunk. Picture yourself in a bar and a person who is shit-faced drunk staggers over and falls all over you. This person is dressed like a bum and smells like shit, so you're worried he's going to puke on you. So you push him away and tell him to get lost. The drunk stumbles out or is removed by security, and by the time the commotion dies down and you go back to your beer, your subconscious registers that something is wrong and you start a mental checklist, patting down your pockets. The realization that you just got conned hits you like a punch in the gut. Your wallet, passport, or camera are missing. How could you be so stupid?

I always carry my wallet in my front pocket because it's harder to grab without me feeling it. Whenever someone intrudes on my physical space, I put one hand on my wallet in my pocket and push the person away with the other hand. This defense applies to drunks, gaggles of punks or hookers, and hot chicks. Still, to this day, even when I'm in America, I reach for my wallet whenever a hot chick starts walking my way, but they usually get it anyway.

The Razor Blade Slash:

Another form of pickpocketing is to slash a tourist's backpack or luggage with a razor blade in passing. On a crowded street, it's easy to give a subtle swipe with a razorblade to open up a gash in a bag without being noticed. It's a two-man job, so the person who does the cutting keeps walking and the other person falls in line behind him and either reaches in to help himself or picks up items as they fall out.

After spending so much time in Third World countries, I've developed a sort of "Spidey Sense" that tingles whenever I feel like a target or I'm in a situation that leaves me easy prey. So on crowded sidewalks or bad areas, I switch my backpack to the front and definitely don't put my wallet, passport, or anything valuable in there. I've even gone so far as to safety-pin my wallet or keys to the inside of my pocket — it's a perfect quick security system. If I'm going into a questionable area I'll put some money under the insole of my shoe in case of emergency.

Beggars:

Beggars are everywhere on the streets of Third World cities. The typical tourist walking by them makes more money in a week than they do in a year, so it's easy to see why they would hold out a dirty hand for alms. The good street worker is an actor who gets dressed up and employs props to effectively convey his role.

Sending children out on the streets to beg is a problem of epidemic proportions in poor countries; the parents know that children will tug on a tourist's heartstrings. In some countries, economic caste systems permanently restrict people's ability to make a living; certain people will be poor for the rest of their lives no matter what they do or how hard they work, as will their children and generations to come. To best prepare their children for this lifelong struggle, parents sometimes injure or cripple their children themselves. Let that sink in. They might scar them with boiling water or acid, or break an appendage and force it to heal impossibly twisted. That gives their children an advantage on the streets as a beggar, and thereby bolsters their chances of making money and eating every day for the rest of their lives. These parents are maiming their own children *and* doing it out of concern for their welfare. We have it so good here it's crazy.

In many international cities, I've found the begging to be so rampant that they're thick as flies. Cairo, Egypt was one such place. First off, Egypt should be way down on your list for places to go. I know, I know … the pyramids. Egypt, and Cairo (Gaza) in particular, is a gigantic shit hole. It's one of the dirtiest, most decrepit, most dangerous places on earth. Every picture of the pyramids shows the vast unspoiled desert as a backdrop, but if you just turned the camera in the opposite direction you'd see a huge slum of shacks, open sewage, garbage everywhere, and burnt-out cars.

The beggars are some of the worst in the world. To be fair, hustling is part of their culture, and they've perfected bartering to an art form. Egyptians haggle over *everything*, and when you're in Egypt it's almost an insult if you don't do the same. I found myself bartering over the price of a pack of gum, both the vendor and I yelling and cussing, waving our arms, making threats against each other's families, faking heart attacks, wishing curses on each other's unborn children, and spending a half-hour making a scene on the street, only to agree on the original price that was quoted, then wishing each *ma'a as-salaama,* God's blessing in Arabic, before hugging, and going our separate ways. It's like that all day.

Everyone demands a tip — *baksheesh* is the Arabic word — for every little thing. The doorman, the security guard, the hotel worker, the taxi driver, the guy who flagged down the taxi, the guy who sold me an apple for one cent, the kids who accompanied me while crossing the street, all wanted my money — it was ridiculous. It got to the point where they'd ask for *baksheesh* for no reason at all — accosting me in such numbers and not getting out of my way so that I couldn't walk down the street unmolested. One guy was such a pain in the ass that I had to pick him up by the shoulders and move him to the side just so I could keep walking.

The Inside Job Theft:

If your hotel room or rental car is burglarized, there's a good chance it was an inside job. Think about how many security guards (who might make $5 a day if they're lucky), cleaning ladies (who work their asses off and make less), or maintenance workers are running around, eyeing you and your stuff, taking note of your comings and goings.

Within a few months of starting our journey in 1999, Shane and I were hit by a maid who stole my silver necklace, and airport workers who opened up our checked bags and helped themselves to his CD player and my new basketball shoes. So what's the best way to combat the "Inside Job" hustle? Be cool with the security guard at your hotel. A lot of tourists don't take the time or effort to recognize and be friendly with the "little" people, so saying wassup and making a security guard feel the love goes a long way, as does bringing him a cold beer at the end of the night, or handing him your leftover pizza, or breaking him off a T-shirt or CD or something you don't really need.

The strategic defense against maids goes a little deeper. Whenever we left our room, we'd leave the TV on loud and the lights on. We called this the "ghetto security system." The things the maid would want to steal — a camera, a laptop, jewelry (don't bring any — I wear a cheap plastic watch abroad), cash, and maybe your passport — can be left in unique hiding places. I leave these things under my mattress, in a bag of dirty laundry that no one would want to go through, behind the bathroom mirror, in the oven or microwave, under a piece of furniture, in a light fixture that can be easily unscrewed, or at the bottom of a box of cereal. The problem then becomes remembering where I hid my stuff!

Deaf Kids:

Have you ever been sitting at a café or on a train and someone comes up to you and hands you a card that says he or she is deaf and needs a donation to go to school or something? This is a common hustle in Third World cities. Another form of this hustle is when an adult has a picture of a sick child and claims to be collecting money for his or her care or a necessary operation — the adult usually even has official paperwork and a signup sheet. The sad thing is that it's all bullshit about 99% of the time, and those hustlers are just good actors. Walk by those "deaf kids" later in the day, and you'll see them cursing and making fun of how stupid tourists are and smoking cigarettes bought with your money.

The Rio Crap on the Shoe Scam:

Some common sense is necessary when traveling as a tourist in Brazil's jewel city, Rio de Janeiro — one of the most dynamic, beautiful, and fun places on earth. But don't dare walk out of the good neighborhoods or anywhere near the *favelas* because you'll end up walking home naked — if you're lucky and not stabbed twenty times within five minutes. Even in Copacabana, the tourist neighborhood right on the beach, there are plenty of hustlers who pick off easy targets — the fat, rich, naïve Americans and Europeans. I was very diligent in looking out for trouble, but one scam in particular was interesting in that it was not technically illegal, yet it was rife with deception.

So you're walking down the street, just minding your own business, when a hot chick with curves that would make a grown man cry walks by you going the other direction. She catches your eye and smiles, and you can't help but turn around and look at the thong as she walks away. Congrats, you've officially been distracted — see how easy it was? When you turn back around, some little Brazilian teenager is in front of you with a wooden shoeshine box. He asks in broken English if you want a shoeshine. Before you can even get your bearings and say "No," he's already on his hands and knees and has the wooden box set up right in front of where you're standing. Of course you protest, because after all, you're wearing sneakers and why the hell would you want a shoeshine, but when you look down you see a big blob of dog shit on your shoe. Gross! How the hell did that get there? You're confused for a second, and that gives the guy just enough time to pick your shoe up and put it on his case and start cleaning before you can even say no again. He quickly wipes off the crap with a rag, and then proceeds to take out some cleaners that he sprays on and shines your sneaks for a couple minutes. You're not too comfortable with it, but he got the crap off and he's almost done by this time.

He finishes the shoeshine show with a snap of his rags and then stands up and demands to be paid. You inquire how much it is, thinking maybe he'll ask for $1 USD, but he informs you very seriously that it's $40. What the hell? When you start to protest he turns his wooden box around, and sure enough, there is a sign that says $40 for a shoeshine. You're pissed, but don't want any trouble and just want to get him out of your face, so you throw him $10 or $20 or whatever you have and get out of there. Think about it: You got hustled, but he didn't do anything illegal, and he made $20 cash in three minutes.

So how does it work? It's a three-person operation — one of them being … drum roll, please … the hot chick in the thong. The second guy is walking a few feet behind you to the side, out of sight. When he sees you turn to look at the girl, he walks by and flings a substance at your shoe with a little slingshot. His accuracy is amazing from years of practice. The dog shit is actually a brown gel. I'm not sure what they use, but from eye level, it looks pretty real.

Gypsies:

If you've never seen a Gypsy up close in person and didn't get robbed then consider yourself fortunate, because they're the most conniving, hustling people on earth. Gypsies are a lost tribe of migrant shucksters with no home, no nationality, no official identity, and definitely no jobs, but damn, they are good at thievery! I would love to spend a year with a Gypsy troupe, traveling around and documenting their various ploys, except that even if I survived it, I'd end up missing my computer, my notebook, my pen, and probably my sneakers.

All over Europe you see Gypsies in the shadows of your periphery — wearing dirty rags and with features so dark that it's hard to see their faces, like trying to read a black map. They love train stations, buses, subways, and markets, anyplace there is a throng of people and enough commotion for them to hit and run. They're as fast as greased lightning from spending a lifetime perfecting the mechanics of their trade. Gypsies work in packs, creating chaos and then swooping in from all angles to strip someone of his possessions before he knows what's happened.

I was in a busy train station in Italy and saw a pack of these hawk-featured, dirt-covered Gypsies walking around. They couldn't have been older than young teenagers, but one girl carried a baby of her own hidden from view, wrapped in rags, and cradled in her arms. Every once in a while she talked to it, touching its nose and rocking it back and forth. Then the girl casually walked up to a gentleman tourist with an expensive camera around his neck and … threw the baby right at him! I couldn't believe what I was seeing. The girl just tossed her baby in its bundle of rags right up at the guy's face. The tourist was in shock and his natural reaction was to lift his arms to catch the poor babe. He didn't catch it cleanly, and to my horror, it fell to the ground and landed hard on the concrete floor. In the split second he lifted his arms, the Gypsy children swooped in, creating confusion as they circled him with their hands all over. It took him a moment to collect his wits and push them away and start yelling at them, but by then the Gypsies had run off, disappearing into the crowd outside, all of this choreographed with amazing accuracy.

The tourist was stunned, as were all of us around him, that these kids had just thrown a baby in the air and let it hit the floor with a thud, and then had run away. A lady went over to check the baby to see if it was OK, but when she opened up the rags, she discovered a baby-sized piece of firewood wrapped in a blanket. Then the tourist realized his camera and wallet were gone.

The Fake Ticket Gambit:

This is popular on trains and buses, and I got taken by this scam when I was riding a rail car from Cairo down to Aswan in Egypt near the Sudanese border. Basically, you're sold a phony ticket and when you get on the train and find your seat, you see that someone else is sitting there. You cross-reference the seat numbers and realize you both were sold duplicate tickets. There's no way to figure out which one is real and which one is fake, and you don't have time to run back to the ticket counter and you'd both have to be present to make your argument, even if they gave a shit.

When this happened to me, I was sitting in a seat and an American college kid walked up to me looking confused and told me I was in his seat. We checked and realized we had both been sold the same ticket. Luckily, there was a seat free so we both got to sit during the four-hour train ride. Coincidentally, he was a freshman at Yale University in New Haven, Connecticut — my hometown and where my mom works. Small world! Cameron and I became friends and traveled all over Egypt together, taking a felucca — a small, open-deck sailboat — back up the Nile from Aswan to Luxor. He kept in touch once he got back to New Haven, and my mom made him a few home-cooked dinners.

The Double Credit Card Receipt Hoax:

One night in Rio, I was in a strip club and used my credit card to pay for a couple of rounds of drinks for Shane and me (and no, there weren't a hundred separate one-dollar charges). The credit card slip came; I signed it; they took it back; I got the receipt; and I thought nothing more of it. From Rio, we had a few travel days that found us in the Philippines a week later. This was before the advent of easy online banking, so the only way you could check your balance was to get a receipt from an ATM. That was an inexact process at best because charges from other countries and banks often didn't show immediately, and I had to apply the exchange rate to convert my balances from the local currency. So the Brazilian *real* might be 3.4 to 1 American dollar in Rio, but the Filipino *peso* might be 29.4 to 1. Those mental gymnastics made it hard to track exactly how much money I had at any given time.

It was a week later by the time I figured out that my bank account had been raided, and I was horrified to see my balance had gone from $7,000 to $500. The next four days were spent arguing over international calls to my bank, filing a complaint, and trying to figure out what happened. The bank came back after investigating with some interesting evidence — there was a $6,500 charge that had been made to an Italian furniture company and a receipt with my signature on it to back it up. I was pretty damn sure I hadn't bought 6K worth of Italian furniture in the last week, nor had I been in Italy — I might have remembered that. To their credit, the bank returned every single dollar of my stolen money — thank god, or my travels would have been cut short by six months. Someone had run my card twice and then doubled up the receipts when I signed, so my signature imprint came through clearly.

Beware of Taxi Drivers:

In most Third World countries taxi drivers can't live on their legitimate wages alone, so they "get things" for tourists: weed, coke, heroin, or a prostitute, for the right price. They also act as "touts" who get paid kickbacks from clubs, casinos, restaurants, massage parlors, and brothels to suggest their place of business and deliver a customer to their door. It's best to use the official taxis that are registered and licensed (there are a lot of gypsy cabs or guerilla cabs who drive people around in their own cars and undercut the legit taxis' pricing). Whenever I jump into a cab, I befriend the driver by asking him his name, where he lives, about his family, and I joke around with him so he feels genuine interest and respect.

Don't Ever Use a Money Exchange Guy on the Street:

I don't know where the scam is here, but I have enough intuition to know that it's better to walk into a bank so you don't get duped.

The "Order Up" Sting:

This is a scam where an attractive lady conveniently bumps into a male tourist walking down the street and strikes up a casual conversation. She feigns interest and eventually invites the over-eager gentleman to a disco or a restaurant. He thinks it's his lucky day and when they get there, she orders food and booze liberally. The whole time his eye is on the prize: getting her back to the hotel, and she alludes that she is on board with this. But when the bill comes it's outrageously expensive, and there's nothing he can do but pay it if he doesn't want to be hauled off by the police. Needless to say, the gal and the restaurant are in on it.

Yes, something like this happened to me. I was in China — far from home, in wintery Beijing — walking down the street, when I met a beautiful local gal who was going to a dance club to hang out with her friends. She invited me along and seemed all warm and fuzzy, so I accepted. We went into the dark club with a labyrinth of hallways and music blaring, and the maître d' was nice enough to seat us in a private VIP room with leather circular couches. It was an elegant setup, and the waiter brought us Chinese beers, shots of a liqueur, and a huge platter of fruit and meats and cheeses. Her friends were nowhere to be seen, and once the platter came in I knew I was being hustled. I asked for a menu several times so I could look at the prices, but no one would bring one. I smelled a rat, but played it cool. The waiter and the maître d' were hovering, and the chick kept ordering more drinks.

When a waiter came in the door, I glimpsed some beefy, crazy-looking dudes in shirts and ties with dragon tattoos on their necks standing around outside in the hallway. Oh shit, those guys were Triads, Chinese mobsters who were known for breaking people's ankles and having their vicious dogs chew off ears for fun. I realized that there were about ten guys and five walls in between me and freedom. Who knew how much the bill would come to — $500? $1,000? Of course, I didn't have that money on me, but I had a feeling they would happily take my credit card or even accompany me to the ATM.

My heart was racing, but I played stupid (which I am surprisingly good at) and pretended to get real loose and buzzed. I still had surprise on my side if they didn't know that I was on to them. I asked where the bathroom was and made sure to seem loosey-goosey when I got up, and purposely left my fleece jacket on the couch with the girl. They didn't think much of it because I left my jacket and seemed eager to come back and drink more and socialize with the girl, so the waiter opened the door and pointed to a bathroom down the hall, deeper in the club. I slapped him on the shoulder, thanked him, and pretended to get the directions wrong and stumbled down the hall toward the front door, pointing to a side closet and asking if that was the bathroom, like I made an honest mistake. The waiter and the maître d' immediately raised their voices to try and usher me back in the right direction, but by then I had a step on them. I dropped my beer bottle and walked fast for the front door. Out of the corner of my eye, I saw the goons come to life and start moving quickly toward me, but once I hit the front door I sprinted down the street and never looked back.

The "I Lost My Passport" Con:

If a distressed family or an old lady comes up to you, dressed respectfully and speaking good English, and claims that they were robbed and lost their passports and need a few bucks for a hotel and a call to the embassy, tell them to fuck off.

Don't Be the Ugly American:

This isn't a scam but a warning. Don't get too drunk — you'll look like a buffoon and make an easy target. Always make a couple of local friends. Before you leave the bar, put all of your jewelry and your watch in your front pocket, or even better, don't wear any. Put your wallet in your sock or in your front pocket, too. Don't take open drinks from someone because it's way too easy to get roofied. Don't pull out a wad of cash — ever. Have some small bills split up in different places on your person and the real money under the insole of your shoe.

And basically, just don't be a disrespectful asshole when you're in another country — be conscious of who you are and where you are at all times. Always be like Fonzie: Keep your cool. Show respect and you'll get respect. Let the people know that you're watching them watching you. And if in doubt, run.

The Shifting Wall Trick:

This ploy usually happens in a spa, massage parlor, strip club, or place where the tourist is getting comfortable and undressed. In any of those places, the tourist will be brought into a private room where his clothes, wallet, passport, watch, etc. are taken off and placed neatly nearby or in a locker. At some point, a secret panel in the wall shifts open silently and someone reaches in and steals those valuables. This trick can be run in numerous ways — I've even seen false openings under bleachers or seats where tourists place their belongings on the ground. If you are lucky they just take your stuff, because I've heard of a tourist who thought he was in a safe, locked room in a massage parlor, but then a couple of guys came in and beat the shit out of him before robbing him.

The Policia Drug Bust Racket:

Of all the places I've been, of all the trouble I've gotten into, this was by far the most elaborate and slick hustle; it was high theater, and I fell for it hook, line, and sinker.

Shane and I were traveling through Bolivia and we made our way out to an island in the middle of Lake Titicaca (on a side note, you should really check it out — it's 15 times larger and at twice the altitude as Lake Tahoe and stunningly beautiful). We took a bus back into La Paz, the main city, and arrived dirty and tired, but happy we took the trip. We walked out onto the parking lot with our bags and flagged down a cab. We threw our bags in the trunk but kept our backpacks with us because they contained our money, passports, and cameras, then jumped into the back seat.

The taxi driver pulled off slowly through the busy parking lot. He was really friendly and asked about our trip and how we liked his country. Before we got out onto the street, he stopped for another tourist and talked to him for a second. The guy was a tourist from Chile, a young, clean-cut man in his 20s who was an architecture student on break, and heading in the same direction as our hotel. The fare to get downtown was sizable, so when the driver asked if it was cool if this guy jumped in and split the taxi fare with us we agreed.

The tourist thanked us and got in the front seat, and we made small talk about where to go and what to do in La Paz as we all drove down the main street that led away from the bus station. A couple of blocks down, there was a police car on the side of the road and two officers flagged us down. The taxi driver complied and pulled over, but seemed pretty scared of the cops. They came over and flashed their badges and identification and started questioning the cab driver, and then told us in broken English that they were drug enforcement officers looking for drugs that were reportedly being trafficked through the bus station. The police officers told everyone to put their hands on the seat in front of them or on the dashboard and not to move.

I was getting nervous because I'd heard horror stories about corrupt cops in Third World countries, but of course we had nothing on us, so I was confident it would get cleared up. They asked everyone in the taxi if they could search our backpacks and we all handed them over. The officer carefully went through everything and then it happened — they found a bundle of drugs in the bag of the guy in the front seat. Fuck! It was a package wrapped in plastic with duct tape around the center so it was hard to see what was inside, but I presumed it was coke, and there was a lot of it.

The cops' demeanors changed and they yelled for us to keep our hands up. They searched everything else and started grilling the Chilean traveler. After a few minutes they pulled him out of the car, cuffed him, and threw him in the back seat of their police car. One officer sat in his place in the front seat and started questioning us. He asked us why we were involved with trafficking drugs in Bolivia and who our friend was. Of course, we made it clear that we'd just met the guy and had nothing to do with any of it, but the cop seemed skeptical. He said if he arrested us we'd be thrown into a dangerous city jail, and with that amount of drugs we could get 20 years in prison. My adrenaline was pumping and I started to feel panicked as I envisioned what would happen to a gringo in a sketchy Bolivian prison. We pleaded with the guy that we had nothing to do with it, and the taxi driver vouched for us, too. The police officers didn't seem like they were going for it, and it felt like a crapshoot whether we would end up locked up in a hellish Third World prison that night or not. But the cops eventually gave in and said that they would let us go with a warning; however, they did take the taxi driver in for questioning and impounded his car.

The taxi driver looked despondent and apologized to us, but honestly, we just wanted to get the hell out of there. The officer opened our backpacks and showed us each item as he placed our things back in — our wallets, cameras, passports, a notebook, a guidebook, and sweatshirts. Then he zipped them up and handed them back to us and told us we were free to go, which was the sweetest sound I'd heard in a long time. We got out, grabbed our luggage from the trunk, and walked away without looking back. One officer stayed in the taxi and drove off, followed by the police car with the prisoner in the back seat. We were relieved and walked as quickly as possible in the opposite direction and grabbed another taxi for the hotel.

Once I was a safe distance away, adrenaline subsiding, my "Spidey Sense" started going off. Check your bag, I told Shane. We rifled through our backpacks and both yelled out in unison. We'd been robbed. Our wallets with all of our money, our cameras, and a nice Walkman from Shane's bag were missing. My pride sank into my stomach as I realized that we'd fallen victims to a grand hoax. The taxi driver was in on the take, the tourist who was a drug trafficker was fake, the bundle of coke was fake, and they were fake cops in a fake car. It was all a carefully choreographed production, and somehow the cop had dropped our items on the floor in the front seat as he pretended to place them back in our backpacks. We had been so scared and had wanted to get out of there so badly that we didn't even question him or go through our bags on the spot; our primal instinct was just to get the hell out of there, and that worked right into their sleight-of-hand ploy.

By the time we got back to the hotel, managed to explain what happened, and placed calls to our U.S. banks to put a hold on our cards, they'd already racked up a bunch of charges. The real police came and confirmed that it was all a bullshit hustle. They took us to the real police station to file a report, and we had to look through about a hundred pages of mug shots. We recognized one of the guys who played the main police officer, and the police said that he was a really bad dude who was wanted for murder, as well as other similar thefts. More than any other scam I've experienced, I felt completely mentally violated by this one, and we had to hit the club and go through a bottle of Jack that night just to feel right with the world again. Game recognize game, I guess.

Mamani Mamani

Peru, August 1999

There's a painting by a Bolivian artist that captures exactly how it feels to be in the mountains in South America. His name is Roberto Mamani Mamani and he's Aymaran, an indigenous tribe of Incas who dwell in modern-day Bolivia, Chile, and Peru. His paintings are simple and yet it's hard to look away from the dazzling colors and symbols of suns, moons, mountains, mothers, and birds; all of the elements of Inca lore that almost whisper a secret of the world from the canvas.

In my favorite painting of his, the pregnant sun takes up most of the sky, almost meeting the earth. The mountains look like they are melting more than trying to climb the sky, curving gently like the lines of a woman ready to be sketched. Nestled into the crux of the mountains is a grouping of little houses with blue and green and orange roofs, a village whose insignificance relative to the rest of the universe is apparent. And then there's a cathedral, with two rounded bell towers adjoining the grand sanctuary, built by the hands of the Spanish, who came to colonize the Incas with intentions of building an empire that rivaled the sun and the mountains, but failed.

That is how I felt when I was in the Andes mountains. The "Spine of South America" runs over 4,000 miles, the world's largest continuous mountain range, and reaches heights of 22,000 feet above sea level, dropping precipitously to the Pacific Ocean off the western coast. For those of you who've never been subjected to high altitude, it plays tricks with your brain in weird ways. There is no experience quite like walking along the cobble-stoned streets of colonial cities like Quito, Ecuador; La Paz, Bolivia; or Cusco in Peru, all of which rest at 10,000 feet or higher in the Andes. To put it in perspective, most of them are twice as high as Denver, Colorado — the Mile-High City. You perpetually feel lightheaded, with a slight twinge of a headache at the back of your skull. Even normal activities like walking up a flight of steps or a slight incline leaves you gasping for breath, and the air is so dry and thin with oxygen that it could take hours to recover. You always feel a little dizzy, like you're suffering from an afternoon hangover after swilling ten mimosas with cheap champagne for brunch. Everyone moves slowly, gliding along as if in a dream, but that's cool because you also feel that there's nowhere more important you're supposed to be. It's either cold or hot outside, or both at the same time, and either way it feels like a blessing, not an inconvenience.

After a few days at 10,000 feet I start getting used to it. I've even lived in a city that high for a few months and loved it. Drinking a few beers actually makes you feel better, like it levels out the delicious vertigo. But any higher than that and my brain starts to disconnect and misfire, and begins to resemble scrambled eggs.

I've climbed a couple of 14'ers in Colorado (the series of 14,000-foot-high mountains called the Collegiate Peaks) and done OK, but when I tried to ascend Mount Cotopaxi in Ecuador, setting out from the base camp lodge at 2 a.m. with crampons and an ice axe, along with fifteen other climbers, my mind just didn't work right. By the time I hit 17,000 feet my consciousness was fading in and out and I saw flashes of light. It became hard to string a series of rational thoughts together. When I forgot who I had come there with the day before, I knew it was time to turn around and head back to the base camp. I felt like a failure until I saw that only five of our original fifteen climbers reached the summit.

But when I was in Cusco, the gateway to the hike to Machu Picchu in Peru, sitting at 11,000 feet I felt like I was in that Mamani Mamani painting. Everyone comes to Cusco for a week or so to acclimate to the altitude, gear up, and hire porters. From there, they head out on the Caminar Inca — the Inca Trail, an improbably windy path through the mountains to the hidden plateau of Machu Picchu.

In Cusco, I was transported to a dream world somewhere in between heaven and earth. It's an enchanting pre-colonial town that crowns the Andes mountains and was settled and fortified by the Incas in the 13th century. I absolutely loved the vibe — everything centered around a big park, the Plaza de Armas, that was lined by internet cafés, bars full of Peruvian students and travelers, discos hidden in alleys, tourist shops, hostels advertising free tea, and grand Spanish-era churches. At night friends met in the park and drank hot chocolate with booze in it, shivering against the mountain cold and sitting on park benches, staring longingly at the thick stars, which seem close enough to touch.

As I walked along the city walls, I ran my hand over the gigantic twelve-sided keystones that still held as strong as when they were placed 700 years ago. Everything appeared to be at a slight angle — whether that was truly the case or I was just feeling a twinge of vertigo from the altitude was hard to determine because there were no straight lines on the horizon to compare it to, so I felt like I was pitching on the waves of a submarine under the sea. Walking up and down cobblestone streets and stone steps all day made my calves ache, so I stopped often to collect my breath and feel the sun on my face.

During the days, Shane and I suffered through full-court basketball games at the local high school, which felt like running with mud in my lungs. In the afternoons, we hit a bar with an old motorcycle theme in the north corner of the Plaza Armas called Norton Rats, where Shane's uncle knew the ex-pat owner and we could play pool and listen to the Rolling Stones with a couple of pints. Or we'd sit outside on the balcony of the bar and watch the town folk sell flowers on the steps of the Church of La Compañía as an old man played a wooden flute. There were good, cheap restaurants in abundance, so I tried every local dish I could, even eating alpaca and guinea pig, though most of the food was a variation of their staples: sweet potatoes and corn.

The young women were strikingly beautiful, with hair black as spilled ink and sultry vampire eyes. The younger generation is Americanized, working in tourism and aspiring to go to college, but their parents are from a different era. The Quechua, a term encompassing a few of the indigenous ethnic groups in South America, still dress in the traditional garb. Men wear wool waistcoats and red ponchos and woven hats with earflaps, called *chullos*, even when it is warm. The women wear bright wool dresses and bola coats decorated with beads, and on their heads bowler hats that were brought into fashion by the British rail workers in the 1920s and never left. Most of the time, people just wear *ajotas*, flimsy sandals crafted from recycled tires.

The indigenous people of Peru and the surrounding countries of Bolivia and Ecuador are dirt-poor, living off the land in small, rural pockets. The post-Colombian-era tribes were so scattered among isolated mountain communities that until recently there'd never been a need for a common identity or even a language they could share. Some would call them simple and passive, but I would describe them as peaceful, and so spiritual that they are blissfully resigned. Still, life is hard for them; most survive through manual labor and tough agricultural jobs, and their life expectancy is short. Their daily life still holds tokens of ancient mysticism and superstition, like drying the carcasses of goats or small game and hanging them up as talismans to ward off bad luck. They've borne the brunt of not only conquest by the Spanish but discrimination and a lack of rights in modern-day Peru, where the education, health care, and economic systems have marginalized them, often to a boiling point, inspiring protests.

After five days in Cusco, Shane and I began our preparations to walk the Caminar Inca, the 88-kilometer (55-mile) roller coaster of a mountain path leading to Machu Picchu. We visited one of the ubiquitous travel agencies that lined the Plaza de Armas and sat down with a bilingual college kid to coordinate our trip. Most tourists spent a lot of money to ensure their comfort on the walk, but if you haven't figured it out by now, Shane and I weren't like most tourists. The Peruvian guy working at the guide shop briefed us on what we would need for the trip: a guide to lead us; porters to carry all of our food, water, and equipment; a stock of carefully planned rations and drinking water; cold-weather and waterproof gear; tents and sleeping bags; and very good hiking boots. That all sounded way too easy — and expensive. We decided to embark on the journey with no guide, no porters, and only our jeans, sweatshirts, and thin jackets to keep us warm. Our waterproof gear included a plastic tarp and garbage bags. We did buy llama hair mittens and hats, and rented huge backpacks that we filled with a tent, sleeping bags, a bunch of canned goods, a few potatoes and candy bars, and jugs of drinking water. My hiking boots were just my brown dress shoes, which had a decent grip on the bottom and doubled as my fancy dancing shoes on the trip. The guy at the guide shop looked at us like we were crazy, and we soon found out why: He was right.

Our last night in town, we kicked it at a local disco and met some really cool Peruvian dudes. They loved that we were heading out to the Inca Trail without the creature comforts that the other pampered tourists enjoyed. We laughed and sang and filled our glasses with beer from pitchers that came to our table faster than we could drink them. Each time, they made us go through the ritual of pouring a little beer onto the floor to bless the name of the Mother Earth in Inca lore, Pachamama. As we grew quite drunk, one of the guys grew sentimental for his traditional Inca ways. He took off his necklace, a braided rope made of llama hide and leather and adorned with green stones, and placed it around my neck. He told us that there was magic in the mountains, and this necklace would give us good luck and help the spirits protect us on our journey. Nice gesture, but I wish he had given me toilet paper instead.

The Incas, or the Quechua, as their culture and language are now called, are spiritual people who believe in reincarnation and have a whole pantheon of gods to appease. They consider this life a temporary passage to a better existence, so it's important to live by the Incan moral code: "Do not steal, do not lie, do not be lazy." It's important that they don't die by fire, nor that their body is burned, because this will prevent their spirit from being free. Their *camaquen*, or dead spirit, needs to follow a long, dark road in the afterlife with the help of a black dog to see the way. Only then will they reach their heaven — fields of blooming flowers and snow-capped mountains as far as the eye can see.

But their theology isn't all warm and fuzzy; the noble and elite in ancient Inca cultures practiced cranial deformation, wrapping tight cloth straps around infants' heads. Their soft skulls molded to the wrappings and left them conical-shaped, signaling nobility and wealth. It's well documented that the Incas engaged in human sacrifice, especially with children, to appease the gods during important events like the death of an emperor or a famine. They chose children who were healthy and fattened them up for months before walking them up to ritual sites high in the mountains. The children were dressed with ornate jewelry and costumes and given a special drink, probably containing coca leaves, to anesthetize them to the fear and pain. The high priests sacrificed them either by strangulation, hitting them on the head, or leaving them on the mountaintop to die of cold and exposure.

The next morning, Shane and I took a train to a village on the trailhead along the Urubamba River, strapped on our packs, and started the trek up the hillside and out of sight of the village. Looking back at my pictures from the beginning of that adventure, I see myself bright-eyed and bushy-tailed, clean-shaven and smiling, as I began a nice stroll up a mountain. The "after" pictures looked way different.

The four-day trip on the Inca Trail started at the ruins of Patallacta at 9,200 feet and climbed steadily by the side of the Rio Cusichca, or Happy River. It's hard to say how many other people were with us on the trail at the same time because everyone was stretched out in a single-file line, but there were probably 50 tourists and 50 porters in our little caravan. The hike was no problem on its own; I was in good shape and acclimated to the altitude, but I underestimated how much our backpacks would weigh. It added up quickly as we threw in clothes and supplies for a fire and a tent, and especially when we put cans of food and water in there (water weighs 75 pounds per cubic foot). We had to bring enough for four days because there was no place on the trail to collect safe drinking water and every stream, river, and lake could be tainted with animal feces. My pack probably weighed 90 pounds on the first day, and walking up the hills felt like giving a petite lady a piggyback ride, which I'd rather be doing than carrying my own backpack. We were the only tourists carrying our own gear and the porters were somewhat puzzled by us.

The porters blew right past us, gliding up the steep mountain effortlessly, even though they balanced impossibly huge loads on their backs, making them look like figures in a Diego Rivera painting. The weight of their bundles bent them parallel to the trail on the way up. Each evening when we arrived at the campsite after a hard day of hiking, the tourists were met with perfectly erected tents, sleeping bags laid out, clean water, bottles of red wine, and a great meal of meat and vegetable stew already cooking over the campfire. They only had to carry a daypack with a small bottle of water and their camera up the trail.

When Shane and I showed up, dog-tired, we still had to go through the long process of trying to find a flat spot that wasn't too rocky, throwing up our ratty tent, scavenging the alpine landscape for some dry wood, moss, or bark to start a fire, and getting a paltry dinner started. Still, we wouldn't have wanted it any other way — we were giving props by doing it old school, earning our journey to Machu Picchu and paying respect to the mountain, the culture, and Pachamama. The porters began to acknowledge our journey and even treat us with growing respect. It was a mutual admiration society because they amazed me; these guys were barely five feet tall, carrying packs that easily weighed as much as they did, and yet they just flew up the mountain. They were super-athletes, and legends circulated about a yearly race where porters set out over a 40-mile course in the hardest terrain with only sandals and a couple of oranges, which they run in marathon time. They were born in the thin air and knew nothing else their whole lives, so their lungs and pulmonary functions adjusted to the altitude, but they also had a little help: They shared their coca leaves with Shane and me.

In Inca culture, coca is considered sacred and possesses magical qualities. They've used it forever for medicine, religious purposes, and also to lessen hunger and pain if they're working in the fields or going on a long journey. The coca plant looks like a blackthorn bush, and is about 7-10 feet high with small green fruit. It's harvested for its alkaloids, one of which is converted to powder form and called cocaine. Needless to say, it's a pivotal plant in South America for several reasons, but the porters took the leaves whole and rolled them into a black tar-like gum that they chewed on and spit out the juice. The gum was bicarbonate that acted like a catalyst to release the narcotic qualities of the leaf. They used it for a little pick-me-up from time to time on the Inca Trail, as well as drinking it in tea form, called *mate de coca*. They were nice enough to share a little with us because we were carrying our own bags, and indeed, it almost instantly alleviated any feelings of fatigue or altitude sickness we felt.

On day two of the Caminar Inca, we walked through the village of Wayllabamba, where the path joined the Mollepata Trail. The village consists of only 300 people who live in tiny stone shacks with thatched roofs. Kids ran around smiling and waving at the hikers as their mothers made maize cakes with a mortar and stews out of small game over outdoor fires. Llamas and donkeys milled about, tied to a tree.

Once we left the village, the trail went west along the tributary to the Cusichca River and then rose to an impossibly steep climb up the Warmiwañusca, or Dead Woman's Pass, cresting at 13,829 feet. The vistas were breathtaking, passing in and out of cloud forests, switchbacks where you could see a panorama of the mountains and valleys below you, dense thickets of jungle with birds buzzing around, and occasionally grassy plains where the Incas practiced steppe agriculture to grow potatoes, yams, and maize.

It's right there that I learned the most basic lesson of supply and demand. They should use this example on the first day of every Economics 101 class. All about the trail there were indigenous women who hiked along to sell water and candy bars to the tourists. Of course, everything had to be hand-carried, so those items were at a premium if you were running low. I came to find out that I could have just packed my bag with Snickers bars, and that would have supplied me with enough calories and protein for the trip but still been light enough to transport. I was at the bottom of Dead Woman's Pass, readjusting my pack and getting ready for the two-hour intense climb, when a lady who was selling her stuff walked by me. I bought a bottle of water from her for $1, thanked her, and fell in line to trek up the steep pass. Everyone was sweaty and exhausted by the time we reached the top. A parched tourist asked the same lady for a bottle of water and she charged him $3, which he gladly forked over. One dollar at the bottom; $3 at the top — a perfect demonstration of value being dictated by supply and demand.

The ascent of Dead Woman's Pass was brutal and most of the tourists, who didn't even have to carry any weight, fell by the side of the path to rest, panting like dogs in the sun. Shane and I managed to get up in great time by being steady — putting one foot in front of the other slowly, but without stopping to take breaks.

Unfortunately, I got stuck behind a donkey the whole way up. When you're in a single-file line, it's very important who's in front of you because you don't want to be trapped behind an annoying chatty tourist, a fat lady who stops all the time, or a pack animal. I had a nice view of the donkey's ass the whole way up and had to bear the olfactory brunt of its mid-walk bathroom breaks.

Once we rose and fell from Dead Woman's Pass, we came to a valley at Pacaymayo, where the river drained. The campground was a field of soggy moss teeming with mosquitos and pools of water. The porters had already claimed the good spots for their clients, so the only place left was on the outskirts, right next to a huge bull with big horns grazing in the grass beside us. He wasn't tied up, so the whole time we set up our tent and made a fire we kept one eye on him in case he decided to charge. He made a lot of noise, but didn't disturb us.

It's there that I ate the mashed potatoes that got me sick. I knew that's what it was because Shane and I had eaten exactly the same things on the journey except for the instant mashed potatoes I cooked up. I knew the water in the swamp would be bad news, but I boiled it over the cooking fire before I put the potatoes in and chowed down. It must not have killed all of the microorganisms because by morning time, I was ill.

I can think of 4,327,499 things that are more fun than contracting giardia lamblia — a protozoa that contaminates water in low areas where grazing occurs — including being audited by the IRS and getting tied to an anthill naked and covered in honey. When we set out on the trail again that morning, I knew I felt like shit and was blowing up the little outhouse bathroom at the campground, but I had no idea how sick I would become. I put on my backpack, which now felt like it weighed a ton, and as we hit the trail I got worse. Every fifteen minutes I had to run off the side of the path and get violently ill. There is no comfortable, convenient place to go to the bathroom on the side of a mountain path; I'll spare you the gory details, but I was so sick that I was getting scared and seriously dehydrated. I tried to keep down as much water as I could, but my body was being ravaged by the hour.

Think about the worst food poisoning you've ever had; then strap a 90-pound pack on your back at 12,000 feet walking uphill, with no toilet and no running water, and you'll get an inkling of what I was dealing with. I got sick all day, and soon I had gone through my roll of toilet paper and also Shane's. I had to use my extra T-shirt, a bandana, then my boxer shorts, then each mitten, each sock, and then tufts of leaves and grass as toilet paper as the day went on.

There was no one who could help me, and it didn't make sense to turn back because we were more than halfway there. Even if we could get word to a hospital, we were so high up in the mountains that I would have to be airlifted out by helicopter. I trudged on, my eyes sunken and my face completely devoid of any color, a zombie falling one foot forward up the trail. No one wanted to be near me in case I started spontaneously vomiting, or worse, and even the smelly donkey kept his distance. Shane was great as usual, offering to carry more of my stuff and sharing as much of his water as he could, but I was pretty sure I wasn't going to make it. I was facing death by diarrhea, an exit so inglorious that you wouldn't even wish it on your enemies. I was racked with fever and delirious with dehydration. I started hearing a haunting voice in my brain: "Don't go toward the light, Norm. Stay away from the light!" *Grandma — is that you?* Or maybe I would see the black dog soon, the one who was supposed to guide me along the dark road to the afterlife. But all I saw in front of me on the path was the ass end of a fat newlywed couple from San Antonio who kept complaining that the food wasn't as good as at Sizzler.

In the midst of all my misery, I managed to lift my head to see some beautiful views. We'd trekked out the other side of the valley up to 12,300 feet by Cochapata Lake, where deer drank and thousands of yellow butterflies fluttered about. In the afternoon we passed the ruins of Phuyupatamarca, the cloud-level town, and had to climb an almost-vertical bluff of 1,500 stone steps. Mist rose from the valley below and shrouded the mountains. It was exhausting, and I have no idea how I got through it, except that my only alternative was just to lie down on the side of the trail and die of exposure like a child being sacrificed to the gods.

And then we were in Machu Picchu, the ruins of an ancient citadel built in the 1400s for the Incan emperor Pachacuti, whom the Incas revered as the child of the sun god, Inti. He and his son, Tupac, the heir to the crown, ruled the vast Inca Empire from this estate. It was built on a narrow plateau with a dramatic drop-off on every side, completely inaccessible except for one winding mountain path: the Inca Trail. The inhospitable topography provided a perfect natural fortress for the emperor and his estate. The city of 140 structures was divided into upper and lower portions, separated for urban and agricultural usage. They had temples, sanctuaries, residences, stables, storehouses, guard towers, and public baths. The water system was an incredibly well-designed series of channels and fountains that supplied drinking water, water for people and animals to bathe, and irrigation for agriculture to the entire complex, all fed by rain water.

Most of the structures had been built with grass-thatched roofs, so only the walls remained 600 years later. They were built with huge stones carved out of the surrounding mountains and placed together so adeptly that they didn't need mortar, adjoined with such mathematical precision that in most places you can't even fit a blade of grass between the seams in the rocks. Like Stonehenge and the pyramids in Egypt, historians and archeologists are still dumbfounded about how the ancient Incas transported the stones to their current location. And just like those sites, every stone in Machu Picchu was placed with religious significance, the ritual stones lining up with key astronomical points in the night sky.

But the empire's use of Machu Picchu was short-lived. Only a hundred years later, as the Spanish began their brutal conquest of South America, the city lay virtually abandoned. Some people say it was vacated because they didn't want the Spanish to discover it, but a terrible smallpox epidemic probably did more to wipe out the population. The jungle overtook the city and it lay dormant and completely unknown to the outside world until 1911, when an eleven-year-old local Quechua boy guided a Western researcher named Hiram Bingham to the ruins.

I could sympathize with the Incas who had died from smallpox. It was an empty victory to have reached our destination, and I tried my best to walk around and get the full effect of the different parts of the ruins, but I had no energy. I lay down on the grass next to a stone wall, too weak and sick to even sleep, and put my hat over my eyes and just focused on my breathing. The tourists hopped around, gleefully snapping pictures and purchasing postcards and trinkets. A couple of shiny new tour buses pulled up an access road I hadn't seen and unloaded the richest and fattest of the gringo tourists. I was shocked — I hadn't realized you could arrive at the ruins by bus without hiking at all. I resented them instantly; I had earned it and suffered and they just took a three-hour bus ride from their hotel and they were there, too. They had thousand-dollar Gortex jackets and hiking boots with metal ski poles to help them walk the fifty meters from the parking lot. The Japanese each wore three $1,000 cameras around their necks and set up tripods to snap pictures of their countrymen at every possible angle, including with me passed out and looking like death warmed over in the background. They thought my lifeless form was part of Machu Picchu, a semi-human remnant of the ancient Inca civilization who was petrified and grown over with moss.

Shane was feeling like a million bucks so he strolled around and enjoyed the well-earned view, but I was firmly planted in my misery. As the tourists stepped around me, I gave them dirty looks and asked for donations of toilet paper. But at least there was something that resembled an indoor bathroom there, though they still had no toilet paper. At that point, I had completely left my pride, as well as half my small intestine, on the mountain trail, so after going to the bathroom yet again, I snaked a hose that was attached outside the bathroom through the window and stripped down and cleaned myself that way. Once I had returned to my position sprawled out on the grass, feeling like I was about to be outlined in chalk, Shane came to check on me. I lied and told him that I was hanging in there, and that I had used the "ghetto bidet" instead of toilet paper. When I explained to him that it was just a gardener's hose through the bathroom window, he laughed so hard that he fell on the ground and actually chipped his tooth on a rock.

All of the hikers from our caravan took a bus down to the village and hopped on a train back toward Cusco. I was still sick, running into every bathroom I could find, but it had slowed down because I was so dangerously dehydrated. I don't even remember getting back to Cusco or getting in my hotel bed, but I came to consciousness a day later. Shane found me some antibiotics to try and kill the parasites, and I spent the next several days in bed, sleeping and recovering on

Gatorade and ice cream bars. I only emerged when Shane dragged me out of the hotel because he needed a wingman on a date with a couple of Peruvian hotties. I remember being in the disco with them and still having a fever and barely being able to keep from passing out. I'm frighteningly thin in the pictures we took that night, the bones in my face and tendons in my neck protruding against my sagging skin. I think I lost about 25 pounds in the ordeal, getting pretty close to my original birth weight. Looking back, I definitely should have been hospitalized, but when you're young you think you're invincible, and you exercise little caution and make stupid-ass decisions. Story of my life. Still, I loved Cusco and I want to go back some day, under better circumstances, to sip cinnamon-spiced rum under strands of white lights on the trees in the Plaza Armas, and pour some out to honor the earth mother Pachamama. I want to feel, again, like I was created by oil and brush amongst red mountains, living in a painting by Mamani Mamani, and visit the ruins of Machu Picchu. But yeah, next time I'm hiring like 10 porters and having a helicopter filled with toilet paper on standby.

The Helicopter Brothers
and Other Madness

Central and South America, May–August 1999

W hen you're traveling around the world you see some strange things and meet some strange people. There is no "normal," no safe place for your psyche to perch and take a rest, so soon it all becomes a chaotic blur. After awhile, you start questioning if you're going mad or if the rest of the world is.

I always wrote — furiously trying to document the snippets of conversations and minutiae that really made the experiences grand before the moments faded and were lost forever. I bought any notebook I could find, often designed for a 10-year-old with Hello Kitty or Ricky Martin on the cover, and when those were filled front and back I scribbled on hotel notepads, napkins, bar coasters, and matchbook covers. I wrote sitting on my bed in my hotel room, during long waits in airports, then on plane rides, in bus stations, and under trees by the basketball court when it rained. I wrote in bars and strip joints, with one eye on the front door, and there was beer and blood spilled on more than one page. Still to this day, I need energy and stimulation when I write — I do better in the middle of chaos with hot music playing than I do in a silent room at a boring desk. By the time I returned to the States, I had filled seven notebooks cover to cover — more than 1,000 pages in all.

Ten years later, I read through these notebooks and I'm amazed, not because the writing is good, because it's not particularly — it's crude and choppy, like the rushed confessions of a prisoner who's going to the gallows in the morning — but by the pace of the crazy experiences that were happening to us, and how the bizarre and dangerous just seemed normal after awhile. So I wanted to share a small collection of these journal entries from Central and South America with you, without dressing them up or crafting a proper story around them, so you can really feel what it was like to be in the heat of battle.

The Favelas

Rio de Janeiro, Brazil

Shane and I took a tour through Rio driving around with a guy from the hotel. He blasted Madonna songs the whole time, but other than that it was cool. He took us to the *favelas* — barrios or ghettos on the very tops of the hills overlooking Rio. They were crazy, self-sustained communities where everyone was dirt-poor and ruled by the drug cartels and violent gangs. The *favelas* had their own schools, stores, and clinics, and people rarely left. We could only go inside the *favela* because we were with our guide, who was from there, or else we would have been toast within five minutes.

The neighborhoods were just shacks along the steep hills, barely remaining standing at impossible angles, and it looked like the only thing that kept them from sliding down a five-hundred-foot muddy cliff was their neighbor's roof below them. I guess they have mudslides all the time when it rains hard, and lots of people are killed or their shacks are just washed away. Everyone threw their garbage and buckets of waste right out of their back window. (Ain't that an accurate metaphor for how life works?) It all slid down the embankment and settled, decomposing in a dump infested with cockroaches the size of rats, rats the size of cats, and cats the size of dogs. The shacks were red clay, faded with the sun, with red tin roofs and laundry lines hanging from every back window. From the distance I could see an occasional spot of blue or white paint, but other than that it was all a red anthill. Most of the shacks had only one light bulb, strung together with electric cords and duct tape, and at night it looked like ten thousand mothers holding candles outside the church, waiting in vigil for the journalists to reappear.

Little kids, none of whom looked like they owned shirts or shoes, swam in a muddy water hole on the side of the road where an industrial drainage pipe spilled over. An old man stood stranded on the median of the busy roadway down the hill from the *favela*, trying frantically to cross. I watched for a break in the traffic where he might make it, but saw none. I wonder if he's still there.

Later on, our driver took us past a shanty town even more poor than the *favelas* — hundreds of people living in tents made from cardboard, discarded corrugated tin sheets, and scrap wood, thrown together in the middle of a muddy field. Laundry hung everywhere to dry and looked like kites when the breeze blew. Our driver said that these people had no schools, no medical care, very little food, and most of them sniffed glue or got fucked up on drugs just to get by. The gangs and drug dealers ruled everything, and someone got stabbed every night. These people didn't have a bathroom — they just dug a ditch and everyone went in it. They're probably the same people I see every night outside of the Churrascaria a Kilo barbecue restaurant we go to down in Copacabana, the tourist neighborhood by the beach in Rio. Whole families wait in the parking lot, swarming like they're at the starting line of a marathon, but following some unwritten rule that they can't step foot near the dumpster until it's the right time. When the restaurant's dishwasher comes at midnight and throws out the garbage, they all run over and jump in the dumpster and start picking out any edible scraps they can find. Whole families get in there together and rip open the bags and eat their dinner right on the spot. That's about all they have to feed their family all day. Fuck, I'm lucky. Except for the nonstop Madonna — no one should have to live with that.

Goaaaaaaallllllll!

Rio De Janiero, Brazil
We managed to get tickets for a football (soccer) match at Maracanã, the stadium in Rio inaugurated for the 1950 World Cup that fit 200,000 spectators and was home to such greats as Pelé, Maradona, and Ronaldo. The hotel arranged for a van to take us over there and briefed us on the match; it would be between Flamengo and Grêmio, bitter rivals like the Yankees and Red Sox. He warned us to be very careful since we were

gringos, and to only wear the red and black colors of the home team so we could avoid trouble from rowdy fans. If the home team, Flamengo, lost, we might have a lot of trouble getting out of there safely, he said. It was just a regular season game, but there were almost 100,000 people in the stands and the place still only looked half full. We had thirty thousand people in our section eyeing us up and down as we walked down to our seats, but once we said wassup to some locals around us and showed them that we were ready to root hard for Flamengo, it was all good. Shane and I rubbed shoulders with the fans, a sea of celebrating fanatics in red and black , and they loved that we jumped up and down and went crazy right along with them when we scored.

In between the stands and the field they had moats, twenty-foot-deep and twenty-foot-wide concrete embankments, and then a strip of concrete that looked like a running track in between. They explained to us that they sold discounted tickets to the poor *favela* kids and put them in that section isolated on that track, where they couldn't spread violence into the crowd nor access the field, but just run around and cause trouble amongst their own kind. Flamengo won 5-4 and we got out all right.

I've Been Up All Night

San José, Costa Rica

There are only two ways to fall asleep in a Third World country and probably two hundred and fifty-seven things that can keep you awake. The first method is to pass out cold due to ingestion of alcohol or narcotics. The second method is to lie down and close your eyes and fall asleep naturally. People have told me that the natural method sometimes works; I wouldn't know.

No matter where you lay your head in a Third World country, whether in an apartment, a cheap hotel, or a hostel, it's impossible to sleep. The combination of noise and discomfort creates an opus of insomnia that would be hilarious if you weren't too tired to laugh. Only during siesta time in the heat of the afternoon or during the rainy season do you get any sleep.

The television blares from your neighbor watching a football match. The cheating lovers in the room upstairs fuck so loudly that plaster dust hits you in the face and you think their bed is going to fall through the ceiling. The maids try to get in your room, hoping you aren't home so they can boost your watch. The parakeet at the front desk that is guarding a bowl of condoms won't shut up. Coils and metal bars stick out of your bed and poke you in the back. Children selling lottery tickets and Chiclets on the street yell over each other, competing for the drivers' attention.

Someone is puking. Someone is crying. Bed bugs, sand fleas, and mosquitoes turn you into a lump of itchy red welts. The drip-drip-drip from the broken bathroom sink is like Chinese water torture. The air conditioner doesn't seem to be working but hums on and off all night. The electricity buzzes and clicks. The misaligned ceiling fan wobbles and whirs. Of course, there are nonstop car horns, police sirens, and the hourly whistles of security guards on bicycles. Dogs bark and cats fight in the alleys. A wife screams at her drunken husband returning home; when she starts throwing pots and pans he slams the door and goes back to the bar. Somewhere there is the screech and smash of a car accident. A motorcycle fires up. Toward the morning, when you're so exhausted that you doze off for a few minutes, the construction crew starts jackhammering concrete at 6 a.m.

So, you see why it is essential to get properly faded before you try to go to sleep? My cocktail of choice was 10 or 12 Imperial beers and a few hits of dirt weed from a Saturday Night Special: an empty beer can with holes poked in it. Under special emergency circumstances, I might add a Vicodin to that. The combination usually numbed me enough to get a few hours of shut-eye.

The Old Spice Mustache

San Pedro, Costa Rica

I was hanging out with my friend Luis "El Toro" Diego and his gringa girlfriend, Wendy, at our favorite little college bar in San Pedro. One of the girls at the bar, a really cute Tica named Alejandra, was sweating me, so we all started hanging out. She was celebrating her 21st birthday, so her girlfriends kept ordering her shots and throwing colorful confetti around, until we were all covered in it. I couldn't believe how many shots she was doing, especially for a girl who probably weighed 100 pounds.

After the tequila shots came out, even I was officially window-licker drunk, but she hung in there like a champ. When the bar closed and they kicked us out she wanted to come home with me, and her friends encouraged her, so they dropped us off at Apartmento Williams.

We started kissing and she wanted to fool around, but she was way too drunk, so I just gave her aspirin and a bottle of water and put my little trash can next to her side of the bed. Around 4 a.m. I half woke up to her stumbling around the room and mumbling incoherently. She asked something about the bathroom and I pointed and went back to sleep. In the morning she looked confused and embarrassed, but I assured her she didn't cause any trouble. She called a cab to go celebrate her birthday with her family and a vicious hangover. I never saw her again, but that's when it starts getting really interesting.

My memories of my last week in Costa Rica are hazy at best. The days were spent playing basketball and trying my hardest to smoke up the huge bag of dirt weed I bought from the Rasta in Puerto Viejo, and the nights celebrating at the bars in San Pedro with El Toro and our crew. I was probably averaging three hours of sleep a night and had completely surrendered to the fact that I wouldn't get a good night's rest in Costa Rica. So every time I went to bed, it was after a night drinking and partying and I mercilessly passed out before I even hit the mattress.

I started noticing that something smelled funny in my room. At first, it was no big deal — the smell of garbage in the midday sun often came wafting up from the street below, but every night it got a little worse. I was too drunk and tired to give it too much thought before I just passed out. I actually started questioning whether I was just tripping and imagining it. A few days went by, and the smell got worse. I did my laundry in case that was what it was. Still bad. I looked for the trash can for evidence of an abandoned late-night burrito, but couldn't find it. Where was that damn thing? Oh well, I drank more Imperial so I could pass out.

Two days later and it smelled like a decomposing baboon in there. What could it be? I closed the window, thinking it was sewage from the street or a neighbor's unit, but the smell got worse and now it was a hundred degrees with no wind. I lit candles. I smoked more weed to confuse my brain so I could get some sleep. It didn't work. The funk was getting so bad that it was almost intolerable, even with the narcotic anesthesia I was giving myself every night. By the fifth day, I couldn't take it anymore. Then I had an idea — I grabbed my Old Spice deodorant and wiped a liberal dose of it on my upper lip. The pungent smell of chemical cinnamon pleasantly distracted my nostrils, blocking out the nasty funk in the room. I lathered more on. Ahhhh, sweet relief — I couldn't smell a thing except for Old Spice and slept like a baby that night, waking up in the morning with a big blue streak caked to my upper lip. I had to put on my Old Spice mustache every night to tolerate the smell, but it worked, and I got through the last days in Costa Rica without dying an inglorious olfactory death.

My last morning in town was spent cleaning the apartment so I would get my deposit back. I was tidying up my room and jammed the vacuum cleaner under the bed, and it bumped into something and made a clanking noise. I got on my hands and knees to look and pulled out the trash can. What the fuck was it doing all the way under there? I looked inside, then gagged and grabbed it, ran through my apartment and out the front door, and launched it off my balcony, almost hitting Perverted Sergio when it landed with a crash. In it was two-week-old petrified puke sprinkled with a bunch of colorful confetti. Cute birthday girl was so drunk that she couldn't find the bathroom in the middle of the night and so puked in the trash can, but shoved it under the bed to hide it from me because she was embarrassed.

After that, I still put on my Old Spice Mustache from time to time, just because I liked it.

Socks and Sandals Are Never OK

Puerto Viejo, Costa Rica

Shane and I jumped a bus to Limón on the Caribbean side, then over to Puerto Viejo. The bus snaked up mountain switchbacks, down thick jungle roads, and through small villages for about five hours. People squeezed in three to a seat on that clunker and it was hot as the devil, so everyone's shirts were plastered to their chests and women fanned themselves with whatever they could find, including their babies. Every once awhile the breeze blew in, but it was all dust from the road.

There were no other gringos on the bus — we were outnumbered 10 to 2 by live roosters and vicious dogs that were barking and trying to bite anyone within reach. When we went through the steep parts of the mountains, the passengers passed puke bags up and down the aisles like firemen with buckets of water. At every stop, vendors rushed onto the bus to sell newspapers, bags of sliced pineapple and mango, fried candy, coconut water, and bottles of Coca-Cola. Shane and I imitated the vendors' yelling: "*Mango mango mango, mangito, buenas y frescas!*"

We passed through rural villages consisting of a few huts that served as auto shops and bars with outdoor lunch counters. Fat men sat out front on plastic chairs, drinking beer with their shirts open, watching the road. As they heard the bus approach, little kids ran into the road and whistled and threw rocks at the passing bus. We got off at one of these villages for a break and the little kids took turns firing a soccer ball at us, trying to hit the gringos — so funny. Hound dogs lay in the dirt and let flies land all over them without bothering to move. Someone told me they were there to guard the cows, but it was too hot for the cows to move, either.

The bus clambered along dirt roads with washouts, potholes, broken bridges, and construction sites that had been abandoned in the heat. All along the main road eighteen-wheelers almost ran us off the road as they passed, transporting their banana harvest to San José. But in the afternoon they pulled over and hitched net hammocks to the bottom of their rigs and slept in the shade.

Eventually, another white guy got on. I knew he was German because he wore short shorts, sandals with black socks, and cursed nonstop at the inefficiency of the Costa Rican transportation system. He pulled cans of Imperial beer from his fanny pack, wiped off the tops carefully with a bandana, chugged them, crushed the cans, and put them back in his fanny pack. We finally got to Puerto Viejo seven beers later.

Please Don't Dance, Sir

Valencia, Venezuela
Saturday night we found a cool bar/restaurant that was packed. The only two free seats at the bar were next to three local chicks celebrating one of their birthdays. And by celebrating I mean doing a lot of shots

and making us do them, too. A band played, the singer belting out in an angelic voice as they jammed out some funky US cover tunes. I got up to dance a little, or at least to sway back and forth and nod my head to the beat, but apparently such displays are frowned upon in Valencia, because the manager came over and told us not to dance. What an odd request when a band is playing! They wanted everyone to remain seated and still. I thought he was bullshitting me, but he was serious. The band was just too damn good and I was too damn drunk, so when the manager wasn't looking, I jumped up and boogied a little and then froze and remained still when he looked over. He knew I was dancing and kept trying to bust me.

That cat and mouse game — me shaking a tail feather for a few notes and then freezing and looking casually at the ceiling when we walked by — went on all night. When the band played a James Brown number, I just couldn't help myself, so I hid behind a big potted plant and boogied my ass off like crazy. One of the girls was digging me and we agreed to meet for a date the next afternoon. I was psyched because she was super hot and looked exactly like Jennifer Lopez.

Church Girls Are Easy

Valencia, Venezuela

The next day, Jennifer Lopez showed up for our Sunday date twenty minutes late at the plaza in the center of town. I must have had some thick beer goggles on the night before, because she looked more like Mark Anthony in a wig than J-Lo. Just kidding — she was cute.

We sat on a bench exchanging awkward small talk (and it was very small considering my lack of Spanish) and watching families stroll through the plaza. Since it was Sunday, the plaza was bustling with activity from some Christian rally. What the hell did they have to rally about? They bellowed messages from a bullhorn, a church dance troupe put on a performance, and some teenagers mimed through a skit. It wasn't exactly the sexiest atmosphere I could think of, so I suggested we go somewhere else … like a bar. She agreed, but took me by the hand and led me to the church instead. Ouch.

We went in and watched the mass that went on for awhile. It really was beautiful, but I can't think of a more platonic first date than a Sunday afternoon with no alcohol at a Christian rally, and then church mass, so I was resigned to the fact that I officially was getting no loving. After church, she suggested I go grab my camera in my hotel room so we could take pics of the plaza. Oh, great. But when we got to my room, she must have been enraptured with the spirit because she attacked me. I've met some kinky broads, but a church fetish? That even freaked me out a little, and that's damn hard to do.

I walked her home through the vacant streets back to her boarding house. Dusk was fading to black, and when the dim streetlights flashed on block by block, they cast ominous shadows against the barred and locked stores. The neighborhood wasn't good, and it got much worse as we walked on. A sketchy-looking guy with his hood up passed by us in the middle of the street. I was conscious of her pace, her grip on my hand, because if something bad happened she would slow me down.

We reached her boarding house and they didn't let guys in, so I said goodbye to her on the front steps while the barrio residents checked me out. I told her I'd call her later that night, but of course I didn't mean it and of course she didn't believe me, and maybe didn't even want me to. She nodded her head and hugged me and let me go without protest. She knew the deal — I was a traveler in town just for a couple days — but I still felt bad, guilty, to be partly responsible for someone else's disappointment.

It was hard sometimes. People always want too much from you — they'll take everything if you let them, and it gets damn sad. No, it was better to be alone, and the streets were my cure. I walked back in the shadows, feeling for the first time like I belonged to that Third World pavement. I tingled with exhilaration, all of my senses acute and alive, expecting danger around every corner but my breathing was completely relaxed. I almost hoped someone would try something so I could spring to action. I could run, and no one would have caught me. Not a single person on Earth could have caught me that night because no one was hungrier, more ready to tackle what life had to throw at them, than I was.

Tourists Dress like Dipshits

Everywhere

Why do tourists dress so damn funny? I understand that you're excited about going to a foreign country, but you're staying in a major metropolitan city and you look ridiculous. Here you are in stiff khaki jungle pants that zip off into shorts, $200 hi-tech hiking boots without a speck of dirt on them, a fly fisherman's vest that looks like something you'd see on *Bass-Lover Weekly* on ESPN the Ocho at 4:30 a.m., metal ski poles just to walk normally — all to navigate the rugged, inhospitable wilderness of … downtown Buenos Aires in between the mall and the McDonalds. And don't forget your dorky floppy hat with roll-out mosquito netting and flip-down Arctic-grade sunglasses. Where did you think you were going, exactly?

But my favorite has to be that funny little money belt that you strap on underneath your shirt or to your leg. It even comes in flesh color and is supposed to be imperceptible to robbers and muggers. Of course, it's the most inconvenient thing on earth if you need to get anything out of there, which sort of negates the purpose. You have to untuck your shirt, unsnap the belt off your fat gut, and fumble with it awhile to get out what you need, and I'm pretty sure everyone within a ten-mile radius can see that whole process, whether they want to or not. Just leave stuff in the hotel room if you need to hide it that badly. And I think by now robbers know that tourists are wearing those, so what's the point?

Dr. Franklin, M.D.

Puerto Viejo, Costa Rica

I saw the town Rasta, Franklin on the dirt road near our hostel. I was walking by myself because Shane had a screwed-up back — he jacked it up playing basketball in Limón and it was really killing him, so I thought I'd get him some weed to ease the pain. Franklin was waiting down the road, wearing only jean shorts and flip-flops, and he whistled for me. I walked up and said hi and he gave a big smile as his dreadlocks swayed to some music in his head that only he could hear. "Jah, love!" he greeted me. He was scarred and calloused, but roped with muscle and full of life. We leaned against a fence and talked.

Franklin was 49 years old and had been living deep in the jungle for the past 19 years. He only came down to the seaside village of Puerto Viejo to move weed. He told me he wasn't a Rastafarian but a Roots Man, which meant he vibed on the natural energy of life. He refused to kill another creature unless it was absolutely necessary, including the ant on his foot or the wasp in his hair. Instead of swatting mosquitos at night, he burned dried coconut husks to keep them away.

My new friend explained how Jah made all the earth, and then created man last. Jah could control the animals, but man tried to be higher than Jah, so man was sent to Babylon. I realized that a lot of his rap was to look and sound the part for the tourists who wanted to buy their weed from an authentic Rasta, but he did have some good points, too. We talked about the hypocrisy of the church, the dogma that focused on the afterlife to placate the people for today so they didn't realize the problems and mistreatment in their lives. Every time I added something to the conversation that he grooved on, he pumped his fist and yelled, "I am the sufferer!" and "Yah, mon, Jah give I the mind and the power!" His belief system was that instead of worshipping some mysterious, invisible God in man's image, he would worship the God inside of nature, and therefore the God inside of himself.

A gaggle of school kids walked by and greeted him warmly. They carried cardboard boxes held over their heads to shelter them from the sun. Franklin walked me to a crossroads near my hostel where four dirt roads met. A crew of his friends and family members were building a new one-room bungalow. It looked to me that they were doing more dancing to the reggae that played from a radio than working. He pointed out which guys were his children and his grandchildren, and they waved and said hi.

Franklin plopped down cross-legged in the middle of the dirt road and motioned for me to do the same. He pulled out a matchbox full of weed and rolled a fat joint. I looked around nervously, but no one seemed to care that we were about to smoke weed sitting in the middle of the road, and Franklin didn't seem worried at all.

I was only three years removed from getting busted for marijuana in Colorado and spending a little time in jail, and still had a suspended sentence hanging over me, so I was sketchy as hell at the idea of lighting up with some stranger in the middle of an intersection. But after a few puffs I realized that everyone knew everyone in Puerto Viejo, and that Franklin selling weed was as much a part of the local economy as the bars and scuba diving shops.

I took another hit. The damp, earthy smoke filled my lungs. He urged me to take another. I coughed. Jah, love! In a sunny haze, Franklin showed me a scar on his neck and told me how a guy tried to harm him because he was a Dreadlock. The guy grabbed Franklin from behind and put a knife to his throat. Franklin pulled out his own knife and stabbed the guy. Jah the merciful had spared him; Jah had given him strength to punish the unjust.

"Love is a powerful, beautiful thing," he said, "but it can be a bad thing, too. I used to have a girl up in the jungle and I loved her, but soon she grew to make me sad and I wanted to die. One night I had a vision of the girl's face outside my window, and then lightning struck. It was a sign that Jah and Lucifer were fighting over my soul like Job in the Bible. I told her to leave, but when she was gone I was lonely."

He looked down the dirt road and then put the joint to his lips. "I found another girl to take her place, but you can't cure poison with poison. So now I believe in myself first and don't look to others for my happiness."

It made sense. I'd been there, too — I mean, minus the lightning and the jungle and the Lucifer stuff. I took another hit. The road beneath me felt like it was rotating toward the horizon. A Brazilian surfer walked by with his girlfriend, balancing his dripping wet board on his head, and yelled, "Fire!" when he saw Franklin. Everything moved in slow motion. Someone laughed and it sounded like wind chimes. The construction workers danced in barbed wire. My body sank into the jungle road while my head drifted toward the clouds. I was the sufferer.

Franklin's eyes were black and against the sun he looked like a lion. He liked it that we thought alike, even though we looked so different. He invited me up to his shack to hang out for a few days and see the jungle. His offer was tempting, and I'm sure it would have been an amazing experience, but I told him that I needed to stay with my friend because he was sick. He told me the herb would cure Shane. I laughed and called him Doctor Franklin, M.D., and he thought that was hilarious and slapped me on the back. I agreed to buy some bud from him and slipped a $20 bill into his hand. He whistled, and a guy on a bicycle appeared from nowhere and peddled by, dropping something in the dirt. Another guy in a woolen ski cap with no shirt on picked it up and dropped it in Franklin's lap as he strolled by. I ended up paying $15 for something ridiculously generous like a half ounce of good bud. Franklin and I rolled up a spliff from my bag and smoked again. I was twisted, but the vibe was good. I had to get out of there before I started drooling and passed out in the middle of the road.

Shane smoked some in the hostel and felt a little better. The next morning, his back had loosened up enough for him to get out and about. We had about three weeks left in Costa Rica, and smoked as much as we possibly could, but we didn't even make a significant dent in the bag. A week before we had to get on a plane for Venezuela, we started handing huge handfuls of weed to waitresses and bartenders instead of a tip, just to get rid of it. Fire!

A Ham-Obsessed Nation

Ecuador

Shane and I were taking a bus to Lake Titicaca and had a few minutes to spare before it departed. We found a deli right outside the bus station that had an impressive menu of sandwiches to choose from. The lady behind the counter took our order for turkey sandwiches and drinks and repeated it back to us:

"Two *jamón* (ham) sandwiches and two drinks," she said.

"No no, turkey please," I responded.

"Sorry, we are out of turkey, but how about some of this nice *jamón*?" She took out a platter with her prize ham from the glass case.

"No thank you, how about two chicken sandwiches instead?" I asked.

"OK, two chicken sandwiches." She got to work making them and we took a seat and started sipping our drinks. In a few minutes, she came from around the counter and placed two plates in front of us containing … ham sandwiches.

"What's this?" we barked at her, "we ordered *chicken* sandwiches."

"Yes, yes — these are chicken sandwiches," she insisted.

I pulled off the bread and took out the ham and waved it at her. "*Jamón, jamón, jamón!* This is not chicken!"

We argued with her for about five minutes until she showed us the order she had written down to prove it was chicken. On her pad it said, "*jamón de pollo*," or "ham of chicken."

"Ham of chicken!?" I yelled. "What the hell is ham of chicken? It's either ham or it's chicken but it can't be both!"

It wasn't fair — you can't just make up a new lunchmeat like that. I calmed down a little and we regrouped and looked through the menu again.

"Well, how about pastrami, then?" I asked.

"We do not have that, but how about some *jamón*?" she said straight-faced, taking the platter of ham out of the case again to show us, waving her hand over it like she was a *The Price Is Right* model displaying the snowmobiles behind door number one.

My head was about to explode. I crouched down to look in their nice shiny glass case to see for myself exactly what other meats they had. The case was empty. No matter what we ordered, she was going to try and spin in to *jamón*. *Jamón de* chicken, *jamón de* roast beef, *jamón de* vegetarian falafel, *jamón de* green salad. We paid for our drinks, stormed out, and found a Wendy's down the street. That damn country is obsessed with *jamón*.

All This for a Pillow?

Lima, Peru

In Peru the police love using tear gas.

I was shopping for a pillow downtown and stumbled upon a university protest. The college kids were protesting a raise in tuition rates, which is a big deal in a country where you have almost no opportunities for education or advancement unless you're part of the 1% of ultra-rich families who run everything. On one side of the wide intersection, the students gathered with crude signs made with spray paint, and bandanas covering their faces to hide their appearance, and the police set up on the other side.

I'd wandered up behind the policemen, barricaded behind riot tanks with water hoses and plastic riot shields and clubs. I walked up next to them, even in front of some of them, and leaned against a building to watch the action. Of course, there was no organization and it was amazing that someone like me could just walk into the middle of the fray without being stopped. The kids would yell and scream and throw rocks and bottles as hard as they could at the cops. Some hit but most of them fell short. The police endured it for the most part, just deflecting the rocks with their riot shields, but if a kid got too close they drew their guns.

After awhile when the students didn't look like they were disbanding anytime soon, the cops fired off tear gas grenades into the throng of students. The streets filled with toxic smoke, and I caught some great pictures before my eyes and lungs started burning, too. I hightailed it out of there before things got really bad.

Rico Suave

Guayaquil, Ecuador

Shane and I made it out to Guayaquil, Ecuador's second largest city right by the beach. Everyone warned us that it was a rough city and that the people were crazy there. The strip of bars and clubs by the waterfront were definitely grimy, and the nicest place we found was a disco that looked like the bar scene from Star Wars. We were chilling and sipping on Polars, chatting up a few local girls and throwing "the biz" at them to make sure they weren't working girls.

In most places, you have no idea if a girl is a hooker, a party girl, or just a nice girl who is genuinely interested, and you certainly can't just come out and ask, so we would run through this charade where we mentioned in casual conversation that we'd both had our wallets stolen or that our ATM cards weren't working or something, and so we only had a few bucks to last us the whole night. If they politely excused themselves to go to the bathroom and never came back, we'd know they had their claws out for us, but if they were cool with it then they were *buenas chicas*, good girls.

So I was about to tell this girl that my ATM card had gotten ruined earlier that day when I jumped into the ocean to heroically save a boatload of orphans who had run out of gas, hoping to combine "the biz" with a story that would endear me to her and earn some coochie coupons. In walks a dude who I swear looks familiar, which is crazy because we're in Guayaquil, Ecuador, but I really think I've seen him before. He has a little city to his swagger, and he's wearing nice jeans, a black T-shirt with a big Jesus-piece hanging from his neck, and a New York Yankees baseball cap. He sits right next to me at the bar and you can tell everyone is sort of making a bid deal about him, and we strike up a conversation because he speaks great English.

It turns out he is Gerardo, the famous singer. Do you remember that song "Rico Suave" in the States back in 1991? It actually made it to #7 on the Billboard charts and made homeboy a ton of loot, which would last him about fifty lifetimes down in Ecuador, even though it was a cheesy disco song. Well, Gerardo Mejía is from Guayaquil originally but was living in LA working as a record executive, and happened to be in town and stopped by the bar that night. He turned out to be a super-cool guy, and was really humble and nice, and Shane and I had a few drinks with him. I was proud of myself for not mentioning "Rico Suave" even once, because that's probably all he ever hears about.

Working on My Third World "Brothel Cred"

La Paz, Bolivia

We were sitting at the bar putting 'em down fast, racing to see if we could finish our beers before they got warm, when the guy next to us, a young Bolivian businessman with his tie loosened, struck up a conversation. He was so drunk he was cross-eyed, but still intent on practicing his limited English on us. I don't know where he learned the language, but judging from what came out of his mouth it must have been at an anger management meeting.

"This bar is SHIT! The people here are SHIT! These girls …SHIT! Another bar…NICE!" he yelled at us. He kept repeating his militant diatribe, cursing out everyone and anything as SHIT at the top of his lungs, and then going back to drinking in silence for a few more minutes. Pretty soon, we knew what was coming and chimed in to yell the SHIT parts along with him, like the chorus of our new favorite song.

He offered to take us to some nicer bars. Since we were drunk and enjoyed his angry ranting, we figured he'd be a perfect road dog for the evening. We jumped in a cab and he gave the driver some instructions, and we ended up in a shady part of town, on a dark street lined with massage parlors, strip joints, and a few tattoo parlors. We were going to find a nicer bar here?

The first strip clubs he led us to were either dead or the cover charge was too high, so he christened them as SHIT. But he said he knew of one other bar that was NICE, so we followed. He led us down an alley and into the open metal door of a dilapidated building. We walked up three flights of stairs and passed some Iranian guys on their way down. Where the hell was this bar? At the top of the steps, there was a small foyer crowded with young Bolivian guys standing against the wall, looking nervous. Where was this guy leading us? In the next room, a dozen chicks sat on long sectional couches. Most of them looked old and round, with makeup like circus clowns even under dim lighting. We were in a whorehouse.

I would have a tough time throwing one of these broads for free, let alone paying for it, and there was not enough alcohol in all of Bolivia to make up the difference. I asked SHIT guy what the hell was going on, but he assured us this was a NICE place. There were a few girls in their 20s in there who were pretty, but they were all flawed in some obvious way, like a big facial scar or teeth so bad they could eat corn through a chainlink fence. The younger ladies had dead eyes — yellow and half closed, like dogs in the rain, and wouldn't look directly at anyone. The older ones had been doing this for long enough that they had grown resigned to it, and bounced around amongst themselves, chatting merrily. All of the ladies wore dresses, lingerie, nightgowns, or bathing suits.

The guys inside the room stared at the prostitutes with guilty expressions but didn't make a move. The whole scene was like a twisted junior prom, with the girls on one end of the room flirting and the boys on the other end, pawing the ground nervously like bulls waiting for their stall doors to be opened.

Someone slammed and locked an iron gate over the doorway behind us. That got my attention, because it was the only way out of the room and we were now stuck in there. I guess they did that to force the hand of the guys in there — shit or get off the pot, so to speak. Our companion went over and talked to the ugliest of the whores, and they walked into the back room together. But the second the iron door opened again, Shane and I bolted for the exit.

On the way down the stairs, we passed a few more groups of young, drunk Bolivian guys coming to get their rocks off. One guy wore a white shirt and a tie and had on a nametag from his job at McDonalds. Wow, "Rafael, Assistant Manager," at least take your damn nametag off before you go into a whorehouse. I hoped he washed his hands before he started making burgers again. We hit the street laughing, glad we had witnessed that place but happy to be out of there, reciting our new mantra: "This place is SHIT! The girls ... SHIT! These people ... SHIT!"

You Can Take the Kid out of New Haven, but You Can't ...

San Pedro, Costa Rica

On the walk home from dinner, we passed six teenagers on the street. They wore baggy jeans and their hats sideways like little hip-hop kids, and had darker skin than most Ticos, so I couldn't tell if they were Nicaraguans or from Limón. They were acting rowdy, swearing and smoking cigarettes and eyeing us up, so I knew there might be trouble. The sidewalk narrowed where we passed a chainlink fence, so Shane and I tried to walk by them single-file. The kids moved over to block us in, squeezing us against the fence. On guy grabbed my wrist out of my pocket, trying to wrench my watch free. I snatched my hand away and walked past them quickly.

Shane and I got free and they talked some shit but didn't follow us. My adrenaline was going and I was so mad that I wanted to go get a baseball bat and go looking for them, but Shane calmed me down and wisely explained that no good could come out of that. I guess you can take the kid out of New Haven but you can't take the New Haven out of the kid! Either way, it probably would have taken me a year to find a baseball bat, and I would have to try to beat them up with a soccer ball instead.

Mother Getting Hit by Car

Heredia, Costa Rica

We were heading to Heredia to a club one night and passed an accident on the side of the highway. Traffic slowed to a crawl, giving me time to see what happened. A pickup truck was pulled over and six Ticos, who looked like poor farmers, stood on the truck's wooden bed. They were leaning over a body — someone who had been hit by a car. Nearby, two little boys sat on a stone wall, the oldest probably twelve, his younger brother sitting on his lap and crying. His whole face was wet with tears, his features melting in sorrow and disbelief. He rocked back and forth, unable to sit still, his mouth opened in an agonizing howl. The older brother wrapped his arms around the younger brother's chest and held him tight, trying to comfort him and keep him from running over to their mother.

There was no evidence that the boys were brothers, or that the person who had been hit was their mother, but somehow I knew. Seeing the kids crying like that felt like someone had stabbed an icicle into my heart. It was a somber reminder that all of our money, our clothes, our flashy cars and big houses and good jobs are no more than an illusion; we are all no more safe than a child clinging to the warmth of his mother's hand as they cross the street.

The Helicopter Brothers

I can't tell you where

Wally, our new gringo ex-pat friend, took us out on the town one night. Back in the States, he bought a ton of cheap land from the government twenty years ago and sold it to the casinos, making a fortune. He moved down here and retired to a life of sun and beer all day. He befriended a local street kid named Tipo and started giving him a few odd jobs to earn some coins. As the years went by, their relationship grew and eventually Wally took Tipo in as a surrogate son. He paid for his college and bought him a truck.

We sat with Wally and Tipo at a posh hotel bar by the sea and drank gin and tonics. Later that night, we went to a casino and played a few slot machines while Wally threw hundred-dollar bills around at the blackjack table. He really liked us because he didn't get to talk to many Americans. By the end of the night, he was pretty drunk and loose-lipped and confided to us that his fortune had been augmented by investing with the Helicopter Brothers.

The Helicopter Brothers was the unofficial name for a charity organization. On paper they airlifted medical supplies to remote parts of Central and South America to help out poor and indigenous people. What they really did was traffic cocaine. It was a perfect front — under the guise of a philanthropic mission, the helicopters had free rein to travel across borders and all of the official paperwork to operate openly. The 'copters could dodge attention more nimbly than a plane because they could fly low and didn't need an airfield to land. Their "donors" gave money to cover the charity's costs and medical supplies and got a robust rate of return. What they were really doing was laundering drug money through this payout and exchange of international currency. It was a secretive organization that supplied no paperwork and hashed out client agreements in back alley bars and at rooster fights.

Wally didn't know for-sure-for sure that the Helicopter Brothers were trafficking drugs, and he'd only met one guy one time on a referral from a friend who set the whole thing up — a mustached guy with dark aviator sunglasses and a knife scar on his face who gave him a slip of paper with a bank account number and told him the terms and then disappeared into the crowd. But Wally wasn't stupid and heard rumors about what the Helicopter Brothers were all about. Still, it was too good not to try.

He started small, wiring over $500 a month, and his investment grew as he saw $680 wired back to his account at the end of the month like clockwork, 36% tax-free *monthly*, meaning he could double his money every 18 months or so. His investments grew to the tens of thousands, and years later he had plenty of money — all cash. His biggest problem was finding a bank to hold it that wouldn't report the deposits so the IRS or US government wouldn't take notice, but was also stable enough that he wouldn't lose his fortune in a coup d'état.

Wally had bags under his eyes and seemed a little nervous until he had a few dozen drinks, but even then he sobered up and spoke in hushed tones when he mentioned the Helicopter Brothers, and quickly changed subjects. But soon he was acting drunk again and seemed like he had to unburden his soul, so he'd come back to that topic and tell us a little more. Toward morning, Shane and I were drunk and sleepy and told him we were leaving for our cheap hotel. He didn't want us to go. Stay a little longer, he asked, in a tone that revealed a glimpse of desperation; he would pay for our drinks — anything we wanted, even coke or women. He didn't want the night to end, he didn't like being alone, and it was nice to have Americans to talk with. He confessed that, even though he had houses and women and nice cars and could sit around getting drunk in paradise every day, he was lonely, and every night he had bad dreams of men with knife scars.

I felt sorry for him, even though I shouldn't have. OK, one more beer, we agreed, but just one while we waited for our cab, and after that we had to go. "OK," he said, "OK, thank you guys," and the waiter was already on his way over.

I have to make sure that my writing about the Helicopter Brothers goes no further than this journal. Maybe I'll rip out these pages and throw them out once I get back to the States. I'd really be worried about my safety if I wrote about it, especially if I ever am traveling through _____ or the port city of _____ again — these people would chop me up and leave me in a garbage can like it was nothing. But that name was just too good, so I had to write it down so I'd remember it. "The Helicopter Brothers" — it's worth the risk.

Jimmy *Tres Dedos*

San José, Costa Rica

We got invited to the American Embassy for the Fourth of July. I didn't know what to expect, but it was an incredible party. As long as you had a US passport you could get in for free, and they had tons of BBQ, all the Heineken beer you could drink, a band, and jump houses and games for the kids. We got nice and drunk and hung with a lot of salty-dog ex-pats.

We met an American who was introduced to us as "Jimmy *Tres Dedos*," or "Jimmy Three Fingers." All I could think when I met him was, "Don't look down, don't look down, don't look at his fingers." Of course I looked down at his fingers immediately, and I gotta tell you I was a little disappointed. He did have three fingers, as to be expected, but he also had a perfectly good thumb. I felt gypped — I thought he had three digits total on that hand, not four, and the way I saw it he was guilty of false advertising. I understand that you could consider a thumb a digit other than a finger, but come on now — that's just arguing semantics. As we got drunker with him I brought up the point, and he was a good sport and laughed it off. I told him that in my opinion he should be called Jimmy *Quatro Dedos*, but come to think of it that just doesn't have the same panache. So I told him there's only one solution: He needed to chop off another finger.

Jimmy introduced us to a friend of his, a beautiful Costa Rican lady in her 30s. We chatted for awhile and she started throwing a full-court press at me to hook up with her 17-year-old daughter. I guess they all want to see their daughters marry a nice gringo because that pretty much ensures economic security for the family. The daughter was stunningly beautiful, but she was way too young and innocent. I liked her mom, though! (Haha.) I declined an invitation for dinner at their house the next night and thought about how sharp a knife we would need when I helped Jimmy cut off his thumb.

I Want to Protest Against Myself

La Paz, Bolivia

We wanted to get out of the city because of all the protests. It seemed like there was a protest every day in La Paz, and thousands of people had surrounded our hotel, yelling and facing off against a wall of military police with riot gear. We'd seen tear gas all over the place and people puking and running, and heard that several protestors had been killed. I wasn't really sure if we were safe, as they had our hotel surrounded as a symbol of international authority.

We asked a local guy and he explained that the poor people had to protest to be heard because they had no voice in the government. It was usually farmers, teachers, students, or coca growers rallying against unfair pay, increased tuition, the government's coca eradication policies, and increases in water tax. The price of meat had doubled and the price of vegetables quadrupled in the last six months, so the poor protested by setting up roadblocks to try and paralyze commerce in and out of the city. They blocked the roads with downed trees, piles of stones, and started burning old cars or barrels of trash. They even boarded buses and started pulling people off, and bad things can happen then. Coca was so important to them — about one in six people made their living with the coca plant — but the government kept pretending to crack down on it in exchange for political favors and foreign aid. But in reality, they were corrupt and trying to make money off of it like everyone else.

In other news, I bit into a piece of chicken on another day and blood spurted out. I didn't get full-on food poisoning, but I was pretty sick. I got sick every damn place I went. I ate cheeseburgers and milkshakes and as many calories as I could and still lost weight, until I was rail-thin.

So between the protests and my stomach, I thought it was best to stay in the hotel. As the sun went down I lay in bed and read Bukowski. He's really my favorite. I just lay there for awhile with the book on my chest and watched the curtains blow in and out and listened to the protestors. The lights flickered. People cheered and then moaned. The lights went out. They had set fire to an overturned car downstairs. It was completely surreal; where was I? What the hell was going on?

Drowning in Rain

Lake Titicaca, Ecuador
We did make it safely out of town with no blockades, but the cab driver was worried the whole time because we were Americans. My stomach was still messed up, so I carried around Maalox, Tums, and toilet paper in my backpack everywhere I went.

We were heading out to Lake Titicaca, and had to take a cab to a bus to a boat to get to the island where we were staying on the lake. I needed to go to the bathroom, but the boat driver told me to hold on until we got to the next village because the bathrooms in our current village were bad, but the next ones would be much better. We finally got to the next village and I ran to the "much better" bathrooms, and they were just horse stables. In each horse stall they had dirt floors and a hole on the floor. That's it. An old lady sat there and watched the whole time, charging me about 10 cents for use of the bathroom. Then she up-sold me on the toilet paper.

Titicaca was an amazingly beautiful lake high up in the Andes mountains. It was so big it blew my mind — it was like looking out at a vast blue desert instead of a body of water. Check this out: Lake Titicaca is 12,500 feet above sea level — that's more than two miles high! The surface area is a jaw-dropping 3,233 square miles. To put it in perspective, our beloved Lake Tahoe is 6,500 feet above sea level and has a surface area of 191 square miles, so Lake Titicaca is almost 15 times as big.

We took a small boat out to this little island of almost vertical green hills, Isla del Sol. There were only a few buildings on the island, a small one-room restaurant that was tipping over and a few huts. A two-story boarding house (I can hardly call it a hotel) stood at the crown of the island. It was a rustic cabin lit by gas lanterns, but my second-floor room was remarkable, with an enclosed porch that had glass windows on three sides so from my vantage point, I could see an almost 360-degree view of the lake.

As evening fell, a tropical rainstorm moved in off the Andes, ominous purple clouds like tidal waves bigger than cities rolling in to engulf us. The sunburnt porters ran around tying things down in anticipation. When the rain came, it was like a waterfall from the sky — a majestic glimpse of nature's fury. The sound of the rain on the tin roof and the wind swaying the trees was almost deafening. I was on top of this tiny green speck of an island, and everywhere I looked for thousands of miles there was water — sky, lake, rain — and veins of lightning illuminating it. I sat and I watched, conscious of every precious breath, a part of something bigger than I could ever describe. I was not scared; the world could have drowned and washed me away, but it was too damn beautiful for me to care.

Sweet Georgia Brown

Copacabana, Brazil
I love Brazil — I never want to leave. The people are so warm and fun-loving. Their spirit amazes me and it seems like all they do is dance, hang out on the beach, party, smile, work out on the beach, and dance some more.

We asked around for a cool club in Copacabana, the beachside tourist neighborhood we were staying in, and ended up at Discoteca Help. Help was a really nice disco right on the beach with American hip-hop, reggae, and Latin music, packed with about five hundred of the hottest girls you've ever seen and only about two hundred gringo tourists any given night. Of course, I realized quickly that most of them were working girls.

I was hanging out at the bar and next to me sat a gorgeous coconut cutie who had some corny tall American dude hitting on her. I recognized him as a prominent NBA player, who I will not name to protect his privacy and cheesy game (OK, it was Matt Geiger). He threw a line at her that went something like, "I want to know what's in here" (pointing to her head) "and what's in here" (pointing to her heart). Wow, that's bad. Dude, I'm pretty certain she's a sure thing — just fork over $80.

His game was so bad that I was cracking up right next to them, but trying not to be obvious. The girl saw me laughing and started laughing, too, and told him to beat it. We talked for awhile and she spoke good English. Her name was Georgia. She was really cool, and we talked a lot and had a great time just on the friendship tip. Sweet Georgia Brown.

We met the next day at the mall to kick it. She asked if I understood that she was a working girl. I said sure, no worries, as long as she understood that nothing was going to happen between us and I wasn't trying to make her. It was all good and we just hung out and had a great conversation over sushi. I learned a lot about what they had to do to hustle in that game, and she was a pretty smart girl.

The next day, Sweet Georgia Brown took me around to some local bars and hot spots. Our first stop was a *therma*, which is like their gentleman's spa and lounge, where you wear a bathrobe and flip-flops and nothing else, but you find yourself dancing to Tupac with twenty beautiful chicks in bikinis and doing shots of rum and smoking Cuban cigars at eleven in the morning. Next, she took us by another place, her favorite bar in a nice neighborhood that had hotel rooms in the back with rubber furniture shaped like a pommel horse, rubber sheets, mirrors on the ceiling, and edible panties next to sandwiches in the mini-fridge. Jesus — Brazilians were off the chain! I'm glad I had her as a friend, but I'd leave the other stuff to dudes who wanted to know what was in *here* and in *here*.

Next Time, Bring Me my Damn Towels!

Santiago, Chile

Damn, we had rough flights getting in; we were so hung-over and operating on no sleep and feeling sick as hell. But there was a dude in worse condition — the back of the plane was blocked off with a curtain and there was a hospital bed behind it with a guy hooked up to an IV. As the plane pitched and rolled, he made weird moaning noises as two nuns worked to keep him alive. I thought it was a direct flight, but it was actually three flights on the same plane, so lots of up and down, which only made me feel worse, but still, I was better than the guy in the back, who probably only had a 50/50 chance of making it.

We only had one night in Chile before hitting Peru early the next morning. We found a hotel downtown that was pretty expensive, but all of the furniture was dusty and it had a weird vibe. The desk clerk didn't seem to speak English or Spanish and had one brown eye and one blue eye like a wolf. We got into the room and the toilet was broken and there were no sheets or towels. I called down to the front desk twice to ask for some, but they never brought them up.

We looked for a bar for some grub and found a whole city block of bars and clubs. Even though it was a Monday, it was packed and we met so many cool people and drank and danced all night — so much for taking it easy. Around 4 a.m., we left and saw a fight between a bunch of sloppy drunk guys and one dude who was swinging a wooden crutch around. Before we knew it, we had to run back to the hotel and grab our bags and head to the airport so we didn't miss our morning flight.

We had paid all that money for the hotel just to drop our bags, and they still hadn't brought my damn towels or sheets or fixed the toilet. Fuck them; I showered and then ripped down the window curtain and dried off, then opened the fifth-floor window and peed right out of it, hitting a satellite dish two floors below. I found that if I hit it just right it sprayed back onto the hotel lobby window.

My Favorite Bar in the World

Quito, Ecuador

We posted up in Ecuador for awhile, in a tiny concrete bunker with no heat, no hot water, and only one light bulb, our only window overlooking a postcard-beautiful valley amongst the mountains 10,000 feet above sea level. Our other roommate was Loco Gringo John, a cool cat we met at the bars one night who was coincidentally from Connecticut, my home state. He was an awesome guy with an interesting look — a shaved head and all ripped up and covered with unique tattoos. He was an atheist but had chosen to enroll in a conservative Catholic college, where he used to drop acid and then sit through mass. Whoa, that's a mind-fuck. He was also one of the nicest guys you'd ever meet.

Our best local friend down there was a Brazilian dude named Santiago. At first glance Santi was imposing — a 6-foot-6-inch man-giant who was as dark and regal as a jungle panther and a monster on the basketball court. But as we got to know him, his intelligence and kindness stood out. — he was in school for architectural engineering and was as sweet as pie.

Every night, everyone in our crew went to the same bar, Arribar, in a funky neighborhood in Quito. Every night, Loco Gringo John, Shane, and I would get fucked up, and every night Santi insisted on walking us home the twenty minutes up the hill to our little apartment. He was like our little-big brother, and was just genuinely concerned for our safety. We thought he was just being paranoid, but there was a reason why the security guards at the Arribar wore bulletproof vests and carried shotguns — someone got stabbed or robbed at gunpoint almost nightly around there. We never had a problem (probably because we were with Santi), but once we had left Ecuador Loco Gringo John got jumped by two guys with knives who robbed him, and then a bus he was on was boarded and robbed by two masked bandits with pistols who started shooting up the place. The poor dude couldn't catch a break. But Arribar was our personal clubhouse, and we danced and hung out and got to know all the local heads really well, so we were safer than Fort Knox while we were inside.

One night, to kick off Carnival, we had a huge water fight with the chicks who worked in the upstairs bar. It was just me and Shane and

Crazy Gringo John and these four Ecuadorian chicas, and we dumped water on each other and sprayed each other with beer until we were all soaked to the bone and smiling ear to ear. It made me happy, and then we went downstairs and danced our asses off to Dawn Penn and Lauryn Hill until dawn.

The streets around Arribar were safe for us when we were together because we rolled thick. I remember clearly one night — one of the coolest experiences I've ever had — about seven of us were at Arribar. Our local friends had a tough time affording the $1 beers, so we'd all leave together and walk down the block to the local liquor store. They'd buy a bottle of Aguardiente, the local firewater, and bring it on the street and mix it with Coke in a plastic bag and pour it into plastic cups, or sometimes just pass it around and take slugs of it straight.

All around us were robbers, drug dealers, hookers, and the toughest gang in town, the Policía; it was about as gritty as you could get. Two men in tuxedos, carrying big instrument cases, walked by. We said hi to them and offered them a drink. They considered it for a moment and then joined our circle and took a slug. Santi asked them where they were going dressed like that, and it turned out they were classical musicians on their way home from giving a concert at the cultural center. They were nice guys, so we gave them another shot of our precious Aguardiente, and on a whim, half kidding around, I asked them to play something. To my surprise, they unlocked their cases and took out a full-sized cello and a harp and started playing right there on the street corner. Those two instruments created the most beautiful sounds my ears had ever heard. I closed my eyes as they strummed a melodic symphony, and the noisy street — car horns, drunks breaking bottles on the sidewalk, lovers quarrelling — all faded away until there was nothing but the music. I opened my eyes, and for the first time that night I noticed the sky was filled with stars. They seemed to grow bigger and brighter like they, too, were leaning in to hear the angelic notes rising to meet them.

When they were done, it was dead silent on the street and everyone on the block was frozen, watching and listening. Then the musicians packed up their cases, thanked us, and jumped on a bus before they got robbed of their instruments. I will always remember that there's some beauty in the world if you just take the time to look for it.

Danger Is My Middle Name
(actually, it's Johannes)

My sister said it best once I was back from my trip, sitting safely in her living room: "How the hell are you still *alive*?"

I don't know — I never really thought about it like that. In the year that I traveled all around the world, fully exposing myself to people and places that a more timid man would judge imprudent (and by exposing, I don't mean I stood on the steps of the Louvre and bare-ass-mooned the good citizens of Paris, though I definitely thought about it), believe it or not I don't feel that I took on extraordinary risks. After reading some of the accounts of my travels, you may think I'm crazy for saying that, but my mindset is explained best by Helen Keller, who said, "Life is either a daring adventure or nothing. Security does not exist in nature, nor do the children of men as a whole experience it. Avoiding danger is no safer in the long run than exposure."

Isn't it dangerous to travel in foreign countries? Yes, it is. But here's the thing you're not realizing: it's damn dangerous in the U.S., too. In some ways, it may be even more dangerous because the violence is more random and often sounds like "Pow, pow!" Never once when I was traveling did I hear of a kid going into a school and shooting the place up; there's no "Bowling for Istanbul." Unless I missed it, disgruntled employees in Ecuador don't show up the day after getting fired and spray machine gun fire at their peers. Senators don't get gunned down randomly at Wal-Marts in Bangkok. Furthermore, would you walk around in the South Bronx by yourself at night? Could a traveler from another country easily see the murder rates in Baltimore and decide that Washington, D.C. was too dangerous to visit? Maybe.

The way I break it down is that there's street crime and then there's political crime. A random dude on the street mugs you with a knife — that's street crime, and the only intent is to take your money or possessions. Political crime is far more nefarious — radical political groups intimidating and even assassinating their opposition, drug cartels kidnapping people, and religious zealots perpetrating acts of terrorism are examples of political crime. *No es bueno.* That's why it's very important to avoid those situations, and that's relatively easy to control — just don't go places where they have a bad problem with political crime. Even today, there's no way in hell I would travel in the countryside of Mexico, and here's a little free advice: Don't hike near the Iranian border without a map. It's not funny, it's not a game, and it's not adventurous — it's just plain stupid, and by extension, extremely selfish.

Outside of being cautious and exercising a healthy dose of street smarts, some things are just out of our control. You can't always prevent things from happening in life, and the perception that we can make ourselves completely safe is false, and often does us a disservice. In other countries, there is no hypocritical cocoon of safety, and therefore people are much more conscious of their actions and the consequences. Conversely, life in the U.S. for the average person has become such a dream world, so anesthetized from the reality of human existence, that we've become docile, our survival instincts muted. Our lifespans may be longer, but our quality of life and happiness suffer dramatically. I believe the real trick is finding the balance between the two paradigms.

So what's the most dangerous place I traveled to? That's a hard question to answer, but if you put a gun to my head (pun intended), I'd say that big cities in South America were the most dangerous for street crime, and in the Middle East I was most at risk of being a victim of political crime.

Remember that Shane and I backpacked around the world from 1999 to 2000, which was a different time in history before September 11, 2001 changed the world. I consider myself extremely lucky to have seen the Middle East when I did, because it probably won't be safe to go to some of those places again for the rest of my lifetime, and maybe beyond. Even back then, there was some anti-American sentiment, but it was nothing like the shitstorm that exploded once good ole George Bush decided to invade Iraq for no other reason than God talked to him directly (not to avenge his father and siphon oil and contracting profits to his corporate cronies). I'll refrain from telling you what I really think about George Bush and the malignant fingerprints he's left on the post-9/11 world out of fear of losing sales to my Republican fan base, because they're the ones who can read the big words *and* afford to buy the book. But no matter who's in office, Americans are extremely ignorant about what our own country is doing every day outside our borders, and the rest of the world is a lot smarter and more sophisticated than we give them credit for.

When I was in the Middle East there were tricks amongst the fraternity of travelers that you could employ to stay safe, like U.S. citizens sewing Canadian flags on their backpacks to divert the anti-American sentiment, or getting your passport stamped on an extra page in Israel and then removing that page when you crossed over to Islamic countries like Syria, Iran, and Jordan, so you wouldn't be accused of being a Zionist sympathizer.

When I was in Israel I learned firsthand the culture of violence and grew to accept it. The potential for political violence and "terrorism" is an everyday occurrence, so people grow desensitized to it, but that's not to say they become complacent — quite the opposite. However, there is a certain fatalism that grows when you live in a country the size of New Jersey and are completely surrounded by your mortal enemies who deny even your right to exist, and that permeates into everyday life. They tell you not to take the bus in the mornings, because if someone plants a bomb it's probably going to be where the crowds flock. They tell you if you hear a bomb go off, run away from the blast, not toward it, because there is usually a second bomb meant to blow up the crowd the first one attracts. When you go into the movies or a mall the police search your bags and backpacks thoroughly.

Military service is mandatory in Israel, even for women, and so every 19-year-old you see is in uniform and carrying an M16 machine gun. They're required to carry these guns with them even when they're going about their civilian lives, so you might be in a disco and see a stack of machine guns by the front door, or in line at a crowded café and the barrel of one of their machine guns pokes you in the back. These measures aren't just precautions; the war is going on daily — not on battlefields but among the populace.

Several times in Tel Aviv or Jerusalem, I saw police and bomb squad trucks rushing down the streets responding to bomb threats. A bomb went off in the seaside resort city of Eilat while I was there, killing a dozen people. On one of my last days in Tel Aviv, I was taking a stroll on the beach near the beautiful Mediterranean Sea. I had my headphones on so was in my own little world and didn't notice that no one else was around. In the distance I heard yelling but thought nothing of it, until four soldiers came sprinting at me with guns drawn, waving their arms and screaming for me to stop. They told me there was a bomb on the beach and they'd cleared the area of people, but I had inadvertently walked right into the middle of it. Oops. How do the Israelis deal with the stress of this everyday violence? They believe in God, they cherish their families, and they party their asses off. I can dig it.

By the time I got to the Middle East I was devoid of most of my possessions, my fear, and definitely my ego, walking around all day with nothing but a backpack containing a bottle of water, a camera, and a notebook, exploring my surroundings and absorbing everything I could. I wore neither a smile nor a frown — my face a reflective mask of serenity. Each step in the ancient sands brought me joy. Each breath was a miracle. I was a seasoned wanderer by that point, a blue-sky pilgrim on a spiritual journey, fully surrendering to the world and willing to accept the outcome. I think people sensed that about me; they saw it in my eyes or noticed how my dusty clothes hung off my sinewy frame, and didn't consider me a tourist. Between the sun and the dirt I was as dark as an Egyptian, but with my short blonde hair and athletic build people couldn't figure out which country claimed me. A few people even asked if I was a CIA agent or a Mossad (the Israeli secret service) operative.

In Egypt I longed to escape the nasty city of Cairo, whose slums I found to be some of the worst in the world as I witnessed them from the safety of a passing train, so I traveled down to Aswan, near the Sudanese border, and took a felucca, a small open-deck sailboat, up the Nile, sleeping under the open skies. I journeyed to little fishing villages on the Mediterranean, every few days taking a bus to the next village until I was so far out that most of the people had never seen a white person, let alone an American. But I felt I could walk the streets any time of day or night with absolutely no concern for my safety.

One incident really illuminated the difference between the perception and reality of safety for me. I was in Amman, the capital city of Jordan, staying in a hotel with a gregarious proprietor who would invite me into his office for tea and a pleasant chat every day. I heard there was a movie theater downtown, so the Arab gentleman arranged for a taxi driver to take me there. The driver was so ecstatic and curious to have an American in his taxi that he raced around the city introducing me to his family and friends, taking me to his favorite coffee shops to offer me samples of amazing Persian coffee. I was in a taxi cab with a stranger in the middle of a strange city in a country that was conservative Islamic, and no one knew where I was or who I was with, but I've never felt more safe or at ease in my life. He got me to the movie with only minutes to spare, and I watched a military whodunit *The General's Daughter* starring John Travolta. It was a typical violent Hollywood movie with a murder mystery, fight scenes, shootings, and a horrific gang rape on screen. When I got out of the movie and jumped back in the taxi, I actually felt scared; there was a palatable anxiety in me that hadn't existed before the movie. It was incredible that my perception of the world around me was so influenced by media, and I only realized it because I hadn't seen a movie or been exposed to American culture in months.

I traveled across the Egyptian border into Sinai and then through the Gaza Strip into Palestine. The Gaza Strip is the most densely populated plot of land on Earth, and if you've seen it at all it's because the media loves showing footage of angry youths throwing rocks at tanks and burning flags, but my experience was different.

The Palestinian people were shocked when I climbed aboard their local bus. Most of them had never seen an American before other than on TV, but they collectively welcomed me, ushered me to the best seat, introduced themselves, and gave me homemade food for the festive bus ride. We arrived at a border checkpoint — a tricky affair because the Gaza Strip is technically within the borders of Israel, but is its own sequestered nation — and got in line to have our passports checked. I got in line with everyone else and was waiting when all of a sudden three Israeli soldiers started yelling at us, vigorously calling someone in line over to them. I looked around — who was it? Well, it was me of course, but at the time I felt so ingratiated with the local people that it didn't even occur to me. I walked over and they quickly grabbed me and escorted me into a separate line by myself to check my passport. They chastised me, saying that I shouldn't be among Palestinians, and took me into a side room and questioned me for a while to find out who I was and what I was doing. If I felt safe before, I certainly didn't now.

There was a time that I did really mess up — I admit it — and put myself in harm's way in such a manner that could have left me in a world of hurt. At this time, I was in Eilat in Israel, heading to the hippie party town of Dahab on the beach in the Sinai Peninsula.

Every time there's a conflict between Israel and Egypt or its other inhospitable neighbors, the borders get shuffled and Sinai changes hands. At that time it was still within Israeli control, so I thought nothing of the bag of weed I had in my luggage when I bought a ticket for a high-speed boat across the Gulf of Aqaba in the Red Sea to Sinai. It wasn't much — about an eighth of an ounce or so, and I don't even remember where I got it from. At the docks, I was shocked to see that the boat was a huge, ultra-modern ship with hundreds of passengers boarding. There were a few military personnel around, but that's normal for that part of the world, so I boarded with everyone else. Halfway through the hour-long trip, they announced that we'd be going through a security checkpoint in Sinai and so we should have our passports ready. To my horror, we docked at an international militarized zone, complete with U.S. Marines armed with machine guns, NATO troops, plenty of Israeli troops, drug- and bomb-sniffing dogs, and X-ray machines. The security made John F. Kennedy airport look like kindergarten.

My stomach dropped — I was fucked. Everyone lined up and had to go through the metal detector, walk right by the dogs, get frisked, and get our passports stamped with bags in tow. The weed was in my toiletry bag and I was sweating bullets, sure that the dogs would get me. I had no idea what kind of hell of a military prison I would end up in for a very long time if I got caught bringing drugs over international borders, but I got lucky and walked through security and by the dogs with no issues other than a minor heart attack. If you ever want to feel *real* pressure, just walk through an international military checkpoint with illegal substances — it will cure your sense of adventure real quick. When I got to my hostel in Sinai, the first thing I did was flush the weed down the toilet. That was just damn stupid of me and violated the two golden rules I've learned to live my life by: Rule #1 – Don't get caught, and Rule #2 – Refer to Rule #1.

* * *

In South America, Shane and I were subjected to street crime more than anywhere else in the world. That's not saying it's more dangerous than Cairo, because it would have been suicidal to walk into the wrong neighborhoods there, too, but we spent a lot of time in big cities in South America, and those are always grimy in the wrong hoods. Most of these cities were complete shit holes with few redeeming qualities, where we'd find only the extremes of the ultra-rich or the extremely poor. Rio de Janeiro, on the other hand, was one of the coolest places on earth, so vibrant and beautiful that I guarantee I'd be living there already if they spoke Spanish and not Portuguese, which is like trying to understand Bob Dylan drunk with marbles in his mouth, but its city streets and favelas were plagued by gangs, drug cartel warfare, and violent street crime.

The good people of Rio exercise all day and night, and the beaches, soccer fields, and volleyball fields are lit up and busy at 4 a.m. just as if it were four in the afternoon. Shane and I were shooting hoops at a huge park complex outside of Copacabana one night, and we met some cool local guys on the court. One was a DJ who spun a lot of hip-hop in a neighborhood called Lapas. He invited us to a party that night, and hip-hop is one of my first true loves, so we were excited to go.

That night we jumped in a cab, but when we told the driver that we wanted to go to Lapas he did a double take. We had to tell him ten times, but still he didn't want to go into that neighborhood. Finally, he agreed, and we found the address on a dark, deserted street of warehouses, but he wouldn't stop the cab for us. We had to scream at him and open the doors while the car was still rolling for him to drop us off, and then he sped off with tires squealing.

Outside the warehouse there were no signs of life, except for a couple guys standing in the doorway smoking weed. We asked them about the party and showed them the flier and they nodded us in. The warehouse was jumping — a bunch of local kids had rented it out and set up huge speakers and a few pool tables, and had brought in tons of beer. There were hundreds of poor Brazilian city kids and not one other gringo, nor one person who could even be described as middle class. Everyone looked at us hard as we walked in — testing us, of course — but no one gave us shit. We found our DJ friend, and he greeted us enthusiastically and introduced us to his friends, and it was all love from there. We didn't have a problem all night, mixing and mingling with these kids, especially when they saw we loved hip-hop as much as they did. We all drank out of 32-ounce bottles that were about 50 cents each, and got properly faded on some wild Brazilian herbs and danced until six in the morning, when we found a cab to get us back out of there.

In retrospect, I guess you could characterize that as incredibly dangerous — two gringos amongst hundreds of impoverished, glue-sniffing, hip-hop-heads in a Brazilian neighborhood that even the taxi drivers wouldn't go into, but once we got some local love, I felt safer than going to Chili's on a Friday night in the U.S.

You do need to exercise street smarts and be conscious of your surroundings every moment in South American cities; everyone is on the hustle, and you have to feel the energy as much as see what's going on with your eyes to keep it moving and stay safe. Walking the streets at night can be most dangerous, when only drunks, crack heads, and robbers are out on the prowl. A local cat advised us to always carry a beer bottle when we walked at night, and if we even heard footsteps we were to crack the bottle on the pavement and wield it as a knife.

Bolivia was poor even by South American standards, though I enjoyed it thoroughly. La Paz, the main city, is at such a high eleva-tion that it looks like they built a city on a crater on the moon. The young people had all of the passion and anger that every generation experiences, but really no hope for the future. They understood that they'd always be poor as hell and had no choice but to scratch and claw for a meager existence the rest of their lives. Their only outlets were football, beer, music, and partying.

We loved going to the bars in Bolivia because people were so friggin' friendly, though Shane and I stuck out like aliens. We'd show up on a crowded Friday night and jump in line with throngs of Bolivians in their early 20s waiting to get in and blow off a little steam. The party would start in the line; soon enough, the local guys would say wassup to us, asking where we were from and what music we liked and start teaching us slang words and the fight songs for their local football clubs as we all slammed tequila shots. Everyone wanted us to meet their friends, so Shane and I were ushered here and there for introductions and shots to celebrate, split up and not seeing each other again for the entire night, other than passing briefly amongst the insanely crowded, hot club. Crowd control was a real problem because if there was a fire they had no ventilation, no sprinklers, no fire extinguishers, and all of the doors and windows were blocked with bars to keep thieves out. So if there was a fire or a fight, people would panic and trample each other trying to get out the door, and it happened all the time that bar patrons would get stampeded or burnt to a crisp.

One particular night didn't end in a fire but in another kind of pyrotechnics. A bunch of crazy drunk guys were causing trouble on the street outside the bar, so the police came. The police represent more of a corrupt establishment in Third World countries than they do safety and service — no one is happy to see them. The youths started talking shit to them and next thing you know, the cops were spraying tear gas to break up the crowd. Tear gas is a son of a bitch — the green clouds float and linger in the air, sticking to flesh and clothing and drifting on the slightest breeze until the whole area is poisoned and unbreathable. One whiff and your lungs are on fire and your eyes feel like someone poured bleach in them. The tear gas wafted into the club and caused a frenzy of coughing, choking, and people trying to run for the exits. Somehow, I got out and ran across the street to the park to fresh air, where people were rubbing their eyes, gagging, and puking. The bar was dead for an hour until it aired out, so someone bought a bottle of rum and a two-liter bottle of Coke that we mixed in a plastic bag, and we sat around drinking under the green moon until it was safe to go in again.

One of the most dangerous endeavors Shane and I pursued was whitewater rafting down Class 4 rapids on the Rio Pacuare in Costa Rica — on a kayak. I'd never been in a kayak before, and we survived the churning rapids on *cojones* and adrenaline alone. For two days, we got dumped into the swirling cauldron again and again, launched off of six-foot waterfalls, circled the deep "holes" that we might not emerge from, avoided the deadly power of fifty-foot cascades, and generally got tossed around like wet rag dolls. When we were done with the expedition, soaked to the bone and utterly exhausted from fighting the river for our lives, all of the indigenous river guides came up to us and signed one of our dry T-shirts with a Sharpie. They were so impressed we hadn't drowned, and had been making bets on our chances the whole time. The adrenaline rush, the flirtation with near death by drowning, was so addictive that we returned the next weekend to repeat our expedition down the river on a kayak. I still don't know how we lived through that one.

As I look back on my travels, I think I was more at risk of cracking my head open being an adrenaline junkie or dying of dysentery than anything else. I jumped out of a plane in New Zealand, skydiving from 11,000 feet; jumped off a mountain in Brazil, hang-gliding down and landing on the beach; and went trekking through the jungles in Thailand amongst poisonous snakes, rivers swarming with piranhas, and wild elephants. I guess I've realized that you can make all of the good choices you want and live your life in a shell, but true safety only comes from going for it 100% balls out, completely surrendering yourself to the inclination that if it's your time to go, then there's nothing you can do about it.

Today, I'm ten years older and content to have my wild days well behind me. Now that I'm conscious and have more to lose, there's no way I'd do half those things again, but ignorance is bliss when you're young and indestructible. Sure, I still travel a lot, and even live in a Third World country at the time of this writing (Costa Rica — back where it all started), but for the most part my experience and prudence (and 10 p.m. bedtime) keep me out of harm's way.

So what's the secret to being safe while traveling abroad? People. That's it. Win the friendship of some locals and you'll always be as safe as possible in any situation. And here's another secret: The poorer a country or a neighborhood is the safer you'll be if you meet the right people, which is cool by me because I prefer to get down and dirty with the everyday folk anyway. I appreciate their values and respect their daily hustle, and if you show just a modicum of respect and humility, they will treat you like the richest king on earth.

On our travels, Shane and I had a formula that worked like a charm: Upon arriving in a new place we'd make a beeline for the local university or park to find the basketball courts and play hoops. Inevitably, we'd meet some cool guys and gain their respect by mixing it up on the courts and showing them that we were as scrappy as any *los pobres* (poor people). I've met some of the nicest people imaginable that way, in very humble surroundings — people I am still friends with today and would trust with my life. Of course, people would test us a little at first, but I just tried to be myself and surrender to the outcome of any situation while keeping my cool, and I think they sensed that trust and confidence. The fastest way to earn an instant bond and ingratiate myself with locals was to ask them about their families and their hometown. Or, if I wanted to be invited over for dinner, date their sister, and have a life-size statue of me erected in their front yard by noon the next day, I could just cut to the chase and ask them what soccer team they liked and tell them I was a diehard fan of that same team.

Walking With Fire

New Zealand and Australia, September/October 1999

I found myself sitting in a small rubber lifeboat crammed in with eight other passengers, Shane by my side, bobbing on the waves of Sydney Harbor on a crystal sunny day. We wore bright orange inflatable life jackets courtesy of Qantas Airlines. With small rubber paddles we rowed as hard as we could toward the skyline of buildings along the shore, which loomed on the nearby horizon but seemed miles away. There were other boats around us, probably ten in all, holding wet and nervous passengers who rowed in the same direction and hoped for a quick rescue. When we were close enough to be seen by someone on the shore, one of the passengers pulled out a flare gun and shot one off, sending a burst of light into the cloudless blue sky. The cavalry came quickly — a column of Australian Coast Guard rescue boats with red sirens blaring. They pulled up next to us and helped the occupants of the lifeboats climb up a rope ladder. One passenger fell in, cursing the cold water, but he was OK, and other than that we all got on board safely and headed for the marina. The concerned Coast Guard guys gave us blankets and water bottles and asked if anyone had any medical issues.

Soon, we were at the docks and were herded into the cafeteria of an emergency shelter. Nurses, doctors, policemen, and Qantas officials interviewed us to make sure everyone was all right and to assess our medical conditions so they could start a report on each passenger. They wanted to hear our stories, for it's not every day they had to pull plane crash survivors from the Sydney Harbor.

A nurse in a crisp white uniform asked me if I was OK. Yes, I was. She asked what my name was, where I had been sitting, and what happened. As I gave her this information she diligently wrote it on a clipboard. I was supposed to ask her about something, something very important, but I was forgetting. I think it was about my wife or something. Yeah, that was it; I was sitting with my wife, and when the plane crashed into the water and we headed for the exit doors we got separated. I was supposed to ask about my wife's whereabouts.

"Have you seen my wife?" I asked matter-of-factly. "When the plane went down she may have been hurt and I haven't seen her since."

The nurse looked at me with mock concern. Did I get it right? Shit, this was bothering me. I put one finger up and told her to hold on a second, then pulled an index card from my pocket. I read it and shook my head in recognition, and then addressed the nurse again.

"Forget about my wife ... ummmm, I don't even have a wife. But I think I'm having a heart attack." I looked at my index card again. "Yeah, definitely a heart attack. My name is Igor Federov and I am a Russian businessman and I'm having severe chest pain and my left arm is numb. I require immediate medical attention and I am allergic to codeine." The nurse looked annoyed — my gaffe had caused her additional paperwork and she had better things to do on this Saturday morning. She scratched out "lost wife" and start filling in "possible heart attack" on the airplane crash survivor report. I sat back calmly and looked around — there were plane crash survivors on gurneys, requesting translators and looking for lost family members, all with straight faces and bad accents. I hoped this would be finished soon so I could go down to the bar in King's Cross to watch the horse races and put back a few pints.

It was all just a drill. Qantas Airlines was running an emergency plane crash response test and needed volunteers. I was doing some work with the Red Cross in Sydney at the time, mostly on land-mine awareness in war-torn countries, but then they offered me the opportunity to help with a harbor rescue drill, so I got on board.

Everyone was preparing for the upcoming 2000 Summer Olympics in Sydney, so fifty volunteers were rounded up and taken out to the center of Sydney Harbor in boats that sunny morning and dropped onto life rafts and left to their own devices. We'd been briefed on the procedure, and each of us had an index card that listed our name, country of origin, and any special circumstances to report. There are two things I learned that morning: that I never want to be stuck on a lifeboat in the middle of the ocean with a bunch of complaining tourists, and that I am not a good actor. I only had one line on my index card and I still got that confused with someone else's and messed the whole thing up. My attempts at a Russian accent sounded like a constipated Ivan Drago. Then again, Shane only did slightly better as a dehydrated Japanese exchange student.

When we were released from duty, we headed down to King's Cross, a funky neighborhood in the low-rent area of the city filled with hostels and backpackers, pubs overflowing with Tooheys beer, and tattoo parlors. Sitting in between the neighborhoods of Potts Point, Elizabeth Bay, Rushcutters Bay, and Darlinghurst, King's Cross is where the action happens — the red light district that's rumored to be the lair of Sydney's organized crime ring. In the Cross, you could get blindly drunk while rooting for the Australian rugby team or watch a chick fellate a live boa constrictor at a strip bar, all within a four-block radius. I preferred the rugby matches. It's also where Shane and I found a cheap hostel, as my money was getting really tight by the sixth month of traveling around the globe.

In the Cross I even dropped my inhibitions and got my tongue pierced on a whim. I figured why the hell not — if I ever wanted to do something crazy like that, the best time was while I was traveling, when my family couldn't see it and I didn't have a boss to answer to. I was sure that getting a tongue ring would attract all sorts of freaky women, but in reality it just grew infected and so swollen that I walked around drooling and accidentally biting my tongue painfully every ten minutes, and I'm pretty sure that's not attractive no matter how freaky you are.

And King's Cross was also the place where, if you were really looking for them, you could see Aborigines passed out drunk in alleyways or selling trinkets from the shadows of the street. No one seemed to notice them, or talk openly about their plight, or even acknowledge them in passing on the street; it's almost like they were an invisible people.

On the way to the pub I passed a man sitting on the ground under a tree. He was painting, a few jars and brushes scattered around him and several canvases propped up for sale. He was dark — his skin so black that he even paled most Africans, his curly hair falling in thick, brown ringlets. He had rounded features and was roped with muscle, wearing only a pair of red running shorts and walking barefoot. He smiled and introduced himself as Neville Oodgeroo Kneebone and showed me his work in progress. The colors jumped out at me — a kaleidoscope of reds and oranges and yellows snaking around the page. There were no lines, just a series of little dots in circular patterns, but if I zoomed out a little it also looked like a map, or an eagle's-eye view of a mountain range, with a kangaroo in the middle. Everything was interconnected yet its own separate form, so I couldn't find where the painting started or finished, but it told a story in its entirety. He mixed and stirred pigments made from smashed ochre, clay, animal blood, and wood ash.

Although the Aborigines had been painting on rock walls and dried bark for thousands of years, it looked eerily familiar. I saw traces of Indian art, or even the roots of symbolism and movement that I recognized in the work of modern artists like New York graffitist Keith Haring. I complimented the Aborigine man on his painting. He tilted his head slightly and looked right through me with his ancient, sunburnt eyes.

The Aborigines may be the most venerable people on earth. The oldest human skull ever found dates back 40,000 years (sorry, creationists), but there's evidence that descendants of the Aborigines date back 125,000 years. To put it in perspective, that's three years longer than Bob Barker was the host of *The Price Is Right*.

Of course Australia is an island, albeit a huge one that's actually a continental land mass surrounded by smaller islands like Tasmania, so the first inhabitants migrated over from India when the two land-masses were closer. For eons, they had the run of the land, living in loose tribes broken further down into hordes, clans, and totemic groups that held as few as ten people, but if needed they would gather up to 1,000 people for meetings. They had no need for a formal, written-out government; economy; or laws, but followed ancient customs and laws mapped out in the stars in the night sky, called the Songlines. They lived in harmony with the land, believing that they *are* the earth just as much as they are *on* the earth — it's all perfectly interconnected in one reality. At one point, there were 750,000 Aborigines speaking 250 languages and dialects — but then the white man came when the first British fleet landed in Botany Bay in 1788.

The British helped themselves to the area known as New South Wales, establishing it as a penal colony in the late 1700s. By penal colony I don't mean they were all dicks, though that may not be too far off, but that the British shipped their criminals to the island for a prison sentence of isolation and harsh conditions. Disease and mistreatment by the white settlers thinned the ranks of the Aborigines to only about 90,000 in 1900, threatening to extinct the race.

The Aboriginal culture was almost wiped out by the British migrants via an integration of the Aborigines into modern society (or attempts at genocide, depending on who you ask) called the Stolen Generation, or the Stolen Children. For a hundred years, from 1869 until as recently as the 1970s, the Australian government and the Christian church forcibly removed Aboriginal children from their homes and placed them in special missionary schools (or prisons, depending on who you ask) with the rationale of converting them to Christianity. The government and church ripped families and cultures apart and basically kidnapped these children to create a permanent underclass that mimicked their Western/Christian belief system.

And then at 18 years old, these children were turned out, lost without the support of family or an understanding of their true culture. Even their names and language were whitewashed. The damage to the psyche of the Aboriginal people was devastating, and many of them ended up in the cities where they faced crime, poverty, drugs, and alcohol addiction. Their identity, their lives really, had been stolen from them.

Nowadays, the Aborigines have regenerated to about 400,000 people — roughly 2% of Australia's population, but they still remain a permanent underclass in modern society. There are few good schools, fewer good jobs, and not many opportunities for the Aborigines. Until recently, they had no political or social voice, but in the 1990s a movement of reconciliation and reprisals started healing those wounds. At least their plight was brought to light, much of it through mainstream exposure to their culture and art. When I arrived in Australia I had no idea who they were or what they had gone through, but seeing the man under the tree and his beautiful paintings stoked my curiosity, and in some small way connected me to their story.

I was beginning to understand just how important each person's life story truly was, how the threads of our individual lives formed a rich tapestry of existence, documenting the course of our past, and as our threads were interwoven, how it showed our future.

When I started my trip around the world, I was just looking for adventure and a big party, but after a while that lifestyle held less and less appeal to me. I was at a crossroads of consciousness, for the first time asking myself some important questions about life and my place in the world. How could I not after everything I'd seen? I began to truly comprehend just how lucky I was to be born to a good middle-class family in the United States. I had plenty of love, support, food on the table, and I never worried about safety or having a roof over my head. I was luckier than 99% of the world, and yet when I traveled I saw so many warm, kind people with so much appreciation and happiness in their lives. It was humbling to see people sleeping on the street, children going hungry, and those with no opportunity for a better existence transcend the "beautiful struggle" of life, as the poet and rapper Talib Kweli describes it. I was beginning to understand that we are all on this earth for just the blink of an eye, but the legacy we leave behind could become eternal.

But there in Sydney, random acts of violence kept stunting my spiritual journey. It was uncanny how trouble found Shane and me no matter where we went. We were coming off some crazy and dangerous experiences in Central and South America, and I thought that the departure to a more "civilized" country would make us safer, but I found the opposite to be true. Jesus Christ, everywhere we went in Australia we got into fights. One day, we were walking across the street at a crosswalk when a car pulled through the intersection and clipped Shane. I was pissed, and went to the driver's window and banged on it for the driver to get out. Shane was OK, just a little shaken up, but the driver sped off before I had the chance to smack him around.

I had the good fortune of meeting a really cool girl in Australia — a Filipino chick named Monina Applebum, but even hanging out with her brought static. We crossed paths in a park one day, and after I mustered up the balls to approach her we hit it off famously. I found her adorable because she was this petite, pretty Filipina but spoke with a thick Australian accent, like the Queen of England had taken over Tia Carrere's body and just come off a three-day drinking binge. Monina and I explored the city, hanging out on gorgeous Bondi Beach by day and partying at the casino at Darling Harbor at night. But everywhere we went, there was always some ornery white boy ready to talk shit about her being Asian, and one night I almost got jumped by five of them just because I was walking with her. The young white dudes in Australia were racist, anti-immigrant, sexist, and they loved to swill massive amounts of beer and display their toughness — not a good combination for the rest of us. I felt bad for the Aborigines who had been forced to coexist with those assholes for 300 years.

There are others who coexist in Australia's shadow, like the nearby island nation of New Zealand. People always lump the two countries together because they are both hidden in that corner of the Earth, so remote that it feels like you might fall off the edge, but they couldn't be more different. I much preferred New Zealand, where Shane and I spent six weeks before landing in Sydney. It's a tranquil nation far south in the Pacific and damn close to Antarctica, best known for sailing, sheep, and rugby. The inhabitants of this bucolic island nation, which is lined with meandering rocky coastlines and impossibly green pastures, call themselves Kiwis after the national bird. There are only a couple big cities in New Zealand, like the capital, Auckland, and even those are spotless and have a small-town feel.

In Auckland we found ourselves in a pleasant routine — every day, we played basketball at the nearby university with Kiwis, Aussies, and a few really cool kids from the U.S., and walked home along the bay and watched hundreds of sailboats practice maneuvers for the upcoming Sailing World Cup competition. At night, we'd grab a few beers at the Anchor Bar near the Sky Tower or hit a Maori bar where they played hip-hop. The Maori, the indigenous islanders covered with intricate tribal tattoos, were some of the nicest folks on earth, but I definitely wouldn't want to cross them (even many of the women were taller and heavier than me), and I quickly became a fan of their All Blacks rugby team and pretended to understand the matches. But no one ever gave us any static.

Shane and I posted up in an apartment in Auckland right near the university and then rented a car and drove to the Bay of Islands, down to Wellington at the southern tip of the North Island, across the channel on an overnight ferry, and explored the Southern Island with stops in Christchurch and Queenstown. Most nights we crashed in cheap hostels or slept in the car, waking up to sunset vistas that were so wild and rugged they almost looked prehistoric. But it was so safe that you could leave your car or apartment unlocked and never worry about it. People always ask me, when we're talking about how I took a year to travel around the world, what my favorite place was. My answer is always the same: There are places I'd want to go just for the experience, because they're so different from the United States, and then there are places that are so nice I'd consider living there. New Zealand was one such place.

However, you'll never hear me accusing Australia of being equally warm and fuzzy. In Sydney, only a few days after almost getting jumped while walking with Monina Applebum, Shane and I were chilling at a disco in King's Cross when Shane, who was always smooth with the ladies, saw a chick he wanted to meet on the dance floor. He went up to her to say hi and touched her on the arm — to ask her the time or to ask if her feet hurt because she had been running through his mind all night, or something like that. Out of nowhere, this diesel psychopath with a shaved head and prison tats ran onto the dance floor and threw Shane back. He started screaming that no one was going to touch his girlfriend and that he was ready to fight. I ran up behind him and got him in a great chokehold. I have no idea where it came from, but it was pure awesomeness — I had his head, his neck, and his whole right arm completely immobilized like he was a dangling puppet. I guess I should have hit him; I have a bad habit of not taking the cheap shot in a fight, and I thought it was going to cost us dearly. The dude kicked and thrashed, ripping my shirt, but he couldn't get free. By now, the commotion brought four huge bouncers, all rugby-playing Maoris (think Samoans), who made me let the guy go and ushered us to the door. As we all marched outside, I thought for sure I was going to have to fight one of the Maoris, so I began mentally preparing to eat my meals through a straw the rest of my life, but they were cool and just wanted to clear the imbroglio out of the club.

Once we were out front, the psycho guy huffed and puffed and jumped up and down and then charged at Shane, who stood there cool as a cucumber and didn't say anything. As the guy came at him Shane executed a flawless side step and used the guy's momentum to drive him into the side of a parked car. The psycho guy's head hit hard enough to create a dent and set off the car alarm, and from there they both went down on the pavement and punched and kicked a few times before the bouncers broke them up again. Nice work, Shane — all those late nights watching Kung Fu Theater paid off, grasshoppa. We walked off unscathed, but the antics continued.

No trip to Sydney would be complete without a visit to the historic Sydney Opera House, sitting on the northern edge of Sydney Harbor and constructed with white concrete shells and pink granite panels to resemble boat sails at full mast, and we decided to attend a performance. The morning of the opera, I went there to purchase our tickets and was looking at some of the posters of past operas in the entrance hall when I heard a commotion. I turned to see a man, a normal-looking white tourist in his 40s, screaming at the top of his lungs at the gal behind the ticket counter. I have no idea what he was upset about, but judging by the way he was foaming at the mouth and waving his arms frantically, he was out of control and about to get violent. The poor girl was petrified because she was stuck behind the open counter within arm's reach of the lunatic.

Everyone in the place stopped and stared, frozen. His rage escalated until I was sure that he was going to attack her — I had to do something. I walked over and squeezed in between him and the counter, blocking her. I asked him what was going on and told him to calm down, giving him a look so he knew that he'd have to go through me to get to her. This brought him somewhat out of his violent trance. He took a step back and continued to yell, but now the gal was safe and he didn't come at me. The police ran in from outside, came up behind him and wrestled him to the ground, and cuffed him. I advised the cops that I thought he was mentally ill but off his medications. When I turned around, the gal was in tears and looked me in the eye and said thank you as sincerely as I've ever heard a human being say those words. In retrospect, I should have parlayed her gratitude into a hot date and free tickets, but back then I wasn't nearly as opportunistic as I am now.

With all of that behind me, I returned with Shane to the opera house that night. It was a classy affair; most of the men wore suits or tuxedos and the women donned cocktail dresses. The opera was "Turandot" by the Italian Giacomo Puccini, a dynamic explosion of color and movement set in an ancient Chinese emperor's court. Of course it was in Italian, which added to the majesty but made it impossible for me to understand. There was an electronic viewing screen where they translated the singing, or libretto, into English, but our seats were so far in the back that it was out of view. No worries, I sat back and enjoyed it … until the Eurotrash dude next to me started in.

He was some swarthy, self-important Italian with a froggy French girlfriend, and upon the opening scene he started whispering to her. I thought they were just getting settled in, and it was only mildly rude, but I soon realized that they planned on talking the whole time. He was translating the opera to her — word for word. Are you kidding me? I "shhhhd" them once, softly. He kept on. I shushed him again, a little more vehemently, but Monsieur Froggy only got louder. So I told them to shut the hell up. He kept talking but did quiet down a little, and I resigned myself to watching the opera next to the most inconsiderate people on earth without letting it ruin my experience. Shane, in the seat next to me, nodded in approval that I had spoken up.

Once the opera was finished the curtains closed and the lights came on, and I turned to walk away without looking at the Italian. I knew my temper and I didn't even want to go there. To my amazement, he grabbed me by the elbow and yelled at me, "Don't you shush my wife!"

Oh boy, here we go. I was shocked that he'd put his hands on me and I saw red, but I tried to be chill about it. I told him something eloquent, like, "Then don't talk the whole way through a goddamn opera next time." We went back and forth a little bit, and I told him that if he ever touched me again I'd knock him back to ancient China. I tried to simplify the problem for him in terms that any third-grader would understand, explaining that we had all paid a lot of money for these seats to listen to the opera, not to hear him talk the whole time.

"Well, if the money you want, then I pay for your ticket!" he exclaimed, turning up his nose at me.

"OK," I responded, holding out my hand. He was stunned by my reaction but didn't say anything.

"OK, dude, give me the money, then. I accept your offer," I said. He hemmed and hawed but of course didn't reach for his wallet. A couple people around us chuckled that I had called him on his bluff and made him look like a fool. It was going nowhere, and the next step was for me to smash his arrogant Eurotrash teeth in, but Shane pulled me away. I knew I couldn't do anything about it, not because I'd even have to break a sweat to mop the floor with him, but because my mom — my dear, sweet mom, who is a huge opera buff — would be heartbroken if her son got in a fight and was arrested at the Sydney Opera House. Love ya, Mom!

I wanted to experience a more tranquil life, to have my environment match the budding spiritual awareness within me. A short train ride away from Sydney found me in the Blue Mountains, where I spent a week at a working sheep farm. Shane had to fly back to California for a week to be in a friend's wedding, so it was a good time for me to find a more peaceful setting. I thoroughly enjoyed my dawn runs through the groves of eucalyptus trees, the misty paddocks wetting my sneakers as I chased after kangaroos that bounded away when they heard me. I watched the Aborigine farmhands going about their work. They seemed most at home, at peace, in the natural beauty of the mountains, never rushed or stressed but fluid in their movements, like they had an extra hour in the day that the rest of us didn't. I watched the farmhands shear sheep and respected how difficult and backbreaking the work was, though it all looked pretty gross to me. The extent of my farm work was struggling to milk a cow and hoping it wasn't actually a bull.

I sat with the Aborigines on the front porch after dinner, when their pipe smoke kept the bugs away and we could watch the stars come out one by one. Each star had a name and a story behind it, which the farmhands talked about like they were long-lost ancestors showing up at their front door. They seemed surprised, but encouraged, that I was even interested in their culture and they told me about some of their customs. They explained the ceremony called the Bora, when a young boy becomes a man; how at a funeral they gather and paint their bodies white and even cut themselves to express sorrow to the dead; and how they may leave on a walkabout, a spiritual journey where they travel long distances on foot out in the wilderness, retracing the steps of their ancestors and the gods during the time of creation. But my favorite Aboriginal tradition was that when you became married, you were never allowed to talk to the mother-in-law directly, nor she to you; all communication had to be through a third party. I think a lot of people in the States could get down with that!

I began to understand what they called the "Dreaming." In the Aboriginal belief system, the world was created in the "Dreamtime," where nothing else existed until their ancestors, called the First Peoples, walked the land, creating everything and naming it all as they went. The Aborigines have always kept history through passing down oral traditions and lore, and their "religion" is really a spiritual connection with the earth and a reverence for the time of creation, the Dreaming. But it is also the present day reality, for there really is no difference between past, present, and future, far or near. Everything is interconnected in space and in time. We are all small, insignificant dots, but if it wasn't for every one of us there would be a void in the painting.

The Dreaming means that nothing in this life is truly real, and everything you can't see or touch is just as tangible as the rock and the tree and the sky around us. It's all just a journey, with no beginning and no end — if you walk about for long enough, you end up back right where you started, and I realized that I was already in the middle of it. I watched the fireflies zip trails of lightning in the evening sky and thought how blessed I was to be on my own walkabout, to experience my own Dreaming.

Less than a year after I left Sydney, the 2000 Summer Olympics went off without a hitch. No Russian businessman named Igor Federov had a heart attack, nor did he misplace his wife. No Qantas aircraft crashed in the bay and needed to be fished out. It was an historic event, christening the millennium and shining a light on a part of the world that was both ancient and new.

Watching it on TV in the United States, where I was safe from Aussie meat-heads taking a swing at me, I saw an Australian woman, a sprinter named Kathy Walker, be handed the torch, and watched her light the Olympic ring at the opening ceremonies. She went on to compete brilliantly in the Games, winning her 400-meter event and becoming the first person ever to light the Olympic flame and go on to win a gold medal. I smiled and got goose bumps thinking about the colorful dot Kathy Walker had just painted in her own Dreaming, and how gracefully she had walked with fire, for Kathy Walker was a full-blooded Aborigine.

Flip-Flop Heroes

The Philippines,
November/December 1999

Everywhere we traveled we played basketball. It served several purposes: It kept us in great shape (there was nothing better than stretching my legs and sweating for a few hours on a hoop court if I'd been cramped up on a plane for seven hours), but basketball was also our ambassador, our way of making friends with the locals and experiencing the culture that we definitely couldn't find at the Hard Rock Cafe. Basketball is not the world's most popular sport — that's soccer (football), by leaps and bounds — so oftentimes hoop games were hard to find. I'm not that into soccer, but they were fanatical about it in any country where they carry man-purses and use the metric system. I never really felt like watching grown men taking a dive on the ground on purpose, clutching their legs while squirming with histrionics more befitting a six year old Girl Scout stung by a bee in an attempt to elicit a pretty colorful card for their opponent, so I stuck to hoops. That search led us to many college campuses, downtrodden public parks, and into dangerous slums. We were among the common people, and our safety was only assured once we earned our respect on the court. We were the whitest things out there other than the backboards, and it was all good.

Shane was a much better baller than me. His game was incredibly efficient, with a deadly jump shot and a vertical leap that allowed him to play above the rim. His motor was always running, and his nonstop hustle when rebounding earned him the nickname "Scrap Dog" back in the States.

When I worked really hard to get in great shape I was, at best, an above average athlete with decent hoop skills, but nothing spectacular — though I was a good passer, rebounder, and all-around team player. Where Shane had pure love for the game, I enjoyed it but got frustrated that I didn't play better. Most of the time I fumbled through it and got by on pure heart and hustle, but in one rare moment one night in Rio de Janeiro, on an outdoor court next to the beach, my potential was revealed: I couldn't miss. That night, I hit jumper after jumper from everywhere on the court, no matter who was in my face. I wasn't even thinking — just letting them fly. I must have hit ten long jumpers in a span of two games. It felt effortless, and I glided down the court in a perfect zone that even had the locals cheering as I swished shots. But after that night my hot hand quickly faded, and soon I was back to the pedestrian, over-thinking-but-gritty player I had always been. That's OK; basketball was still a hell of a lot of fun. I'd met some of the coolest people on basketball courts all over the world: Big Santi and Crazy Gringo John in Ecuador, Luis "El Toro" Diego and Tony "the Tiger Tico" in Costa Rica, Ben in New Zealand, Frank Captain in Australia, and DJ Lapa in Brazil, and those friendships opened the door to experiences that no other tourist could fathom.

Our search for a great hoop game, for sublime athletic bliss, never led us further on a wild goose chase or was more rewarding in the end than in the Philippines. I didn't know much about the country but assumed that it would be well developed because of the U.S. military influence there. That notion was quickly dispelled when I looked out the airplane window as we landed amongst pockets of shantytowns and garbage dumps. Manila looked like a city had once been there but a nuclear bomb had detonated and decades later, the jungle was taking over. It didn't seem like people had homes; they were always on the street working, eating their meals, falling asleep in the back of their cars or on park benches, and probably even making love out there. The traffic made Los Angeles' highways look like country roads on a Sunday afternoon. Several times, we hopped in a taxi and asked the driver to take us to some tourist destination only to get stuck in a maze of gridlocked traffic for hours, the driver honking and yelling and nudging and rolling onto the sidewalk, but unable to make forward progress. Eventually, he'd give up and we'd have to turn back. We kept the windows rolled up because of the pollution that turned the sky a hazy, pea-soup color. People on the street wore bandanas over their faces to try and keep out the belching black smoke, and even the shoeshine boys wore ski masks as they whistled and snapped their rags.

The tropical sun burned through the haze and made everyone wilt by noon. Women carried umbrellas on the street to try and block the sun's rays. To take refuge from the heat, we visited the local shopping mall to let the AC wash over us. The place was gigantic and every day we strolled around, never buying anything but spending a few blissful hours in the cool temperatures. I guess that young gringos with white skin were a rarity around there because families or teenage girls would stop us and want to take pictures together. Little kids ran up and touched my arm hair, amazed that it was blonde. I found everyone to be so warm and friendly, it was touching. I seriously think Filipinos are the sweetest people on earth — much more agreeable than my stern and cranky German stock. That's the same experience I've had in the United States, where new Filipino friends have treated me like family instantly (shout-out to my peeps Gale, Joyce, and Charito!). At the mall, I'm sure they didn't suspect that I really couldn't afford to buy anything and was just exploiting their free AC, but it was an ego boost just the same. In my six weeks in the Philippines, I didn't purchase anything other than a notebook to write in, but I was never happier on my trip around the world because I was completely devoid of material desires — there was nothing to do but enjoy the people around me and feel blessed for what I already had.

It was early November, but the whole city was already decorated in Christmas lights. The Philippines is a devoutly Roman Catholic country and they don't celebrate Thanksgiving, so the Christmas festivities start months in advance. The entire city glowed with strands of blinking red and green lights, which looked surreal when it was one hundred degrees and there wasn't snow within five thousand miles.

We searched high and low but we couldn't find a basketball court. We asked the porters in our hotel, waiters at the bar, and even at the sporting goods store in the mall, but no one could give us a definitive answer as to where we could play hoops in Manila, though they were nice enough to sell us a red-white-and-blue rubber ball that looked like a holdover from the ABA. But then, one night, we found a bar packed with patrons jamming out to a great band on stage jumping seamlessly from the Rolling Stones to the Black Eyed Peas to the Beatles and back to Britney Spears, often sounding better than the original musicians. The table next to us was filled with college kids with "Pinoy Pride" on their jackets who invited us over to drink with them. We asked them if basketball was popular in the Philippines, to which they said gave a vigorous "yes" and yelled, "Michael Jordan." OK, at least they knew what sport we were talking about. They told us about a place we could play. Really? Shane and I perked up. We tried to piece their words together with their heavy accents and inebriated slurring in between singing along to a Ricky Martin song, and I understood the name "Angeles City," and something else about "Rodman." Rodman? Was that the name of a neighborhood or a park or something? Or were they still reciting their favorite Bulls players? They assured us that Angeles City was where we wanted to go, and that it was close.

The next morning, we headed to the bus station and walked around aimlessly, looking for the correct bus and repeating the name "Angeles" to anyone who would listen. We had to squeeze in three to a seat on a sweltering converted school bus with sparkly diamond plating, Filipino flags, and colorful stickers plastered on every inch of the outside. I was jammed in between a mother breast-feeding her baby and a farmer holding a cage with a live chicken in it. At least it was going to be a short ride, like our friends in the bar promised.

Seven hours later we arrived in Angeles City, my shirt soaked in sweat and baby puke, our faces blackened with diesel fumes. We found a cheap hotel with white tile floors and walls like an insane asylum where I changed my shirt, and we hit the streets to look for the basketball court. We asked the first person we ran into where the court was, and he pointed to the ball and said, "Rodman!" and motioned for us to head up the street. There it was again — this "Rodman" talk. Was it a Tagalog word or something? I was hoping it meant "props and free beer to all gringos over 5 feet 7 inches tall," but I wasn't holding my breath. We walked up the road into the heart of Angeles.

It was only dusk, but the streets were already packed with paunchy, middle-aged white guys in socks and sandals arm in arm with attractive Filipina ladies, walking into bars. It seemed like there were hundreds of bars, all blasting dance music and advertising the coldest beer with chromatic neon signs. What was this place all about? We went into the first watering hole and bellied up to the bar, ordering San Miguel drafts. It looked like a strip club, the whole back side of the room taken up by a stage with brass poles and mirrored walls. A tattoo chair sat in the middle of the dance floor just in case a drunk patron wanted to make yet another permanent bad decision.

The bartender was a burly gringo wearing a Hell's Angels leather vest. He told us that we were now in Balibago, the seediest nightlife district in Angeles City. Years ago, the town had catered to all of the American GIs from nearby Clark Air Force Base who wanted to do nothing but drink, fight, and fuck when they were given 48 hours' leave. Angeles had all of that, every go-go bar filled with party girls, prostitutes, and dealers with hash and heroin smuggled in from Thailand. You could find anything you wanted and the law was nonexistent.

Clark Air Force Base was a stronghold in World War II for Allied planes to launch campaigns against the Japanese, but in 1991 nearby Mount Pinatubo erupted in a volcanic blast that did serious damage. Soon after that, the U.S. lowered its flag and vacated the base, and the grounds stood abandoned for years, open to looters and any drug traffickers who wanted to set up shop. With the GIs and their dollars gone virtually overnight, the town went from a bustling bazaar of sin to a sad shell of its notorious infamy. There were the same number of bars and the same number of hustlers and girls trying to make money, but only a few hundred, instead of thousands, of drunk patrons every weekend. Years later, it did start to fill up again, this time with American ex-pats and perverts, those too socially unacceptable or too broke to ever pull a date in the U.S., let alone pay their rent.

Our biker-bartender excused himself and walked to the end of the bar to ring a cowbell at full blast about ten feet from my head. I almost fell off the stool as the ringing echoed in my empty brain. On cue, a dozen attractive girls in their late teens or early 20s walked out onto the stage in red or white bikinis with a numbered card hanging off their g-strings. They looked like a busload of Hawaiian swimsuit models lining up to buy ham at the deli counter. The bad disco music went up three notches and the girls started to writhe and gyrate, laughing and teasing one another by trying to pull off each other's tops. A withered white guy in an Army jacket smoking a cigar in the corner signaled to the bartender which number he wanted, and the girl came down off the stage, took him by the hand, and led him out of sight through a bamboo beaded curtain.

That was Angeles. There really was nothing else to it — just party after party, day after day, bars filled with countless girls and nasty American dudes with a couple dollars to throw around, because they definitely weren't spending them on gym memberships or dental care. You could find a donkey show easier than a church service, and the girls did things with beer bottles that would make Ron Jeremy blush. But they were just doing what they had to do to survive, and probably sending most of the money back to their poor families in the country. They were still filled with laughter and had joy in their eyes, but the gringos just looked damn pathetic stumbling around half drunk with pickled yellow skin, chain-smoking over warm beers in the noon heat. Even the streets all looked the same, and the sun never seemed to shine through the haze.

To this day when I see a gal in the States who is half Filipina and half white or black, and she's in her 30s or 40s, I can ask if her mom was from Angeles and about 90% of the time I'm correct, leaving her amazed, like I'm the best psychic since Aunt Cleo. Usually, they don't have a clue what Angeles is all about, or that their mom was probably a bar girl who got knocked up by a rambunctious GI with a few bucks in his pocket.

Over the next few days, we hung out at bars with nonstop thumping music and neon lights casting shadows on so many hot young Filipina chicks that it all became a blur. We drank with muscled-up Special Forces soldiers on weekend leave from all sorts of dangerous hot spots in the Pacific Theater. Shane and I looked younger than our ages, and we were athletically built with short haircuts, so the soldiers would inevitably ask us where we were stationed. When we denied being in any military service, they sized us up with newfound curiosity, falling silent for a few sips of whiskey before asking again, this time in hushed tones. No seriously, we weren't in the service, we'd say. We were just travelers backpacking around the world. Yeah, right — in Angeles? They weren't buying it, and every time we denied the obvious, they mentally promoted us to a higher rank in a more secretive unit of the military. Eventually, they came to the conclusion that we were CIA agents and bought us tequila shots and treated us with reverence. The CIA? Come on, now — with my rap sheet I probably couldn't even get approved for a library card, but I took the free shots anyway and declined the lime and salt; Special Ops soldiers like myself don't need training wheels.

We kept asking around for a basketball court with no luck. It was apparent that there was plenty of ball-handling going on in Angeles, but it wasn't on the hoop court. I wore a New York Knicks jersey around town, and everywhere I went the girls giggled and pointed and said, "Rodman" to me. What the hell was it with this Rodman thing? This was a Knicks jersey, and I *know* Dennis Rodman never played for the Knicks.

Finally, we'd had about enough of that little brown sin city, so we planned to take a bus out of there the next day. On that last night we were chilling on the street, eating roasted chicken and rice we bought from a vendor for $2, when I looked up. A tall black gentleman was sauntering down the street with a woman on each arm, wearing a Chicago Bull's jersey with number 91 on it — Dennis Rodman. He had to be about 6'8" tall and was the spitting image of Dennis himself. I hollered over good-naturedly that the Knicks were gonna win it all that year, and he looked back and smiled. That's how we got to meet Philander Rodman, Dennis Rodman's biological dad. He was a super nice guy, and we bullshitted on the street a little before he invited us back to his bar.

Philander was an interesting cat: He had 27 children — count 'em, 27 — though he'd had fallen out of touch with or didn't support a number of them. Shane and I hung out with him in his bar all that night and the next afternoon. It turns out he was a local legend in the

Philippines, blatantly living off his son's fame, even though he was publicly estranged from Dennis. He told us about his plans to write a book about their (lack of a) relationship. Philander was perpetually accompanied by two middle-aged Filipinas who catered to us and pandered to his every need, and as far as I could ascertain he was in a romantic relationship with both of them. Just when I was pegging him as a … well, as a philanderer, he told us that some of his 27 children were adopted and that he ran several charities that bought wheelchairs and medical care for Filipino orphans who otherwise couldn't afford it.

We asked Philander where we could play hoops — who would know better? He thought for a while and told us that there wasn't much basketball in Angeles, but further south in the country, like in Davao or Cebu City on the Visayan Islands, we might find some basketball tournaments. Cool — finally we were making progress. Philander offered to drive us to the airport and was so hospitable that he wouldn't even let us carry our own backpacks, instead piling our 75-pound packs onto one of his 4'10" Filipina wives to carry. We jumped an island-hopper flight down to Cebu City, watching hundreds of small tropical islands sprawled out in the ocean below us.

Cebu is a sunny colonial city with 400-year-old Spanish ruins on its turquoise waterline. Even though it is the second-largest city in the Philippines, it's much more mellow than Manila. We managed to find a local sports store and asked the manager where we could play basketball, but he just pointed to a banner hanging on the wall and shoved a sign-up sheet in our faces. What was this? He wanted to enlist us to run the upcoming Cebu Marathon. Shane and I looked at each other in disappointment — still no hoops, but the entry fee was only $10, and we didn't want to be rude, so we signed up. I'd never run a marathon in my life, in fact the furthest I'd ever run was a few 10K races. These days I was more about pushups on hotel floors, half-court hoops, and steadily hydrating with beer. But why the hell not — it was only 26.2 miles, right? The store workers applauded when we handed the signed forms back to them, like they had just discovered some Kenyan super-runners. How long did we have to train? I inquired, hoping the race was at least a couple weeks away. It was the next morning. Oh, shit. They told us we had to be at a local Italian eatery at 6:00 that evening along with all of the other racers to go over the details during the pre-race meal.

Back at the hotel, I carefully planned my race attire. I took off the long basketball shorts, Knicks jersey, and cheap Reebok sneakers I was wearing and threw them on the bed. From what I'd seen on TV, when people ran marathons they wore impossibly skimpy nylon outfits. I didn't have anything skimpy, but I could easily cut off my one pair of jeans and make some nut-hugger jean shorts. Also, wasn't I supposed to put Vaseline and Band-Aids on my nipples or something? Or was that for ravers on ecstasy who danced all night long? I was getting mixed up, but thought it might be best to keep my jeans intact and not show up at the starting line looking like Richard Simmons going to a rave. I rifled through my luggage to find an outfit that would be more appropriate for running a marathon. I pulled out all of my clothing options and laid them on the bed carefully. What I decided on was a pair of long basketball shorts, a Knicks jersey, and a cheap pair of Reeboks. OK, problem solved.

We found the restaurant and walked into the midst of 500 Filipino guys, each one shorter and in better shape than the next, all ready to run the race the next day. The room fell silent when we entered as they sized up their new competition. They started whispering amongst themselves and pointing at our legs. We were the only white guys in the room, and they thought for sure that our long legs gave us a decided advantage to win the marathon. I'm not that tall by U.S. standards — about 5'11" (6'3" with the afro) — and Shane is a leggy 6'2", but compared to 5'4" dudes I must have looked like Carl Lewis. The activity in the room throttled back up again as they huddled together and readjusted the odds, hashed out new strategies, and cursed the gringos who surely must be professional distance runners who flew in just for the race.

I can confidently say that my favorite part about a marathon is carbo-loading the night before. We sat at long tables, and of course they gave us white-skinned distance-running superstars the head of the tables, and the waiters brought out huge bowls of spaghetti. Everyone dug in and I was loving it — an all-you-can-eat that rivaled Tuesday nights at the Olive Garden. I ordered baskets of garlic bread, meatballs, and sprinkled Parmesan cheese on everything. The other runners stuck to spaghetti with little sauce and water, and looked on in amazement at my eating display. Surely I must be an Olympic-caliber athlete the way I was carelessly ingesting calories, because no amateur in his right mind would eat all of that bad stuff the night before a marathon. Half of them probably considered dropping out when I had the waiter bring me a bottle of cabernet and toasted to their health.

By midnight, I was stuffed and quite drunk, with stained red teeth. The other runners retired to their hotel rooms one by one until just a few of us were left. It occurred to me that we didn't have many details on the race, so I asked the guy next to me what time it was starting the next day; maybe I could sleep late and get in a nice breakfast before heading out. He pointed to his watch and told me that the race started at 4:00. Four o'clock, huh, that's pretty late in the day to be starting a race that could last five hours. No, no, he told me, 4:00 a.m. Oh, shit, the race was starting in four hours.

Shane and I got a few hours of sleep, but I was still tipsy and red-toothed when we arrived at the starting line in the pitch-black morning. They started the race so early so the runners could finish by the time the sun really started blasting the pavement. They signed us in at a registration table and helped us safety-pin our race numbers to our shirts, which made me sort of feel like a bar girl in Angeles. Maybe a nice gringo would come take me away from all this so I wouldn't have to run. We tried to hide in the back of the pack, but our competitors wouldn't have it, ushering us to the very front right under the starting-line banner.

Bang! The starting gun went off and 500 Filipinos bolted into action. My first reaction was to duck for cover because where I'm from, when a gun goes off it's not for a road race. I started off number one, but within ten seconds I was number 124. A wave of humanity pressed against my back, everyone charged with adrenaline to launch into the 26-mile endeavor, but as the street turned and widened the runners spread out into loose groups, each at their own pace. This was way different than running a few miles for exercise or sprinting up and down the hoop court. I tried to keep up with Shane, but after three miles I couldn't keep kicking with him and he left me in the dust.

We were leaving the city and heading into smaller towns, and then into the countryside lined with sugar cane fields and chicken farms. I thought I was doing pretty well, especially considering that I was still slightly drunk and filled with enough pasta to make Tony Soprano push back from the table, but those little Flip runners kept blowing right past me. Around mile seven, my face was a lovely purple color and I was breathing like a water buffalo giving birth. The real marathoners were just warming up and left me in the rear-view mirror with scornful looks, not because they condemned me for being an inferior athlete, but because they had so grossly misjudged me as the Great White Hope Olympian.

All of the men under 30 years old had long since passed me, but over the next few miles phalanxes of older men with graying hair, portly women, and then a few wheelchair athletes passed me. I swear I saw a pregnant woman smoking a cigarette and pulling a rickshaw lap me around one remote village. I kept laying one foot in front of the other, but my legs were like rubber so it was all a struggle. My back was tightening up and my feet were killing me, not just from the pounding on the pavement, but because my skin was rubbing inside my shoe the wrong way and causing agonizing pain. It was at that point that I realized if I was going to finish this race, my mind had to take over. I would do this, I told myself — I would run this marathon. No matter what, I wouldn't stop. I was going to make it a seminal event in my life by transcending the limits of my physical body and setting my soul free.

Have you ever heard of "runner's high," where you get in such a groove that your breathing becomes meditative and you actually feel like you're floating outside of your body, the miles melting away effortlessly? Yeah, well, I never got that. Maybe those cheesy breadsticks were weighing down my soul, but all of a sudden it sounded a lot better to kick back on my fluffy hotel bed and watch SportsCenter while eating coconut pancakes from room service than run around out in the jungle. I flagged down the first taxi that passed and collapsed into the back seat, sweating and panting, and told the driver to high-tail it to the hotel. I ducked down when we passed the streets near the marathon's course so they wouldn't see me trying not to puke. I limped into the hotel and up to my room and ordered breakfast and a pitcher of pineapple juice from room service, and carefully unlaced my sneakers. I had doubled up my socks, but they were still soaked with blood.

Shane limped in an hour later, looking a lot better off than me. We checked the course map and figured out that he had run an amazing 19 miles before stopping, and I had made it 11 miles. Not bad for a couple of gringos who hadn't trained at all, but we still hadn't found a basketball game in the Philippines.

Our six weeks in the Philippines were drawing to a close, and we had a flight scheduled to take us to Thailand for Christmas and New Year's Eve within the week. We got a ride on an island-hopper flight back up to Manila and put down our Lonely Planet Philippines guide in favor of an unopened Thailand edition. I had pretty much given up on our hoop dreams, but we still carried the red-white-and-blue basketball around Manila with us, whether out of habit or hope I cannot say.

We made one more visit to our favorite mall, where we sat down to eat at Goldilocks. Our table was filled with steaming dishes of lumpia, pancet, and chicken adobo as Shane and I discussed our plans for Thailand. The basketball rolled off the chair where we had placed it and across the floor, and I gave chase. I followed it to a table in the corner of the restaurant where an old bearded man had picked it up and was playing with it and laughing. He only spoke Tagalog, but his teenage daughter translated for him when he asked us if we were basketball players. Why, do you know a place we can play? I asked, just kidding around. Sure, she responded, he knew a nice court where they played basketball.

We were stunned and questioned him optimistically, but after being burned so many times before we were skeptical. The old man gave us a good lead on a guy he knew who was in a basketball league, and from there we followed the trail to his home, over to his neighbor's house when he wasn't there, and eventually to a garage mechanic's shop littered with abandoned car parts and stray cats. Was there a court here, we asked? No — this was where the guy's cousin worked. The cousin came out and talked to us for a while in Tagalog and pointed in the other direction. The old man's daughter, translated that we were supposed to head deeper into Manila and look for a certain market. What the hell did a market have to do with a basketball court? Was there someone else to ask there? Were we going to run into Larry Bird's dad, or have to join a triathlon? Who the hell knew, but we set off alone that way, too lost to go back, with nothing but faith and some bad directions.

We found the market after hoofing it for miles, seemingly backtracking and crossing in and out of increasingly crappier neighborhoods. It was deep inside the city, an open-air bazaar at the intersection of four roads and a nearby bus stop. People unloaded fruits, vegetables, cigarettes, and clothing from their motorcycles, bicycles, and pickup trucks and sold them from rickety wooden stands or on cardboard right on the street. As far as I could tell, there were no other Americans within miles, nor any familiar faces or police. All of a sudden, I felt pretty conspicuous in this dangerous Third World city with my wallet, passport, and camera in my backpack. The locals looked us up and down like we were an oddity and then went back to their business of buying and selling things to make a living. We asked a bus driver where the basketball court was and he pointed across the street. I was excited — we had finally found it! We'd have a proper basketball court to run up and down and play full court games all afternoon. Then I saw what he was pointing at.

The "court" was just a rusted iron rim with no net and a wooden backboard slapped together from the tops of packing crates. It hung at a slight angle around nine and a half feet off the ground, nailed to a wooden electric pole right next to the busy street.

That was it? That was the best basketball court we could find in all of Manila? Even if we could find people to play on this beat-up homemade rim, our "court" would be right in the middle of the street where the traffic zipped by. We looked at each other, stunned, and burst out in laughter. How could we not? I grabbed the ball and put it back in the backpack, ready to start walking to find a taxicab and take the long journey back to our hotel. But Shane grabbed the ball and had another idea.

We dodged our way across the street and stood almost directly under the hoop, the only place we wouldn't get run over. Shane threw up the first layup and it rattled in. I collected the ball and did the same on the other side. A few people looked over, thinking that either we were touched in the head or were attempting suicide-by-traffic. Shane and I kept taking a few dribbles and putting up layups and baby hooks right under the basket. I strapped my backpack around the electric pole so it would always be in view while we played. A vendor next to us selling magazines laughed good-naturedly when I missed a layup. I handed him the ball and waved him onto the street to try a shot himself. He was hesitant to come, but Shane and I dragged him out after he had laughed at us. He took a shot and it flew over the whole backboard and bounced into the market. Some of his friends around his stand laughed at *him*, and he called for the ball so he could shoot again.

Now we had three people shooting hoops and a handful of bystanders. Our new Filipino friend got a little braver and stepped out into the street to shoot a jump shot. The cars honked but slowed and swerved around him. At least he had carved out some space to dribble and take ten-foot jumpers. More heads turned. I made a jump shot and heard some gleeful applause behind me. Four dirty street kids sat on the curb, cheering on our game with big smiles on their faces. We pulled them into our circle and showed them how to shoot the ball, and as they missed we lifted them up so they could put the ball in the basket at point-blank range.

Out of nowhere, three older teenagers appeared, wearing ratty hoop shorts and flip-flops. They looked a little rough, with knife scars on their arms and broken noses, and for a moment we didn't know if they were there to rob us or to kick us off their turf or what. I passed the basketball to the biggest one and motioned for him to shoot. A smile appeared on his face as he took a couple dribbles and nailed a fifteen-foot jumper. We had some competition.

The guys turned out to be friendly, and they pushed the gathering crowd back so we had more room to play. We split up our six players into teams, four of the six around 5'6" tall and wearing flip-flops, and set the lip of the sidewalk as the baseline. We were going to play to 21 by ones, but if you hit a shot past the manhole cover it was a two-pointer.

By now, most of the vendors and market patrons had wandered over to see what the commotion was. I checked the ball to my opponent at the top of the key (the middle of the street) and the game started. He immediately blew by me and executed a flawless reverse layup to score. Wow, this guy was good! I had assumed that it would be a crappy game because they would be falling all over in flip-flops and they were all short, but actually these guys were great athletes. They cut, ran, jumped, and D'd up just like they were wearing the newest pair of Jordans. Believe me, it's a little embarrassing to be outrebounded by a guy half a foot shorter than you wearing flip-flops, so I stepped up my intensity and soon we were hustling, scrapping, and sweating at full speed. A kid whistled every time a car came through that didn't want to swerve out of our way, or a bus that would surely squash us all, and we would scramble to the safety of the sidewalk. It was a great game and we managed to win by only a few points.

I paused to catch my breath, but three new muscular Filipino guys in flip-flops stepped on the court, ready to play next. I looked up while panting for oxygen and was amazed; it seemed that every man, woman, and child within a block of the market was standing in a big crowd around our game, cheering on the local players and celebrating every good move or made shot. Someone had even moved his pickup truck to block oncoming traffic on one side of the street so our game wouldn't be interrupted.

We played four more games against these Filipino guys — exhausting, sweaty, hotly contested matches at full throttle. They weren't the most skilled players but hustled like crazy because they were playing for pride, representing the heart of their people. I won some and lost some and didn't play particularly great that day, but it was a victorious moment for everyone involved nonetheless. I could feel the love emanate from the rowdy crowd, who were pleased to be thoroughly entertained by their flip-flop heroes.

Soon, all of us were spent and thirsty, and the bystanders wandered back to their jobs in the market or got on with their day. It was approaching five o'clock and the rush-hour cars had to get through, so the court disappeared and the street became a traffic thoroughfare once again. We congratulated our newfound friends and gave them homie hugs as they said goodbye. The street kids were still around, so we grabbed them and put them on our shoulders and had a lady snap a couple of photos with my camera. I gave one of them the ball and we walked out of the market with the locals yelling goodbye and slapping us on the backs. We were still hopelessly lost on the way out of the barrios of Manila, and as the sun went down Christmas lights quickly clicked on one by one, but this time it didn't matter; we had finally found our basketball game and the soul of the people at the same time, and I was in no rush to walk away.

The Afternoon Ice Cream Club
Thailand, December/January 2000

All of the backpackers stayed on Khosan Road, a row of dingy hostels, seedy bars, and internet cafés that catered to the young party crowd in Bangkok — a mélange of sweat-soaked T-shirts, bad house music, and hashish smoke. Always the iconoclasts, Shane and I had a cab driver take us on a random jaunt through the city and yelled "stop" when we were in a neighborhood where we saw the fewest people who looked like us.

It turns out we'd chosen a district called "Little Arabia" on Sukhumvit Road, a part of the city reserved for Muslims and Arab businessmen trading spices, fabrics, and knockoff merchandise. One whole city block was consumed by a massive sky-rise advertised as the "Grace Hotel," and we sauntered in. The Grace Hotel was like a city unto itself — a fifty-story-high complex with bars, restaurants, a disco, a bowling alley, a movie theater, shops, tailors, barbers, saunas, massage parlors, banks, and an Arabian cabaret inside. The other patrons were all from Saudi Arabia, Iran, Iraq, or Turkey, dressed in traditional Muslim garb, and they bartered and closed business deals night and day without having to leave the hotel.

We visited every nook and cranny of the "Lack of Grace" hotel, as Shane aptly called it, which was a homogeneous slice of the Middle East surgically removed and transplanted into the heart of Bangkok.

We had no idea what an Arabian cabaret was, so one morning around 6 a.m. we took the elevator down to the bottom floor to check it out. We walked out into a strange room with red carpet covering the floor and all of the walls, but no furniture. Dividing the room, which was as big as a basketball court, was a floor-to-ceiling glass wall. On the other side we could see the identical red carpet room except with red carpeted stages and wide steps. Everywhere you looked there were Thai women in bikinis sprawled out sleeping, all with numbers pinned to their thongs.

A fully clothed madam greeted us and chirpingly told us that we could pick whichever women we wanted for special massages. She started clapping and yelling to wake the girls up. Oops. We took a step back and told her that we'd made a mistake and that we were just looking to see what this place was, but she wouldn't hear it. She clapped louder and the girls began to wake up and come to life, groggily looking up and starting to line up against the glass wall. We apologized profusely and begged her to let the girls sleep, but by then they were all getting in their lineup behind the fishbowl, hoping to be picked. Those poor girls must have been so pissed off that we wasted their time and woke them up just to look but not spend, and they'd probably just gotten to sleep an hour before. We bowed out and retreated back to the elevator, embarrassed. After that, we were sure not to hit the button on the elevator that took us anywhere near the "Fishbowl," as we called it.

A short walk out of the hotel into the Arab district led us into so many open-aired bazaars and restaurants with Arabian food that we could try a different one for every meal and never double back. The food was amazing and super healthy: saffron rice with grilled vegetables and exotic curries, served steaming in huge mounds. Actually, in Thailand I ate very little Thai food, which is one of my favorites. It wasn't for lack of trying, but believe it or not there just weren't that many Thai restaurants there in their own country. Thai people are so passionate about their amazing cuisine that they rarely go out to restaurants — declaring that they can make it better themselves at home.

As Shane and I wandered through the Arab District and the main city we talked about doing something special for the upcoming millennium. In a week it was going to be New Year's Eve 2000, a huge deal if you remember, and the international news was rife with concerns about how the Y2K computer bug was going to wipe out the world's financial records and set us all back to the Stone Age. (In retrospect, that may have been preferable to the current world financial situation.) We decided that we'd do the new year right by renting tuxedos and going out to a nice dinner and then hitting the town partying. Some of the best tailors and garment shops in the world were in Bangkok, so we started dipping our heads into one after another and asking if they rented tuxedos. No one rented because it was just as cheap to get a tux custom-made, so we ended up getting measured and fitted for our own. A tuxedo along with cummerbund, shoes, shirt, and bowtie, as well as two custom-made business suits, cost me something ridiculous like $150 USD and were ready within three days.

Bangkok, a megalopolis of 9 million people, buzzes with human energy. The official name of the city is "Krung Thep Mahanakhon Amon Rattanakosin Mahintharayutthaya Mahadilok Phop Noppharat Ratchathani Burirom Udomratchaniwet Mahasathan Amon Phiman Awatan Sathit Sakkathattiya Witsanukam Prasit," which is in the *Guinness Book of World Records* as the longest name of a place on Earth. The city's mere presence was a monument to contradiction, displaying both the elegance of a great culture and the depravity of a nation struggling to find commodities more noble than sexual tourism and knockoff purses. But Thailand, or the Kingdom of Siam as it used to be known, is the only country in Southeast Asia never to be colonized by a European country, and their beautiful culture reflects that independence and autonomy. Even the language is soft and beautiful; the feminine form of hello in Thai, "*Sa wat dee kahhhhh*," sounds as silky as a brown woman slipping out of a hotel towel.

The country was ruled by benevolent monarchy under King Bhumibol Adulyadej, but unlike most royal families or dictators, I got the sense that the people loved the king out of respect, not out of fear, and indeed, you'll still find his photo in most Thai restaurants even in the U.S. The king and his son put their international educations to good use, adopting progressive programs to modernize agricultural practices, health care, and amnesty for the poor. They actually gave a shit about their people and their country, so much so that the king rewrote the constitution to *welcome* criticism and dissenting opinions of his rule, and therefore spread his power. That is extremely rare, not only in the world today, but throughout the course of history.

And yet Bangkok is a city of sin that makes Mardi Gras look like an Amish picnic. In the world-renowned red light district of Patpong we found ourselves awash in a sea of neon, every inch of the sidewalk filled with vendors selling knockoff purses, sunglasses, shirts, watches, shoes, and T-shirts. Touts tried to usher us into the hundreds of bars and strip clubs that bumped disco music and one-upped each other by advertising donkey shows, ping-pong ball shows, and a lady who could pop balloons from five meters away by shooting darts from somewhere other than her hands. To round out the surrealism, little kids walked down the sidewalk with malnourished elephants on leashes, offering rides and photo ops to the tourists. You could take a Tuk Tuk — a motorcycle with two-wheeled passenger platforms built on the back — through the city for a few baht coins, whizzing through the open night air with a buzz off Singha beers, laughing and taking in the scenery. It was so full of noise and dazzle that I could barely sleep after getting out of there, my brain wound up.

But surprisingly, I wasn't feeling like partying in Bangkok. That's what I had wanted out of my trip around the world when I first embarked, and Bangkok was supposed to be the epicenter of the international party scene where anything goes, but suddenly I had less desire to rip it up every night. When I looked back on the trip so far it wasn't the wild nights and good times that stuck out for me, but the human connections with good people, their warmth and spirit despite poverty and struggle, that resonated the most within me.

It wasn't a conscious plan, but our focus began to shift to more philanthropic priorities. It started small: One day in Bangkok we were playing basketball at a local park and there were a couple grimy little kids hanging around watching us, a cute little girl with pigtails toting around her toddler brother. I'm not sure if they were street kids but they obviously weren't in school or being supervised by their parents. We were overheating from playing hoops (for the record, I had a triple-double that day: 13 turnovers, 11 fouls, and got my shot blocked 19 times), so we bought a few ice cream bars from an old man with a cooler on his bicycle and gave one to each of the kids as well. They were thrilled, huge grins breaking out on their faces. We walked away as they ripped off the wrappers and raced to eat them before they melted in the tropical midday sun.

The next day, we were leaving the park after playing hoops again, and sure enough the girl and her little brother were sitting on the outskirts of the park under the shade of a tree. This time they were with another little boy who was dressed in filthy rags and had no shoes on his feet. They didn't ask for anything; they just watched us and smiled with gratitude for our gift from the day before. Shane and I were heading across the street but stopped and huddled for a minute, then turned back to the kids and whistled and waved them over. They sprang up and sprinted over to us like little Usain Bolts. They thought we were just going to buy them another ice cream bar, but we had something better in mind. There was an American-style ice cream shop on the block, so we marched down there and opened the front glass door for them, the frosty air giving us sweet relief from the heat. The kids looked hesitant to come in, but we urged them to enter and let them know it was OK.

It was a nice establishment, the gals working behind the counter wearing white shirts with little paper hats as they scooped away at the buckets of ice cream inside a glass cooler. When they saw us walk in they smiled, but that turned to trepidation as they saw the dirty kids trailing in behind us. One gal came around the counter and started yelling at the kids, pointing them to the door, assuming that they were beggars who had followed us in off the street. We let her know that they were with us, and she backed off after giving them dirty looks, for normally these kids wouldn't be allowed in the ice cream shop as they were bad for business.

We sat down at a table and the kids followed suit, their feet dangling off the chairs and not quite reaching the floor. The waitress brought us menus, and our little friends opened them up but couldn't read the writing. Luckily, there were colorful pictures next to each of the items. They didn't really know what to do next so we encouraged them to order anything at all they wanted, and I pointed to the picture of the shop's biggest ice cream sundae. They looked shocked at their good luck, and carefully touched all of the pictures with their fingers and chatted in

Thai before each settling on variations of the four-scoop banana split sundae with extra toppings. When the sundaes came to our table, it was so funny to see the kids mesmerized by the huge treats in front of them, but it didn't take them long to attack them with oversized spoons. In fifteen minutes we were all up to our ears in ice cream, holding our stomachs. The kids had melted ice cream, hot fudge, and whipped cream all over their hands and faces. They were in great moods and laughed and gave us huge smiles as a thank you. We paid the bill and went out onto the hot sidewalk, waving goodbye to them and walking back toward the Grace Hotel.

The next day it rained so we didn't play basketball, but we passed through a street near the park on the way to a museum and saw the kids again, soaking wet and obviously looking for us. Huge smiles hit their faces when they discovered us. This time they had another little one with them who looked like the girl's little sister and couldn't have been more than 5 years old. They didn't ask for anything — just waved hi to us and sat there in expectation. Ah, what the hell. We waved them over and the whole lot of them broke into a run, the little girl practically being dragged by the hand by her older sister to catch up with us. We hit the same ice cream parlor, and the gals working were torn between being happy to see us and pissed that we were bringing in dirty street kids. Forget them. Everyone got menus and counseled each other about what the best options were, and compared notes on their sundaes from the day before. The kids weren't used to using a spoon or utensils to eat, so almost as much ice cream got spilled as ended up in their mouths. Once again we all chowed down on huge frozen creations and made a blissful mess before parting on the street. The Afternoon Ice Cream Club was officially born.

I admit that it would have been better to give those kids some money or more responsible to buy them healthy meals, but they'd get healthy meals other times in their lives; there's something to be said for giving someone a gift that is pure joy. Human beings need certain things to survive, and just as much as food, water, and shelter, we need hope to uplift our spirits and love to nourish our hearts. In a lot of ways that's harder to get than the basic necessities. When I traveled, I was shocked at how many kids were left to their own devices to survive.

Everywhere I went, but especially in the cities, I encountered scores of dirty children wandering the streets, many of them homeless, living in makeshift cardboard tents under bridges and behind bus stations, oftentimes with no parents so the older kids had to raise the younger ones. They sold bubble gum for pennies a day or ate out of garbage cans. When they got so hungry they couldn't stand it, they sniffed glue or huffed gasoline out of rags, a cheap high that sated their hunger and fogged their brains for a few hours of relief. They had to beg and hustle right in the midst of busy traffic belching black smoke, hookers, pimps kidnapping kids into the sex industry, touts trying to get people to come into their bars, drug dealers, and gangs. It's a very dangerous way for children to live, and at best they're seen as cheap labor; if their parents work until 4 a.m. they're usually required to work right there next to them, or catch a couple of hours' sleep curled up on a piece of cardboard right on the sidewalk.

But children also have the most indomitable spirit. In my opinion, adults are scumbags — we've all made our bad choices and know right from wrong and sold out a thousand times, but children are still innocent, even though they have to suffer for everyone else's choices. Yet they still show joy just to be alive. The street life was all they'd ever known, so they just assumed it was "normal" and it became a game that they grew good at playing. I realized how ridiculous it was to judge people from my safe perch in the United States unless I saw how they lived and walked a mile in their shoes.

Every afternoon, more kids showed up, each one dirtier and poorer than the last. The original members invited their family and friends but still looked to us for permission like it was too good to be true, and they didn't want to invite half of Thailand and risk us shutting the whole operation down. We didn't have to say anything when we greeted them on the street — we just gave them high-fives and turned to walk for the ice cream store, the kids skipping and singing as they followed. The word was out on the Afternoon Ice Cream Club and everyone wanted in on the delicious secret. There were no minutes, no membership dues, and no agenda. We didn't have special jackets or Grand Poohbah hats. The only rules were that you had to order whatever you wanted, as much as you wanted, and stuff your face. Seconds and thirds were fine — they had complete carte blanche. It made me happy to hook these kids up; it grounded me like I was a part of something real instead of the nihilism of partying and spending all my money on booze and strippers, like all of the other travelers in Bangkok.

Before New Year's Eve, Shane and I traveled south, trying to evade the excesses of Bangkok. We went to Phuket for Christmas, a nice beach community that would be devastated by a tsunami only four years later, killing more than 5,000 people. We found our way across the island chain of Koh Samui and then on a smaller boat to Koh Phangan — home to the historic Full Moon Party and in the cluster of tropical islands where the movie *The Beach* with Leonardo DiCaprio had just been filmed — for a few days.

Years back, a few Brits had started a once-a-month party on the beaches of Koh Phangan, and the tradition grew until 30,000 backpackers and partyers overtook the remote island regularly for a Bacchanalian festival of house music, ecstasy, and raving on the beach. The final Full Moon Party before the millennium brought in an even bigger crowd and the small, isolated island, with only a couple of hotels, cabanas scattered along the beach, and a row of bars and restaurants, was overrun with scumbag drunken Euros looking to get as fucked up as possible. Even the boat over there was crammed past capacity so people had to stand, and on the island there were thousands of backpackers who didn't have a room, and were just trying to get any cheap buzz they could. They loitered around the falafel shop, asking each other for spare change and bumming smokes, sleeping on the beach after spending their last money on beer and ecstasy.

Shane and I were abhorred by the behavior of these travelers who had absolutely no regard for the local people or their culture. They threw their empty beer bottles on the ground, smoked like chimneys and discarded their butts everywhere, and disrespected the local workers. The vibe felt weird as the hours led up to the party — escalating with a scary energy that just didn't add up to me: There were 40,000 or more travelers all tripping their balls off on ecstasy, coke, and heroin, getting shit-faced drunk, recklessly stumbling around the island, wandering around alone at night, and jammed in the back of every speeding pickup truck. But it was completely out of control, utter chaos, and there were no police on the island, no authority of any kind, and no hospitals or fire departments. The potential for some very bad stuff to happen was hard to ignore.

Shane and I went down to the beach to witness the party and listen to the DJs, but our hearts weren't in it. The way we saw it, what the hell was the point of traveling to such a beautiful place if you were going to act like an asshole and trash it? And there's never an excuse to disrespect the local people.

We were relieved to survive the party, and did catch a cool Muay Thai match our last night, set up in a boxing ring right out under the stars on the beach. I'd never seen Muay Thai before, but I was impressed by the religious and dance-like rituals of the fight, and also the way the participants battled with bare knees, elbows, and kicks as well as with gloved punches. This was before anyone had heard of the UFC, or before MMA was a household word, so it was pretty amazing to see fights at such close quarters with dudes beating the snot out of each other, but with a good vibe and reverence for their art form. All around me drunken Brits, Swedes, and Aussies with bad haircuts howled for blood, but I felt a connection with the flowing, charming Cobra dance of Muay Thai.

Shane and I retraced the steps of our journey off the island, taking a boat across the sea to Phuket and then a northbound train back to Bangkok. On New Year's Day we visited the Buddhist temples, which were lined up in a row along the Chao Phraya River in downtown Bangkok like monks waiting patiently to pray. They told us that it was good luck to start the year that way, so we burned incense in front of golden statues of Buddha and rolled prayer globes for the health and happiness of our loved ones along with throngs of chanting Thai visitors. The temples were unbelievably detailed and colorful, mosaics with golden spires sloping toward the heavens so grand that I felt like I was glancing into a postcard. At the entrance, a mountain of shoes and flip-flops piled up as the spiritual seekers entered barefoot to show respect for the holy place, but never worried about them being stolen.

From the temples we jumped on a water taxi, a jalopy of a boat that didn't look seaworthy, and took a tour of the floating markets and villages along the river. There were whole communities built on docks and boats tied up, and our driver told us many of them were Boat People, refugees from Asian conflicts in Vietnam and Cambodia who had escaped by boat and lived as floating migrants ever since.

After the Full Moon Party and a bustling New Year's Eve in Bangkok, we wanted to retreat to a environ more placid, to truly enjoy Thailand's breathtaking scenery and warm culture without a ping-pong ball show or more Eurotrash dirtballs putting their cigarettes out on a statue of Buddha. We took the train north to Chang Mai, a rural province close to the borders of Burma and Laos. We hiked and camped in the mountains, riding elephants and navigating down a river on a small bamboo raft by pushing off with a long pole. Our guide told us that those areas in the jungle were within the Golden Triangle, an area spanning Burma, Laos, Cambodia, and Thailand, where most of the world's opium was grown. Farmers grew the poppy plants in the mountains and then hauled them to southern Thailand for processing and shipping all over the world, mostly on (or in) human drug mules on international flights.

We didn't see evidence of the drug industry, but did enjoy the tranquil countryside and warm, soulful people who welcomed us to sleep on bamboo mats on the floors of their stilted bamboo huts. I loved Chang Mai. We took a deep breath up there for a week and even found an orphanage where we volunteered for a few days.

Most developing countries have few social services, and the government certainly isn't going to take care of people, so the common folks have to survive just by the support of their community. This orphanage was set up on the grounds of a Buddhist temple within groves of shade trees and rock gardens, where monks in orange robes walked slowly amongst the grassy compound. Temples in Bangkok were majestic towers, colorful like peacocks taking flight from gold-covered domes, but up in the mountains things were simple: They had an open-walled wooden building with bamboo floor mats where they could pray and meditate in silence. The orphanage consisted of two concrete rooms on the corner of the compound. A few ladies supervised and helped the kids all day in one room and then they all slept on the floor in the other room. I don't think they got many tourists to visit, because no one really knew what to do with us when we offered to volunteer. To them it was unthinkable that their guests do any sort of manual labor or menial tasks.

They invited us in and we sat down in two little plastic chairs as the kids stared at us intently, hesitant to approach. Then, Shane took off his baseball cap and put it on the head of a little boy who was standing there watching us. The whole top half of his head disappeared in the hat, and he looked around to see who had turned the lights off. The other kids burst into laughter and instantly felt comfortable now that they saw we were goofy. We played with them all afternoon, which I think was a great break for the exhausted ladies who ran the orphanage. More than anything, these kids never got physical affection; they didn't have mothers or fathers to hug them or cuddle them, so they clung to our arms, hung off our legs, and gang-tackled us, piling on and climbing all over as they laughed hysterically. A few of them had white powdery stuff on their faces and I asked a Thai lady who spoke a little English what that was. It was white ash that they ground up and put on their skin to lighten it. It's strange because in the U.S. we all want to be tan, but in most foreign countries the darker you are the more you are perceived as poor or common, so they were trying to give those kids some help in what were to be very hard lives by lightening their skin a little.

The kids were so damn cute and we started to see their personalities come out. Our favorite was a little plump-faced dude who was pure comedy; when someone did something funny, all he could do was throw his head back, eyes closed, and chuckle uncontrollably. Everyone laughed more when he laughed. The orphanage ladies had to grab him every few hours to clean him off and change his underwear because he kept pissing himself. But he didn't care — he thought it was the funniest thing ever, and would throw his head back like a little Buddha and laugh his ass off. We named him Leaky Boat, and played with him as much as possible at arm's length, trying to keep him from rolling around on top of us.

At the end of the afternoon, we said goodbye to Leaky Boat and the other kids at the orphanage. I was sad that I would never see them again, and sad for what they had to face in life and that I couldn't help more, but they all lined up and vigorously waved goodbye. Shane let

Leaky Boat keep his baseball cap, more because he had gotten it wet than out of generosity, and we headed out of Chang Mai, and the city of Krung Thep Mahanakhon Amon Rattanakosin Mahintharayutthaya Mahadilok Phop Noppharat Ratchathani Burirom Udomratchaniwet Mahasathan Amon Phiman Awatan Sathit Sakkathattiya Witsanukam Prasit, knowing that we'd left it a little bit better than we found it.

The White Ghost
Japan and China, January/February 2000

"**R***espect ghosts and gods, but keep away from them.*" —Confucius

The most beautiful thing I saw in the entire world was not a majestic purple sunrise on the rocky shores of southern New Zealand. It wasn't the heavenly view from Machu Picchu, nor the golden pyramids of Egypt, nor even the "Mona Lisa" hanging on the walls of the Louvre. And no, the most beautiful thing I laid eyes on in my year of traveling around the world wasn't a woman, though a few did come close. Surprisingly, the thing that filled me with the most "beauty and truth," as Keats would say, was an in-flight movie on a rickety old Air China DC-9.

Yeah, I know — crazy, right? The messed up thing is that the movie was in Mandarin, so I had to endure squinting at subtitles to understand what was going on. But man, I'm telling you — this movie touched me. I found myself balling, tears streaming down my face unchecked, even though I was packed in with a hundred Chinese men who just looked at me funny and readjusted their surgical masks and white gloves lest they come in contact with my bodily fluids. I swear to you that I wasn't going through man-opause or having an emotional breakdown triggered by seeing the gelatinous mystery meat they were serving on the flight. No, this movie was just damn sublime.

I had no plans to watch it when the screen first flashed to life, but the opening image of a young man walking to a destination unknown, alone through the snowy, desolate plains, caught my eye. Maybe I would watch it a little just to put me to sleep.

The movie starts with a young man coming home to a small village in the mountains of northern China where he grew up. His father has died unexpectedly and he has come back from the city to comfort his mother. He finds a sad vigil outside the schoolhouse where his father served as a teacher for all of his years. In these modern times, no one observes the ancient customs to mourn and bury the dead anymore, but his mom is adamant that they do just that for his father. No one believes in ghosts anymore, but his mom says that if they don't honor him, he will become Gu Hun Ye Gui, a ghost who hasn't been properly cared for by his family, doomed to loiter on earth forever, blocked from entering the spirit world with his ancestors where he belongs.

The son, Yusheng, tries to talk her out of the silly old ritual, but she won't waver in her resolve. Yusheng thinks it is ridiculous because by ancient rite, they have to find men to carry the coffin for miles in the winter snow to its resting place. And even if he could find the 32 men needed to make the journey, he would have to pay them a small ransom and supply them with rice wine to keep them warm. Yusheng is frustrated, so he goes into the schoolhouse to sit by himself, remembering his father and thinking about his courtship with his mother. It is a story that everyone in the village knows well ...

I was enthralled. The simple elegance of the movie couldn't have been more in contrast with my surroundings. The old DC-9's prime of service had been way back in 1965, and by the looks of it not much maintenance had been done since then. Unbeknownst to me at the time, Air China was one of the shoddiest airlines in the world. The plane we boarded looked like it wasn't even adequate to practice drink cart procedures for flight-attendants-in-training, let alone safely fly us from Tokyo, Japan on a northern trajectory past the inhospitable, barren plains of Mongolia and then across the Korean Peninsula to Beijing. The interior cabin was yellowed with age and cigarette smoke. The drafty floor was covered with the original blue-patterned carpet, frayed and stained by years of vodka, coffee, and vomit, and some of the seats were held together with duct tape. Somehow, the pilot maneuvered this bucket of bolts airborne and we cruised uneventfully for an hour before the storms rolled in.

Lightning flashed all around us, illuminating huge black clouds as big as cities that threatened to envelop us. Driving rain and wind battered the side of the plane horizontally, and water was actually trickling in through the seals of my window. The plane pitched violently, dropping my stomach to the floor, and when we hit a particularly bad patch I saw a petite Air China flight attendant fly right past me. The movie screen went blank, and the pilot got on the loudspeaker and spoke in Mandarin for what seemed like ten minutes, leaving my fellow passengers nervous and chatting vociferously with Buddha. He then delivered the same diatribe in broken English, and I could see why they were concerned:

"Uhhh hello there, this is captain Sheng Xu with Air China, part of the United Star Alliance. We're so glad to have you aboard today. We are currently diverting off our course slightly to get around some thunderstorms over Mongolia. They have the potential to be dangerous — we might hit high-pressure air pockets that cause the plane to lose altitude up to 2,000 feet at a time, causing us to experience up to three G's of force, which can shoot you right out of your seat to the ceiling. You could crack your head open, or get thrown to the back of the plane and snap your neck, or collide with someone else and knock them unconscious and cause great bodily harm, so please fasten your seatbelts. I understand that you have physiological needs, but this is important. Thank you and have a nice flight."

I buckled my seatbelt so tightly that it cut into my large intestine and instinctively looked for Shane. If this was going to be our last goodbye I wanted to confess that it was I who had stolen the French fries off of his plate when he got up to go to the bathroom back in Brazil, and not a crazed gang of switchblade-wielding midgets who had the munchies because they were blitzed on caipirinhas, like I had originally told him.

But Air China had split us up and seated him somewhere deep in the recesses of the plane close to the bathroom, so instead I buckled the seatbelt for the old lady sitting next to me — a yak farmer with a mustache thicker than I could ever grow who had no clue what was going on. I glanced up toward the cockpit to see if Satan was flying the plane.

The pilot's speech did nothing to inspire confidence that we would arrive in one piece. It's not that I'm scared of dying, per se. I mean, of course I want to keep kicking as much as the next guy — I have a lot of shallow sex and beer drinking left in me — but I don't want to go out like *that*. My father died in a plane crash. Among other things, including being an engineer, an accomplished artist, and an amateur musician, he was a pilot and actually built and flew a couple small planes. One of them was a single-person plane similar to a Cessna, and out on a skyward jaunt one sunny day the engines failed completely and he crashed and died, leaving nothing but a seven-foot crater in the pavement and a young wife with two babies at home.

So dying in a plane crash wouldn't bother me so much as it would really shake up my mom and my sister, and I would like to spare them that trauma if at all possible. I said a quick prayer to God, Buddha, and whoever else was listening to at least let me land safely, at which time they would be free to arrange for me to be stampeded by wild elephants or overdose on Viagra during a weekend with Anna Nicole Smith if that was their fate for my demise.

Despite the rough flight, I was excited to leave Tokyo. I found the culture too cold and materialistic for me, a strange algorithm of ancient social norms that exuded no human warmth. For instance, it was OK for businessmen in suits to pass out drunk in their own puke and sleep all night on the sidewalk or a train platform, and you could buy anything from 500-page Anime comic books to used schoolgirls' panties in the vending machines, but it was gravely frowned upon to use someone's first name casually. Huh? Sure, I had fun kicking it in the more traditional city of Kyoto with my buddy Casey from Boston, and I thoroughly enjoyed going to the Kabuki theater with Shane (who fell asleep and snored loudly through the whole performance, pissing off both the theater patrons and the actors whose monologues he interrupted), but for the most part, it lacked friendliness. And it was expensive.

Tokyo, the most densely populated city on Earth, cost so much that even a "room" at a business hotel ran me $250 a night. The room was actually a cubbyhole, a round, person-sized tube in a human kennel where businessmen stayed when they were coming into or going out of town. Upon entering the hotel, I put all of my possessions and clothing in a locker and got a key, some fuzzy slippers, and a kimono to wear. I asked for an extra large kimono, but apparently they only come in one size: big enough to go to the knees of the average diminutive Japanese businessman, but on me it barely covered my man-junk. I had to keep pulling it down to avoid flashing the all-female staff, who followed me around giggling, pointing, and laughing to themselves when my kimono slipped open or I had to bend down and pick something up. I felt like Sharon Stone with a penis. I found my "room" — the third tube high on a catacomb of humanity that extended to the ceiling — just wide enough to slip into without touching the round plastic walls, and I had about six inches' clearance above my head. Inside was a little reading light, a three-inch TV screen that looked as big as a movie theater because it almost touched my nose, a tiny mirror, and an alarm clock. It was actually pretty comfortable, even though my feet stuck out the bottom and I could hear every snore and cough of my neighbors'.

But before I could officially escape from Japan, I had to land safely in China, and from what it looked like, that wasn't a sure thing. The rain and lightning crashed down relentlessly, but eventually we pulled out of the storm and the pilot stabilized the old DC-9. They re-started the movie:

The story of their love is legendary in the village. The young man's mother, Zhao Di, was 18 years old and living with her blind mother when a young man appeared from the city to be the new schoolteacher. Zhao Di was the prettiest girl in the village and soon began pining just to be near the handsome outsider. He took notice of her attention and they grew closer. Their young love was left unspoken because it was still a time when marriages were arranged, but their gravity was so intense that everyone understood it was fated by the gods. But then, one day, Communist Party men in gray uniforms with red buttons arrived from the city and took the young schoolteacher away for questioning. It was the early days of the Cultural Revolution, and any intellectuals or those who were not Party members were under scrutiny for treason to Chairman Mao. Before they could take him away, Chang Yu rushed to Zhao Di's side and professed his eternal love and promised to return for her as soon as he could. Then he was escorted away by the Party men ...

When we landed, I dried my tears, hugged the old lady next to me, wiped my nose on her yak-hair tunic, and walked out onto the metal staircase leading us to the tarmac. I faced the frozen elements in nothing but short sleeves and thin jeans, shaking like a leaf. We had landed in the midst of the worst blizzard Beijing had seen in thirty years, but somehow Shane and I managed to wander through customs and grab a taxi to a hotel in the center of the city without getting hypothermia.

Beijing, also called Peking, was shrouded in a blanket of fresh snow, drifts sitting placidly on every street and rooftop, burying any bicycles that hadn't been used in the last two days and frosting the shopkeepers' windows. I couldn't tell if it was still snowing lightly or if snow was just blowing off the rooftops, but thick crystal flakes drifted down all day long. The cold was like a starving wolf, chasing us around the streets, finding us when we ducked into foyers of buildings or escaped into storefronts that mercifully offered cups of hot tea, but once the wolf caught up and bit us he wouldn't let go. Shane at least had a winter coat, but I was properly dressed to hang out on the beach in Thailand, not walk around all day in wintery Peking, so every time I left my hotel I put on every piece of clothing I owned: three pairs of shorts, nylon tracksuit pants, a pair of jeans, four pairs of socks, three T-shirts, two short-sleeve shirts, and a sweatshirt, so bundled with layers that I wobbled around like the Michelin Man float at the Macy's Thanksgiving Day Parade. I found a knockoff North Face ski jacket and mittens at an outdoor bazaar and those helped a little, but even indoors it was only a few degrees warmer than outside, so the only way to try to keep from freezing was to keep moving.

Do you know what I noticed about Beijing? I didn't see any churches or dogs. It's funny how you take for granted certain things always being in your periphery, and then one day they're gone. The churches were nonexistent, or underground, because China was the last powerful

Communist country built strictly in the Soviet image and any religion other than the most traditional of Buddhist or Taoist following was considered a political threat and met with clandestine detention and electric clubs for its practitioners. Remember, this was back in 2000, only a decade after the bloody civil revolts in Tiananmen Square, and the world was still crawling out from the shadows of the Cold War. I assumed they ate the dogs.

Soldiers in full military dress practiced their formations and flag-raising exercises every day under a 50-foot mural of Chairman Mao. Western influences were still strictly regulated; all of the television stations and newspapers were run by the state, and no one except the biggest international hotels had any access to the internet. In a country of more than one billion people, with thousands of years of rich history like a hand-spun tapestry, the cold post-modernism of Communism was withering up and dying right before my eyes. Everyone knew it was inevitable that they would be opened up to the rest of the world and would soon be drinking Pepsi and wearing the blue jeans that they manufactured in sweatshop factories, but that didn't stop the government from sabotaging its own demise any way it could, like scratching every American music CD that they allowed through customs.

But most of the populace still operated on the level of consciousness of scrambling around, trying to feed themselves and live through another day. Everyone rode bicycles, even through the snow and on highways, and outside every store or alley there were hundreds of bikes stacked up without locks, but never stolen. People attached wooden decks or carts to the backs of their bikes and carried around firewood, buckets of clean water, bags of coal, carcasses of dead animals to be slaughtered right on the streets, or their family members. Red banners and paper globes hung off doorways and rooftops for good luck.

Shane met a pretty Chinese chick and started hugging up with her daily, so I was on my own a lot of our remaining time in China, which made for a challenging visit. This place was so beautiful and mysterious to me; I might as well have been on a different planet. Of course, all of the writing was in Chinese characters, so I couldn't even identify a street sign, the name of a hotel or restaurant, or figure out what denomination of money I was handing to someone when I bought noodles or tea. I'd just walk into any little restaurant, have a seat, and point to something on the menu or at someone else's plate and hope for the best. After the meal, I'd hand them a fistful of yuan bills and let them take what they wanted. I'm pretty sure I ate some horse, dog, turtle, snake, and who knows what else, but the way I see it it's no uglier than a cow or a lobster.

When the sun fell behind the walls of the Forbidden Palace, vendors lined up their bicycles with food stations on the back under a lone light bulb, selling everything edible you could imagine. There were hundreds of these carts side by side, stretching for a mile on each side of the street, and I walked up and down trying a little of everything for a few yuan. At night, I retraced my steps to my hotel and bundled up under every blanket, towel, and curtain I could find in my attic room, the wind howling against the rice paper windows until dawn turned the world golden once again.

When Chang Yu was taken away, Zhao Di braced herself for the wait. She kept herself busy cleaning the schoolhouse and repairing its paper windows. Chang Yu was gone a long time. Her heart grew sad in his absence and soon she could not even eat or sleep without his love. She couldn't stand it anymore, so she ran up to the road that led out of town toward the city far away and waited there for him to return to her. She didn't move from that spot, even when her friends and family came and tried to talk her back into the village. The snow blew across the plains and piled up against her like it was trying to freeze her heart. For three days and nights, she stood there until she was covered with snow like a statue, and so feverish that she collapsed. They carried her back to her bed and lit a fire and tried to attend to her so she would not die ...

I visited Tiananmen Square on a rare sunny day, which looked exactly like a square in Leningrad where they would have military parades with missiles instead of floats. There was a lovely Chairman Mao museum that had his embalmed body, in full Party uniform, eerily displayed in a bulletproof case. It's not every day that you see a malevolent dictator who's been dead for a quarter of a century frozen under glass.

I skipped the adjacent Chairman Mao gift shop, where people racked up their credit cards for T-shirts with his likeness or plastic Little Red Books hanging off key chains, and bolted that creepy scene as soon as possible and went in search of more traditional Chinese culture.

One of the most interesting forms of entertainment in Japan and China are the bathhouses. In the U.S. they have a questionable reputation, like massage parlors, but in China and Japan public bathhouses are an enjoyable part of family life. Most Chinese take a bath in the evening but don't have heated bathrooms in their homes, or it's too expensive to pay for the electricity to heat the water, so for three yuan (36 cents), they can go to the public bathhouse to clean up and relax. Since Shane and I were always freezing cold and didn't have much money, we hit the bathhouses regularly. We paid at the front desk and then put all of our clothes and possessions in a locker and donned just a towel and flip-flops. The first room had rows of hot, steaming showers packed with little middle-aged Chinese men sitting under the water on wooden stools with wooden-handled brushes. When we walked in they peered over, curious to see white guys undress and compare the size of their "Great Wall" to ours. I don't think they were too impressed, but for the record it was a little cold in there. From the shower room we went into a bigger room with dry saunas, steam saunas, ice-cold pools, a regular hot tub, a super-high-temperature hot tub, and even one infused with herbs.

In the back corner there was a tub by itself, the only one that no one was going into. What was it? I asked Shane. He had no idea, either, so we tried to ask a few of the Chinese men, but we couldn't understand their animated responses. Curiosity won over prudence, as usual, so we went over to take a closer look. It looked like a regular hot tub with nothing special about it, though there were a few cracked and broken tiles around it. Shane put his leg in first, and reported that the temperature was good, but suddenly yelped and jumped out, stringing together curses with his laughter. He'd been shocked — there was actually an electric current running through the hot tub. I didn't believe him, so I had to get in there myself. Sure enough, I could feel an uncomfortable electric buzzing throughout my body that turned into stinging pain after a few seconds. I jumped out as well and we laughed our asses off.

Was the tub supposed to be like this? Was it some ancient Chinese wisdom that electrocuting yourself is good for your health? Or was this tub under construction and in need of repairs, and they failed to put up warning signs and block it off?

This was too random to ignore, so I jumped in again up to my shoulders and spent the next quarter-hour testing how long I could stay in there, Shane timing me with the clock on the wall. The pain was moderate for the first five seconds, but after that it became pretty intense, and around the 20-second mark all of my muscles began to lock up and palsy. My record was 23 seconds, at which time I was gyrating uncontrollably with muscle spasms and my screams of pain sounded like Rambo passing a kidney stone. I tried to get out of the tub, but my arms and hands turned inward and my legs wouldn't respond, leaving me in fits, stumbling like a newborn deer. I fell out of the tub with a grunt and cracked my hand on the tile, landing buck-naked in the fetal position before Shane could help me up. I was bleeding all over the white tiles, and my jaw muscles were still locked up. The Chinese men in the bathhouse looked on intently but did not comment on my antics. To this day, I wonder if they're telling folk stories about the white guy they witnessed set the electro-hot-tub endurance record, or if they thought I was an abject moron and I single-handedly set U.S.-China relations back a decade. I'd have to put my money on the latter. When I emerged into the Beijing evening an hour later, the dry winter air steamed off my skin and I was finally warm.

The love of her life, Chang Yu, heard a rumor all the way in the city that she was sick. A political tribunal was scheduled to judge his guilt or innocence, so he wasn't supposed to leave, but when he heard that she was sick he bolted for the village without permission. Like in a feverish dream, he appeared at her bedside. They professed their love to each other, and he promised that he would come back for her no matter what happened. He waited that night by her side until her fever broke; then in the morning, he had to go back. Since he had left without permission, he was in serious trouble and the tribunal ordered him detained for two years.

The seasons changed, but Zhao Di waited patiently for his return. Every day after her chores were done she walked to the end of the road and faced the city, watching for him to reappear on the horizon. For two years, she stood out there in the rain and ice and driving snow, intent on being there to greet Chang Yu when he returned. No one tried to talk her out of it because they saw her resolve, but when it was cold they brought her hot tea or draped a blanket around her shoulders and then left her be. Their love became legendary in the village. And then, one day, Chang Yu came walking back, appearing like a dot against the horizon, and found her there, waiting. That same day they were married in the schoolhouse under hand-sewn red banners, which were supposed to bring them good luck and blessings so they'd never have to part again ...

Shane and I signed up at our hotel for a tourist excursion to the Great Wall of China an hour outside of Beijing. The previous night Shane had been on a date with a chick from Beijing and they ended up doing shots of rum all night long, so he had a hangover you could donate to science. But we'd already paid for the trip so he wanted to be a trooper and come along, even though he only had two hours' sleep and looked a nice shade of green. They packed us in the van with a dozen other tourists so it was ridiculously tight, and they cranked up the heat as we sputtered onto winding roads.

I was amazed that only a few miles from the modern city people lived in such primitive conditions. Most country-dwellers lived in little one-room stone huts and farmed a rocky patch of earth or kept a few goats and chickens to sustain their family. The huts had thatched grass-and-mud roofs and many of them had caved in during the snowstorm. Women with rosy red cheeks bundled up and lit cooking fires, and pounded meal with mortars in their front yards. The men, dressed in traditional fur and animal hides like Mongolian warriors, appeared at the edge of the paved road holding up freshly hunted ducks, fish, and small game to sell to the passing drivers. I even read in a national newspaper that the Chinese government confessed that hundreds of thousands of their countrymen were still living in caves — and that's just the number they admitted.

Shane had no choice but to endure the heat and the bumpy ride inside the airless van. I knew he wasn't doing well when he rested his forehead against the seat in front of him and started to moan. Eventually, he couldn't take it anymore and he yakked. We were packed in there like sardines and there was no place to move, no bag to puke in, and he couldn't even move enough to puke on the floor, so he just vomited in his mouth and then swallowed it. I was flabbergasted, disgusted, revolted … and utterly impressed. I begged him to learn to recreate that feat at will so I could book him on David Letterman's "Stupid Human Tricks." From that point on Shane was my new hero, and I vowed to tell my grandkids about his remarkable performance in the van.

We arrived at a spot on the Great Wall popular with tourists and we spent the next few hours hiking up and down the embankment on top of the wall, sliding and scampering in the snow. The views of the countryside were breathtaking, and because of the cold most of the other passengers stuck close to the van, so as Shane and I hiked further out we were in complete solitude except for a little old man with a long beard sitting on a set of stone steps, laughing cheerfully as he smoked opium from a long pipe. He smiled at us like we shared some ancient secret that need not be spoken, though I would have preferred he share that opium pipe. Puff, puff, pass, brotha!

Back in the fifth century B.C. they began building the Great Wall out of stone and earthen bricks to protect northern China from invasion by Mongolian warlords and nomadic tribes. It was built and rebuilt all the way through the 16th century A.D., though most of it was fortified during the Ming Dynasty. It stretches an improbable 3,800 miles from the eastern edge of Shanhaiguan to Top Lake in the west. Some of the walls rise to 40 feet high, and in other places they are crumbling and no taller than a person.

The Great Wall snakes up and down hills and mountains, across rivers and deserts, and it's the only manmade structure visible from the moon. The emperors used prisoners and indentured servants to build it — they rounded up the best craftsmen and masons from all over China and forced them to work the rest of their lives on the wall. There was built-in accountability that they did a good job, for failing to do so would mean that invaders could get in and topple the empire, so each brick a mason placed in the wall had his family name etched in it so that later on, if a section crumbled or proved to be shoddy, they could track down the responsible craftsman, as well as his entire family, and cut their heads off.

Sitting in the schoolhouse, Yusheng reflects on this story of his mother and father, and his frustration softens. He understands why she wants to honor her late husband with the proper traditions, so he goes to the mayor of the village and gives him all the money he has in the world to buy a coffin and hire the men for the ceremony.

The day of the funeral, Yusheng walks his mourning mother up to the schoolhouse. They only expect the few people who were hired for the funeral, but are greeted by hundreds of Chang Yu's former students waiting for them. They all want to lend a hand carrying the coffin through the snow to the burial site, and none of them will accept any payment for their help. They even bring their own rice wine and rice to offer Yusheng and his mother. The next day, Yusheng goes to the schoolhouse and teaches one day of classes to the young pupils to honor his father's memory ...

On a day the snow stopped falling from the slate-gray sky, I walked to the Forbidden City in the center of old Peking. This vast, ancient city-within-a-city was the ceremonial and political home to 26 emperors through the Ming and Quing dynasties. The entire complex was surrounded by a 25-foot-high wall and a 100-foot-wide moat to protect it from outsiders, and indeed, it survived bloody occupations by the Japanese, Taiwanese, military warlords, and the Communists. During my stay, artists and craftsmen pulled up on their bicycles and worked on the sidewalks outside the wall, cutting hair or painting pictures right outdoors, and early every morning citizens practiced Tai Chi in perfect unison.

The Celestial Emperor, the Son of Heaven, never stepped foot outside of the Forbidden City his entire life. His wife and family lived within the city but in palaces apart from him, balancing out the Yin and the Yang. The Forbidden City and Imperial Palace within are about eight million square feet, or 178 acres, with 980 buildings and 9,999 bays. It was quite possibly the most ornate, grand architecture that I'd ever seen. Every single color, tapestry, gate, waterfall, mural, rooftop, bridge, koi pond, garden, and statue has religious and astronomical significance, and God is definitely present in the details. The Chinese emperor's court was closed off to the outside world for centuries, following the belief that the primitive ways and culture of foreigners would taint the chosen people of heaven.

I wandered around the Forbidden City that whole day, transported to an ancient place of honor and beauty where the past was just as real as the present and echoed eternally in the silence. On my way out of the city, I saw two men playing music. One sat on a chair playing a rickety wooden violin while his partner stood next to him and sang a traditional Chinese love song. I pulled out my camera to snap a photo, but they stopped playing and yelled at me. They called me a *gweilo*, the word for "white person" or, literally, "ghost man," and ushered me away, still protecting their Forbidden City from foreigners. I took the picture anyway and walked on.

Was I a *gweilo* — a white ghost? It was hard not to feel like one. I was alone in that ancient place, enveloped in a blanket of white, like gently blowing curtains. I felt as if I were becoming invisible, that the wind and the snow could gust right through me. Did I even exist? Far from home and family, who would even know if I was gone? I hoped the spirits of my ancestors were protecting me, too. When my life was over, I wanted to be able to say that someone waited at the end of the road for me, that I had honored my family and treated others well. I hoped that people would show up at my funeral and carry me the rest of the way home in the snow, like in that beautiful in-flight movie that I will never forget.

Zhao Di is happy because the love of her life is honored. His soul will be at peace for eternity, and he will not be a ghost roaming around, a Gu Hun Ye Gui, who has died far from home or was forgotten by his family. She, too, can rest, and no longer has to stand vigil at the end of the village road, waiting for the second half of her heart to come walking home.

Popcorn Zealots

Israel/Palestine,
February/March 2000

P eople freak the fuck out in Jerusalem. It happens every day. To state it more eloquently, a common phenomenon is for tourists to go completely rubber-room insane and become religious fanatics literally overnight. It happens with Christians, Jews, Muslims, agnostics, people who like Adam Sandler, and especially atheists who had absolutely no religious inclinations before stepping off the plane. One day, he's an insurance salesman from Des Moines who hasn't set foot in a temple since he got drunk on screwdrivers and did the electric slide at his friend Barry Mendelstein's bar mitzvah in 1989, and the next day he's single-handedly starting a crusade against the Infidels. Something takes over their brains, suddenly and absolutely, and spins people out to the point where within a week in Jerusalem, they sell all of their property, deplete their bank accounts, donate their clothing, file for citizenship, enlist in the army, and become orthodox followers of their new religion. They never half-ass it — these "popcorn zealots" place themselves in the torrent of religious fundamentalism as if a switch has flipped in their psyches.

The frightening thing is that I can understand why; I felt it, too. Jerusalem holds a certain magnetism that is unlike any other place on Earth. I'm not a religious person at all — I've even been wrongly accused of being an atheist in the past. I tell people I was raised Catholic but

I've since reformed, but the truth is that I very strongly believe in God without accepting the dogma of manmade religion. Still, the ancient city of Jerusalem drew me in and wouldn't let go. For a culture and anthropology buff like me it was pure heaven, but further than that there's a certain preternatural connection between the known and the unknown, the pantheon of gods and prophets and mortal men, heaven and earth, in Jerusalem. Everyone feels the buzz of spiritual electricity. In fact, it's the crux of the world's three major Abrahamic religions: Judaism, Islam, and Christianity, so the stronghold of Old Jerusalem has been the antenna of the conscious spiritual universe since the birth of mankind. Human beings have always looked skyward and asked the questions "Why are we here?" "What's the meaning of life?"and "Is there something bigger than me out there?" but it's only in Jerusalem that they've actually received answers.

Of all the places I visited on my trip around the world, I would categorize only my experiences in the Middle East as irreplaceable. Everyone should go to Jerusalem once in their lifetime — no matter what your politics, ideology, or nation of origin. Few foreigners realize that Israel is a country only one and a half times the size of Connecticut and surrounded by its sworn enemies — Lebanon and Syria to the north, Jordan and the West Bank to the east — landlocked except for the Red Sea in the south and a priceless 10-mile strip of the Mediterranean Sea. It didn't even formally exist before 1948; the British occupation of Palestine was not a happy marriage, so the United Nations partitioned a portion of those lands for an independent Jewish Zionist state. The very next day, all of Israel's neighbors attacked in protest, starting the Arab-Israeli War and displacing more than 700,000 Palestinians who have a legitimate beef for crying foul. This pattern of bloody wars and conflicts, attacking and defending, feuding over and then annexing land with only a few fragile months of peace in between, has been the reality for every day of the young country's existence.

Despite its diminutive size, Israel spends more on national defense than any other country in the world and every citizen, man or woman, needs to serve a few years in the army. But Israeli politics and Israeli religion are two different entities, though they are intertwined tighter than Alan Iverson's cornrows. About 75% of the country is of Jewish descent and 20% is Arab, but it gets way more complex than that. There are Israeli citizens who are secular, and Christian Israelis, and Christian Palestinians, and Christian Arabs, and even Muslim Israelis. I could go on and on. The foundation of all the conflict is that Jerusalem is anointed as the Holy Land for the world's three Abrahamic religions, each of which has an historical imperative to make a case for owner-ship of the soil and the holy relics that sit upon it.

Over its history, Jerusalem has been occupied by the Jews, Zionists, Muslims, Assyrians, Babylonians, Romans, Greeks, Sassanians, Persians, Byzantines, Ottomans, Turks, and most recently the British, many of whom have cruelly sacked the city, slaughtering its occupants and burning its holy sites. Interestingly enough, I read somewhere that of all the conquerors the Muslims were considered the most humane and tolerant of religious freedom.

The wave of modern Jewish migrations to Israel started in the 1880s as a response to the diaspora, which found Jews populating many countries far from their home. The Zionist movement called for Jews to return and reclaim their holy land and establish their own state. As anti-Jewish sentiment grew in the first three decades of the 20th century in Europe, and then as Jewish persecution followed dur-ing the Holocaust and World War II, the numbers of refugees moving back to their homeland exploded.

But this isn't about the Middle East, or Israel, but about how Jerusalem makes people snap like a cheap suit. Even documenting that phenomenon is too ambitious a project, for someone could focus on just one small corner of the old city and spend a lifetime unearth-ing its mysteries. But no matter who you are or what your beliefs, the one consistency within all theologies, throughout all of history, is that Jerusalem has heaven on speed-dial, and the degree of that consensus is downright scary. No wonder it attracts, or converts, the wackiest of the wacky.

Rarely does this "possession by the gods" happen quietly; it's usu-ally accompanied by a divine vision only the person affected can see, or a voice from God that only he or she can hear — or even better, the epiphany that *he or she* is a prophet or Jesus Christ reincarnate, or even the Big Man himself. How convenient. I guess no one has an epiphany that they're a dental assistant from Coral Gables, Florida, who lives in a two-bedroom condo and peruses AdultFriendFinder.com before going to bed by 10:30 every Friday night. No, being a prophet entrusted to deliver a personal message straight from God's lips racks up way more cool points. Don't get me wrong, a lot of people go to Israel and stay there for nationalist or religious reasons that are completely understandable, and even commendable, but for those popcorn zealots who just flat out lose their shit, I really don't think that the shift to an alternate dimension is conscious and carefully orchestrated. I guess that when the spirit calls you, resistance is futile.

If you were to put all of these nut jobs in a lineup, my personal favorite would be the street preachers. There's nothing like someone with a loud voice who's vowed to infect the rest of the world with his own delusions of grandeur. I loved spending sunny afternoons in Old Jerusalem, sitting on a park bench by Avenue Ben Yehuda with a falafel and a bottle of grape juice and watching the street preachers do their thing. There is no more creative and passionate salesperson on the planet than those peddling salvation, and hoping to be paid by divine commission. You never know what you're going to see, and that's the charm. Every Friday in the center of town there's a fat guy in suspenders with a Southern accent and a booming voice yelling about the coming of the Apocalypse. On the opposite street corner, right outside of Ben and Jerry's, is a swarthy-looking fellow in a green suede suit with a bird feather in his hat proclaiming to be Jesus. Mind you — not the second coming of Jesus, or Jesus-like, but *actually* Jesus. I'd love to call "bullshit" and test his biblically documented carpentry skills by throwing down a couple of two-by-fours and a Black & Decker drill and telling him to build me a birdhouse posthaste.

On another corner, an Orthodox Jew rails against the moral dangers of the internet, music, movies, porn, and the genetic impurities of McDonalds. He totally had me until he attacked my quarter-pounder with cheese. An old guy with a beard down to the ground, naked except for a burlap sack, stands in the fountain and screams that we have to build an ark to survive the coming flood. A tattooed man dressed like a Roman soldier in golden armor waves a plastic sword, trying to rally his countrymen to swarm the gates of Damascus on a rusty bullhorn. Waitress — I'll have two of whatever they're drinking, please.

Some of these fruit loops are more organized than others: The African Hebrew Israelite Nation of Jerusalem even has glossy business cards and a secret handshake. Also known as the Black Hebrews, this group of about 5,000 men believe they are direct descendants of the Ten Lost Tribes of Israel. Of course, those from mainstream Judaism don't want anything to do with them, nor do they even acknowledge them as real Jews, but that doesn't stop the Black Hebrews from touting a genealogy that can be traced from the lost tribes of Judah to West Africa and then to Chicago, Illinois. The group's founder, a steel plant worker named Ben Carter, had a "vision" in which the Archangel Gabriel revealed all of this to him. I'm not making this shit up. I had a similar "vision" after dropping mescaline and drinking 23 Jack and Cokes while wearing disco clothes at a casino in Lake Tahoe, but you don't see me bragging about it. Oh, and one more thing to tally up under the column of "ain't that convenient": the Archangel Gabriel told him that it was OK for the Black Hebrews to each have seven wives and mess around with married women. Good times.

I tried to write these zealots off as a rare few bad apples, but it seemed that for every street preacher who *didn't* need a prescription for lithium strong enough to date-rape a rhino, there were three more kooks wearing Kentucky Fried Chicken buckets on their heads reading a scroll listing all the reasons why Britney Spears was the devil. Well, actually, they had a good point on that one.

Within an hour I could collect some great information, and a stack of corresponding humble literature, all about the end of the world; how to convert to the one true religion; why Christians need to die; why Jews need to die; why Muslims need to die; why Scientology is evil; a checklist for what to do when the plague of floods and locusts hit; why Lenny Kravitz is actually the King of the Jews; that abortion is abhorrent and pro-life is the way to go, but then in the next breath that all homosexuals should be killed; that it's not too late for personal salvation; that the Beatles were really biblical prophets; that cloning is the beginning of the end of mankind; that the holocaust never happened; that the holocaust was funded by Wal-Mart; that a spaceship is going to come beam us all up on 12/12/12; that we all need to recant, repent, repatriate, and reregister to vote in Sodom and Gomorrah; and that there are secret Satanic messages if you play *A Charlie Brown Christmas* backward. It was wild; all of these guys peacocking with absolutely no shame in their game were pure entertainment. But there was one thing I noticed that consistently irked me: Who the hell made their signs? They were always super shoddy, looking like they'd been slapped together on the top of a soggy cereal box with a Sharpie in a dark closet. Have some pride in your visual aids if you're going to be a psychotic religious megalomaniac — spend the time to make a nice PowerPoint presentation, or go to Kinkos and get something printed in color and laminated, for Christ's sake. I'm just saying.

My personal introduction to Jerusalem occurred on my 28th birthday, on February 9, 2000, when I landed in Israel late at night with absolutely no idea where to go or what to do. That same morning I had gone to the airport in Beijing, China and asked them when the next flight to anywhere in the Middle East was.

I had become frustrated because Shane and I had developed such different agendas for the trip, and trying to run in two different directions at the same time was leading nowhere and wearing on both our nerves. So I decided it was time for me to move on, which I'm sure he didn't mind. In retrospect, I think that was a healthy decision for both of us because he wanted to explore European cities more, while I wanted to challenge myself by venturing to the most remote places in the Middle East I could find. We were both seasoned adventurers and it was time for us to fly solo. It's amazing that we still respected each other and had a solid friendship after being stuck together 24/7 for eight months under the most trying circumstances. So I gave him a big hug and wished him well and boarded the plane, but I missed him instantly, like a familiar appendage had been chopped off.

The plane ride was excruciatingly long — 16 hours spent flying all the way across Russia to Germany, and then connecting on a flight that took me to Jerusalem. Somehow, I found a hostel with a light on at 2 a.m. The next morning, I rubbed my sleepy eyes and wandered out to take a walk. I still didn't have one shred of information about the country, language, culture, or any of the sights to take in. I strolled down a pedestrian avenue that had a high wall made of huge old stones on one side. All of the Jews, dressed in black with hats with curly hair dangling from above their ears, walked one way, and the Arabs in robes with head wraps walked the other way. I entered an enormous old iron gate and found myself in some sort of ancient sandstone city. I wandered in the general direction that most of the tourists were headed, and when I saw a bunch of them get in line outside an old church I took my place right behind them. A young couple was getting married inside the church when I walked through. Judging by the way the other tourists snapped photos and spoke in hushed tones, the church was obviously historically significant in some way, but I had no idea what I was seeing as I tagged along.

After the church, I jumped into a pack of Orthodox Jews who were walking somewhere in the city. They ended up at another huge old wall where hundreds of their brethren mingled and prayed, swaying as they chanted, and kissed the wall. Security guards with M16s checked people out before allowing them passage to the wall. There weren't any tourists in line through the security checkpoint, but I got in the queue anyway. There was a cardboard box filled with yarmulkes and I noticed that everyone was wearing one, so I grabbed one and put it on. I liked it because it conveniently covered my bald spot. Maybe I was on to something; I could just convert to Judaism instead of paying for Propecia every month. Hey, if Sammy Davis, Jr. could do it, then so could I. The guards looked at me in my yarmulke, in line with all of the Orthodox Jews, and let me pass without question.

I walked up to the wall and watched everyone praying. It was a good scene, except that it looked like everyone was cramming little pieces of paper into the cracks of the stones, and I thought it was a shame that they allowed people to litter like that.

Only afterward, when I bought a Lonely Planet travel guide and did a little reading, did I realize I had just kicked it at the holiest spots on earth. I revisited those sites armed with a new appreciation and a guidebook.

That church? That was the Church of the Holy Sepulchre, built on the exact spot where Jesus was crucified, his body was placed in a tomb, and where he rose from the dead three days later, as per the New Testament.

And the big wall? Well, that was only the Wailing Wall, one of the most revered places in Judaism. Tradition teaches that the Wailing Wall, or Western Wall, was part of the First Temple that was built by King Solomon. Over the centuries, the temple was sacked and demolished except for the Wailing Wall. It's said that the Divine Presence rests upon that wall, and that the return of Jesus and salvation of humankind requires the temple be rebuilt.

I had a lot to learn. For the next two weeks, I wandered around Jerusalem taking in every sight and sound like a religious scholar. The more I learned, the more I was spun into its gravity. People see TV clips of suicide bombers and youths throwing rocks at tanks in the Middle East and think that's what it's all about, but in reality every person you could imagine, from every race, nation, creed, and religion, rubs shoulders and goes about their daily business in Jerusalem. Of course, security measures to prevent terrorism are ubiquitous, and the place buzzes with the nascent undertone that all hell could break loose at any minute — and it often does. But somehow that just makes the holiest place on Earth glow that much more. I saw police bomb squads respond to scares, or heard about suicide bombers every day I was in Israel. Security was heightened because the pope was making a visit to the Holy Land in a few weeks. But right after I left the country the Camp David Accords fell through, sparked by bloody rioting between Jews and Palestinians, and the Middle East once again fell into the throes of an all-out religious war.

A good example of why everyone is so cuckoo for Cocoa Puffs about Jerusalem is the Temple Mount. It's a mega-sized stone plateau built by Solomon, son of David, and later fortified by Herod the Great, to raise the holy sites built upon it above the surrounding Jerusalem. All three religions attach the highest significance to the Temple Mount and its buildings, consistently saying that it's the origin of the world and that the Messiah King will return to save humankind there. As you can imagine, that makes them just a tad territorial and contentious; a lot is at stake here, and no matter who you are there are two other religions standing in the way of reclaiming that real estate. Today, the Temple Mount is the home of the Dome of the Rock, where God ordered Abraham to sacrifice his son Isaac, and is also the site of the great Al-Aqsa Mosque.

I had the opportunity to walk through tight security checkpoints and gain entrance to the Temple Mount, which was controlled by Muslims, and into the mosque during prayer time. These silver and gold-domed sites were incredible, some of the most ornate and beautiful structures I've seen. The Church of the Holy Sepulchre and the Wailing Wall had better hang some nice wallpaper and repaint their bathrooms if they want to keep up with the Muslims in the decorating department. In Islam, the Al-Aqsa Mosque is the third-holiest site behind Mecca and Medina, and is distinguished as the place where the prophet Mohammed took a flying horse on the Night Journey from Mecca to the current site of the mosque. A golden ladder dropped down from heaven, and when he climbed all the way up he was granted divine wisdom from Allah. When he climbed back down and returned to Earth, he had with him the words that became the Koran and the basis of Islam. How cool is that? I wish I had a golden ladder to take me places, but instead I have a golden Kia Rio rental car that my 13-year-old nephew makes fun of because its tires are as small as pizzas and it doesn't even have power windows.

I walked the Via Dolorosa, where Jesus was paraded and tormented. I hiked up Mount Sinai where Moses received the Ten Commandments and smoked a joint at dawn with some Canadian backpackers (I mean *I* smoked the joint — not Moses, though you can never really be sure what was in his "burning bush"). I climbed Masada and witnessed the stronghold where 500 Jews held off 100,000 Roman soldiers for a week and then carried out a suicide pact instead of being captured. I laid eyes on the breathtaking St. George Monastery, a catacomb of churches carved out of rock hanging right on the face of a cliff, reached only by a pedestrian bridge across the Valley of the Shadow. I spent a night sharing a hotel room with two Persian Air flight attendants in the hippie seaside town of Dahab, and trust me when I tell you it was a religious experience: I think I said "Oh, god" no fewer than 57 times. I floated on my back in the Dead Sea, the lowest and most saline body of water on earth. I took a taxi into Palestinian-controlled Bethlehem where the Church of the Nativity stands over the manger where Jesus was born. The driver put a Palestinian flag in the back window of his car and urged me to get out by nightfall for my own safety.

But the most telling parable about the complexities and contradictions of Jerusalem, and how mankind will always screw up something that's supposed to be pure, is to look behind the scenes at the Church of the Holy Sepulchre. Even fellow Christians can't play nice amongst themselves, so since the beginning there has been backstabbing and slimy politics in play between different sects to wrest control of the church. These days, the church in Jerusalem is owned by four separate Christian sects: the Greek Orthodox Patriarch, the Eastern Orthodoxy, the Roman Catholic Parish, and the Oriental Orthodoxy. The priests, monks, and friars from these four separate churches fight bitterly over control of every single day-to-day detail, down to who gets to screw in a light bulb. Even the most trivial decision about scheduling a service or what color to paint a chair is preceded by arguments, written petitions, council meetings, and formal mediation. There's no governing body that has authority over the church, so any decision needs to pass by unanimous agreement. As you can guess, that's almost downright impossible, so often, needed repairs go untended for years to the point where the deterioration of the church reaches a critical state. Back in 1852, a little wooden ladder was placed on a window ledge for a basic repair, but the priests soon got into a contentious disagreement about who had the authority to place it there and the definitions of common grounds within the church. They never got it solved; instead exhausting themselves until they moved on to the next irrelevant dispute, so the ladder sits there still to this day.

Apparently, their petty agendas are way more important than preserving the holiest site in their belief system. It's downright comical how quickly people *from the same religion* completely forget the premise of their whole calling to the cloth. It even gets to the point of fistfights amongst the priests, as it did in 2004 when someone left a door to the Franciscan chapel open by accident and a rival faction within the church took it as a sign of disrespect and started a brawl. The police actually came and arrested some of these troublemaking priests. On Palm Sunday in 2008, a bare-knuckle brawl broke out when a Greek monk was ejected from the building after his mass went over the allotted time. Later that year, on a Sunday morning no less, a donnybrook erupted between Greek and Armenian monks over who would deliver the main sermon for the Feast of the Holy Cross.

That's what I'm talking about! If my church services looked like Raiders games, I would have gone way more often. When I was growing up, my church didn't have fistfights or cool stories about flying horses or little hats you could wear to cover your bald spot; I just sat around on an uncomfortable cold bench and prayed that it would be over quickly before I fell asleep and started snoring. Give me some of that old-time religion any day! I might be tempted to head to Jerusalem, freak the fuck out, begin writing a newsletter of nonsensical rantings, and pass it out on the street. I could even call it "Pushups in the Prayer Room."

The Blind Man and the Mosque

Jordan, March/April 2000

At five in the afternoon I heard the buzzing of a microphone coming alive somewhere in the city, and then the most beautiful chanting drifted down from above. It was a sing-song, haunting prayer in Arabic. "Allllahhhhhu Akbar. Allllllllllllllahhhhhhhhhuuuu Akbarrrrrr." I looked around, but the streets were empty. The man's voice sang like that for ten minutes, and then the microphone clicked off and it stopped just as abruptly. It happened again later that day, and then at 4 a.m. when it woke me up. Normally at 4 a.m. I'm just finishing up my dream of getting mistakenly locked in a women's prison in Sweden and beginning to dream about being the starting point guard for the Knicks, but that morning I didn't mind being awoken — the chanting was beautiful as the purple sky softened before dawn, and I felt the spiritual energy of the voice even though I couldn't understand what he was saying.

And then one day I saw where it was coming from. I had to squint against the sunset, but on the horizon in the center of the city was a thin tower that spindled skyward from a domed mosque below. A solitary man in traditional robes was in the tower and he began to sing in Arabic, which was projected to every corner of the city through a microphone and huge speakers. I came to find out that he was called the *muezzin*, the Islamic religious cleric who is chosen to lead the

181

prayer from the mosque five times a day and for Friday services. The tower he was in, with an ornamental half-moon crescent at the top, was called the minaret. A *muezzin* was chosen for his good voice and skills in orating the prayers in Arabic. It was an ancient and revered profession, calling people to the mosque for prayer since the time of Mohammed. Often, they enlisted a blind man to serve as the *muezzin* so he couldn't peep into windows and private courtyards from his vantage point high up in the minaret.

"Alllllahhhhhhu Akbarrrrrrrrr." "God is the greatest." It became a welcome part of the day, as I closed my eyes and let the blind man's voice settle down onto me on the surreally placid streets.

Jordan, officially called the Hashemite Kingdom of Jordan, is a small Islamic nation nestled between Syria, Saudi Arabia, Iraq, and Israel. That's a rough neighborhood if ever there was one. The country is somewhat of a contradiction, ranking low on international watchdog lists for countries that ensure freedom and human rights, but modern and progressive by Middle Eastern standards. About 96% of the population is conservative Islamic, yet the 4% Christian minority has religious freedom and is welcomed into society, even holding posts high in the government and business community.

I had only been in Jordan for a few days, and so far it was all so unexpected, strange, and magical. I'd taken a boat across the Dead Sea and arrived at the port town of Aquaba with no clue where to go or even where to stay. Aquaba wasn't a tourist spot, so there were really no amenities for foreigners and very few people spoke English, but I managed to find a hostel that took me in and went walking around to explore the town. Most of the grown men wore the traditional robes, called a *thawb*, and plaid cotton headdresses called a *keffiyeh*. The women looked like … well, I don't know because I really didn't see many women. They rarely went out in public, and when they did they covered themselves completely in *niqābs* with only their eyes peeking out. When they needed something from the store, they'd lower money down in a bucket on a rope from their upstairs window, and little kids would grab the money and run to the store to buy whatever the woman needed, and then put it back in the bucket to be pulled up. The streets were immaculate, without even a speck of trash, and I was told that the punishments were strict for littering, and that is why it just didn't happen. I made a mental note not to drop any gum wrappers so the authorities wouldn't have to cut off my pinky with a dull scimitar. I couldn't even read a street sign or what store was what since it was all in Arabic, but soon I was welcomed into Jordan with open arms.

At dusk one day, I walked by a house whose front door was open. A family sat at the kitchen table, and when they saw me walking by they came to the door and called me inside. I was hesitant at first, but they ushered me in and pulled up an extra chair. They didn't speak any English, but somehow we managed to introduce ourselves. They put a plate in front of me and the man of the household literally shared some food with me off his plate. Right then and there those people had my heart. I will never forget that, and that's the real Middle East, the soul of the people that you don't see on TV or in the news.

It was like that everywhere I went. A taxi driver my age whisked me around town, blasting his one Doctor Dre tape over and over, showing me off to his friends but not wanting to let me get out at my destination because he was so excited to hang out with an American. I found the local post office so I could send a postcard to my family back home. There were no other customers, and the man behind the counter sold me stamps and then asked me to stay for tea. He led me into the back of the post office, and I sat there with eight other Jordanian postal workers sipping tea and chatting for an hour.

With a little help from my new friends, I learned a few phrases in Arabic: "hello," "thank you," "come here," and "God willing," so I could at least greet someone properly. I found the written language to be so beautiful that when I ordered a Coca-Cola at a café, I'd sit outside and meticulously draw the ornate letters in my notebook. It didn't matter to me which words I drew — names off of store signs, soda bottle labels, car license plates — because the beautiful script was all unknown to me but made for a wonderful art subject.

One day on the beach, I ran into a Muslim man about my age who owned a small juice stand. His dad was a farmer who lived in the country and every morning, he would drop off fresh fruit to his son in Aquaba. The son made the best fruit smoothies, and I started hitting his spot after running on the beach every morning. Even though we couldn't really talk, there was still an understanding and we communicated fine through hand gestures, our tone of voice, and drawing pictures in the air of what we wanted to say. He was the nicest guy, and every day he fed me and showed me all over town and wouldn't accept any money. I started helping out around his stand by sweeping and mopping up first thing every morning, and then he would send me to the local bakery to pick up bread. He wrote what he wanted on a piece of paper and I was so happy to be able to help out and be a part, no matter how small, of the local community. The folks at the bakery looked on in disbelief at an American running errands in an Islamic port town, but after the first few mornings they knew I was coming and greeted me with hot tea. When I brought the bread back, my buddy would break it up and we'd hand it out to about twenty little street kids who milled about. He explained that they were orphans — Afghan refugees from the war with the Soviets. They had nowhere to sleep and no parents, and if he didn't feed them scraps of bread they might not eat the rest of the day.

Everyone kept talking about a place called Petra, so I had to visit it to find out why. Petra is the site of a partially excavated ancient city carved out of the cliffs. In Arab legend, it is the exact spot where Moses struck a rock with his staff and water sprang forth from the ground. I got a room in a hostel in the charming village nearby, a half-mile stroll away, and walked to Petra every brisk morning. I first passed through the bottom of a narrow gorge called the Siq that was only 10-20 yards wide, with rock walls climbing straight up on either side for hundreds of feet. The magnitude of the gorge and the size of the rock-carved city within was breathtaking.

The entire city was hand-carved out of the red sandstone rocks, its buildings up to ten stories high, complete with domed roofs and unbelievably intricate architectural details. To try and compare its grandeur, visualize Manhattan buried in a sandstorm and then dug up thousands of years later. You probably have seen one of the most memorable of these red rock buildings in the second Indiana Jones movie, which they filmed in front of a magnificent structure called the Treasury.

Petra was first used as a city by the Nabateans in sixth century B.C., but its first origins are older than that, even going back to the

18th dynasty of Egypt when the Horite and the Edomite tribes roamed the earth. (Coincidentally, a friend of mine was at Mix dance club in Sacramento last Saturday, and he said the Horites were out in full force — but that's another story.)

The stronghold of Petra was a major trading route along the desert valley that stretched from the Dead Sea to Aquaba. In its golden age, the city was an architectural marvel, complete with public buildings, a huge amphitheater, and an intricate water system carved right out of the rock. Surrounded by thousands of miles of unforgiving and hostile terrain, water equated life, and the Nabateans engineered a way to control flash floods, divert waterways, and fill up cisterns and dams, creating a livable oasis.

Unknown to the Western world for centuries, Petra was "discovered" in 1812 by a Swiss explorer. Almost 200 years later, in the spring of 2000 when I was there, only 30% of the ancient city was excavated, but it had recently been named one of the new Seven Wonders of the World. I hiked around for days amongst those soft, rolling red hills, meandering through caves and huge, grand buildings, marveling at the details and even sketching some of them. The entrance by the Treasury Building was crowded with tourists trying not to fall off of their camels, local guides, food peddlers, and donkeys carrying explorers — a pilgrimage into an ancient world that came with the dawn and left by sundown. The further I hiked out into Petra the more blissful solitude I felt, until the hills, and the city it hid, were all mine and there weren't any tourists in sight.

After a relaxing week in Petra, the usual Arab hospitality led me to friendships with a bunch of local guys my age who worked at a souvenir shop. I spent many fun afternoons with them, drinking tea and smoking apricot tobacco out of hookahs and shishas and shooting the breeze. They were a blast and a lot smarter than the other tourists gave them credit for. Whenever a tourist couple would pass, they would yell out, trying to guess what country the couple was from, and then in their best faux-Middle-Eastern-English accent ask the man how many camels he would trade his girlfriend or wife for. Of course the tourists would decline, but they really didn't have the right to be offended because they were in a foreign country, so the number of camels offered for the girl, given at full volume for the whole street to hear, would escalate from 2 to 10 to 20. Then they would add further insult by rescinding that last offer when they realized she was only worth 10 camels.

The guys from the souvenir shop wrapped a *keffiyeh* around my head to shade me from the sun when we kicked a soccer ball in the street. They told me I should head to the desert if I wanted a true Jordanian experience, and maybe there I could find some camels to bring back for our budding tourist camel/wife exchange program.

The Arabic name for desert is *wadi*, and I traveled to check out a void of desert called Wadi Rum in Southern Jordan. Wadi Rum, also called "the Valley of the Moon" in English, is an expanse of barren, arid land cut out of granite with sandstone cliffs on either side. It's best known for being the locale where British officer T.E. Lawrence led a ragtag group of Arabian tribesmen against the massive invading armies of the Turks and Germans, successfully driving them back and protecting their homeland in the Arab Revolt of 1917. His swashbuckling adventures of battles with scimitars, sandstorms, and camels in the middle of the unforgiving wasteland were told and retold in the Western world until his legend grew into the famed "Lawrence of Arabia."

I had to take a train to a van to a four-wheel-drive truck to arrive in the tiny outpost of Wadi Rum, an enclave of about 30 people living in box concrete houses with dirt floors. I met my guide, Mohammed, a dark-featured man of indeterminate age who looked like he just stepped off a movie set. It seems like 80% of the men in the Middle East are named Mohammed, either for their first or last name, and quite a few are actually named "Mohammed Mohammed." The running joke is that you can yell, "Mohammed!" in a crowded place and bet on how many guys will turn their heads. My Mohammed equipped me for my expedition, handing me a sleeping bag, a box of firewood, and a box containing some food — onions, potatoes, a few cans of chili and hash, four jugs of water, olives, and flat bread. That was all the rations to last me three days.

After drinking tea sitting on the floor of Mohammed's home, where I also noticed he had a fax machine and a mobile phone with a remote transmitter, we packed into a pickup truck with his brother, Mohammed, and went further out into the desert. There was nothing but sand and low brush as far as the eye could see, with red cliffs looming on the horizon. We stopped at a patchwork tent for more tea, bread that was baked on coals buried in the sand, and fresh olives. The small meal was surprisingly good. We jumped on a couple of camels, and I managed not to fall off mine as it stood up with double-jointed legs. After a herky-jerky ride for an hour across the sand and rocky crags, we ended up at a huge outcropping. They showed me a cave — really just an area where the rock formation extended overhead to keep the heat in and provided some shelter from the wind and the animals. We dismounted, put all of my equipment and boxes on the sand in the cave, they wished me luck, and both Mohammeds rode off. I stood there and watched them, not sure what I was supposed to do. They yelled back that they would be back in three days to get me and if I wanted to, during the day I could walk west and I might run into some Bedouins.

That's it? No map, no guided tours of the mountains, no phone for emergencies? They even forgot to tell me where the closest Starbucks was. And what the hell were Bedouins? Hopefully that was the name for a movie theater chain that served beer and cheeseburgers set up all over remote deserts in the Middle East. At least leave me a camel to talk to or cuddle with. I had only known the Mohammeds for two hours and I missed them already.

And there I was, alone. We say the word "alone" a lot, but I'm not sure we appreciate the magnitude of what true solitude means. It's like a giant mirror, which only reflects back whatever is inside of you and echoes your thoughts until they fade into infinity. But I only had 72 hours to kill there in the desert; this would be a breeze.

I moved all of my rations to the back of the cave and arranged everything by day. That took about nine minutes. Only 71 hours and 51 minutes left. I went to take off my jeans and put on shorts, but one leg got caught and I hopped around and almost fell, then looked around to check if anyone had seen my embarrassing clumsiness, and finally got them on. That took three minutes. I threw a water bottle and my camera into my backpack and went out to explore. I hiked around all afternoon, getting a sense for my surroundings but frequently checking landmarks so I could find my way back. I climbed to the top of a huge rock precipice that went almost completely vertical, and from there I had a 360-degree view for hundreds of miles, from the Red Sea all the way to Saudi Arabia. And there wasn't a single human being in sight.

Things are simplified in the desert; I sat up on that bluff and just looked out and breathed deeply. It was very meditative, with nothing but my thoughts and the sun overhead. It felt like I was up there forever. My mind recounted everything I had seen that year of traveling, and then turned to all of my friends and family back home whom I missed, and then, like watching a movie, I saw my life unfold in front of me in reverse until I relived childhood memories. I laughed, I cried, I talked to myself. I hallucinated that people from my past were there, and then argued out loud with them when I realized that they still owed me money. I yelled at the wind and went silent and looked around when the wind didn't answer back. I realized I was as alone as I'd ever get, so I took off my clothes and lay naked on the rock to sun myself.

I thought about my survival; if I was out here too long, I'd have to start digging up bugs to eat and drinking my own urine to keep from dying of dehydration. Maybe I should get started now to conserve my water rations? Ummm, nah — pass. As the sun started to move down to meet the slate outcroppings on the horizon, I thought I should get safely back to my cave before dark. I put on my clothes and headed down and found my cave just in time — the landmarks were already shifting and fading with the sun's abrupt departure. I looked at my watch: I'd been gone for a grand total of 43 minutes. Seventy-one hours and seven minutes to go. Oh boy.

But after that, I settled in nicely. Once the sun went down all the heat from the earth escaped into the crystal sky, so I made a big fire and drank some tea and ate a few olives. The fire was beautiful — I could be happy just sitting there and watching it forever. I sat back on my sleeping bag roll and stared at the walls of the cave. To my amazement, there were petroglyphs — ancient carvings in the rocks depicting human beings hunting antelopes and worshipping the sun. After dinner, I turned around to face the desert and gazed up at the stars, so thick in the sky that it looked like I could reach up and pick them like ripe fruit. At the same time I felt both eternally connected and infinitely small. I grew a little scared: What if someone came up here and wanted to rob me or kill me? What if an animal came in here to eat me? I was completely vulnerable and powerless, but I was happy and just accepted my fate. I put another log on the fire and wrapped myself in the sleeping bag, huddling against the freezing inky darkness. At times, the new moon shivered white light out into the desert and the sand looked like waves in the ocean, and I felt like the lone survivor shipwrecked on a tiny island in the middle of the vast sea. You have never spent a night so lonely, so humbling, but so utterly beautiful at the same time, as you do by yourself in the middle of the desert.

I don't know if I slept or if I just dozed and shivered, but the first kiss of light at dawn was never so welcomed. I extinguished my fire with sand and took a hike to warm up and watch the sun rise. At midday I set out west. I walked at a good pace across the center of the desert valley, sometimes on hard-baked clay and sometimes on sand so loose I sunk in like it was powder snow. I walked steadily for two hours in the direct sun, though surprisingly it wasn't too hot. I was looking for Bedouins, whatever that was. I assumed they were some sort of desert-dwellers, but I didn't know what I was supposed to be looking for exactly. What if I got lost or was on the wrong track — how the hell would someone find me out there in the middle of nowhere? I started questioning myself and was thinking about turning back when there, right about ten yards ahead, was a young man in a white head wrap with a bundle of firewood in his hands. Funny, the desert was completely flat, but I hadn't seen or heard him come up to me — he appeared out of nowhere. He smiled at me and I said hello in Arabic, and he motioned for me to come over to him. I had found the Bedouins, like finding a needle in the middle of a haystack — or more accurately, they had found me.

The Zalabia Bedouins, a nomadic tribe of sheepherders, have lived in those deserts for eons. What looks like a desolate canvas of sand to us is a teeming civilization to them, vibrant with the cycles and struggles of everyday existence. To them the desert is a woman, and they listen closely to the wind in case she wants to tell them her secrets. You or I might last a few days out there, but they've lived completely self-sufficiently for countless centuries. The young man didn't tell me his name, but I could see how names would be sort of irrelevant out there. He walked me toward an outcropping for about twenty minutes until we reached his village.

The entire community consisted of 15 goatskin tents propped high on poles made from dried tree branches. Some of the Bedouins were dressed in traditional Arabic robes, but others wore a hilarious mish-mash of secondhand Western clothing — one guy sported black-and-white checkered pants that you might find on a restaurant chef, a red smoking jacket, shiny black dress shoes, an "I heart New York" T-shirt, and a woman's white fashion belt. Robust, olive-skinned mothers milled around busily, packing up their blankets and cooking pots into bundles. At the edge of the circle of tents, a flock of goats brayed and shoveled their noses through the sand looking for buds of grass to eat. One of the Bedouins spoke a tiny bit of English, so he explained that they were relocating their village that morning. The Bedouins survived by grazing their sheep in parts of the desert where no one else could exist, and when the precious greenery in one oasis was all chewed down, they would just pack up and move somewhere else. The whole process of breaking down and packing up their village only took half a day. Everyone threw bundles on their backs and walked in a caravan, single-file across the desert with their goats and camels in tow, leaving no trace of their past camp. They didn't want or need any more possessions than they could pack up and carry as fast as a sandstorm or a flash flood could strike. Despite their harsh lifestyle, I was amazed by how warm and generous these people were; it was almost like they didn't have the capacity to be angry, or the vocabulary to express negativity. They walked me around and pointed out their children and grandparents (and by the looks of it, they were all related somehow), and then sat me down in the last bit of shade for tea and bread that had been buried and baked in the sand. After that, I helped them pack things up and played with their children while they were busy, and soon they were ready to move.

I walked with them for a while and then they pointed to the far-off rock outcropping where I needed to head to get to my camp. I found my tracks from that morning and headed down for a minute before turning to wave goodbye to them. But they were gone, and once again I had only the sun and the wind as my companions. I got back to my cave just as the sunset's red shadow melted features of old men's faces onto the rocks. It would start to get cold again soon, so I collected scraps of wood and got them smoking by the third match. I wanted to stay close to the fire that night. I looked to the sky, but the stars weren't out yet, only the light of Venus sparkling against the purple sunset. I no longer felt lonely, no longer felt small, because I was a part of all this, and it a part of me — there was no difference.

The wind was picking up, and when I listened closely enough I swear I could make out the voice of a blind man in a mosque chanting from somewhere far off, "Allahu Akbar."

The Richest Urchin in Cairo
Egypt, April 2000

I shot up with a start, soaked with sweat and completely lost with the vertigo that a deep sleep had brought me. I had no idea where I was. Actually, I had no idea where I was, no idea when it was, and no idea *who* I was. It was a horrible feeling, and I was still breathing heavily as my half-asleep mind spun in panic to try and lock onto some detail of my life, but I could not.

I was in a dark room with the curtains drawn, the busy worka-day noise of diesel trucks and motorcycles drifting in from the street outside. It was oppressively hot, the only breeze in the room coming from a wobbly ceiling fan. I rubbed my eyes and tried to focus, but I still felt like I was falling down an elevator shaft, desperately trying to grab hold of something to slow my fall. Was I in the South Islands of the Philippines? No wait, in Chang Mai? No, I'm pretty sure that was last week. That meant I had to be in Bangkok, right? But I had been in Bangkok twice already, so that couldn't be it.

I swung my legs off of the creaky bed and put my feet on the floor. I couldn't even remember the date or be sure of what month it was; maybe it was March? Or February? I wrestled to pull off my shirt, but it stuck to me because it was so wet with sweat, and then I threw it on the green tile floor. I had been traveling way too long — it felt like wherever I went I left a piece of me, and pretty soon there would be nothing left if I wasn't careful. I rifled through the drawer on the cheap nightstand by the bed. There was a menu and a letter in some language I could not decipher, a book that looked like a Bible or a Koran — I couldn't tell which — that I pushed to the side, and a pad of stationery. It listed the information for the hotel on the header: the Nuweiba Hotel in Cairo. Damn, I was in Egypt — I hadn't even been close. In that dizzying kaleidoscope of my year backpacking around the world, I'd seen and heard and felt so much — maybe more than any one person was meant to in such a short time — that my psyche couldn't keep up and process it all, but at the same time my spirit was vaulted to heights that I never imagined possible. What dream was this — what dream of a life that I was walking in? There was something I was missing, but I couldn't quite wrap my head around it.

A few days later I took a train from Cairo down to Aswan, near the Sudanese border. Traveling within Egypt was always a tricky endeavor: I was advised not to take the train, nor sit near the windows, because militant Islamic fundamentalists would often take pot shots at the tourists, hiding in the sand dunes with rifles and causally sniping. Then again, taking a car ride between cities was even more danger-ous. Egypt has the highest rate of road fatalities in the world and they drive like absolute maniacs, literally speeding up and swerving to *try* to hit pedestrians. They could care less about lanes and stoplights or even going the correct direction down the street, instead cursing and honking and jamming five lanes of traffic into a two-lane road, running smaller vehicles, donkey carts, and old ladies carrying firewood off into the ditches. So when I had to get down to Aswan I thought my odds of survival were better in a window seat on the train. We were scheduled to depart at 6 a.m. but I was there early, just in case they scammed me with a fake ticket again. I carried an oversized backpack that held all of my possessions in the world: a few pairs of clothes, notebooks bursting with my words, and souvenirs like Turkish rugs and jade statues. As dawn broke on the train platform, columns of light marched over the dusty skyline, armies sent to warm the earth and send steam rising from the cold metal train cars. One by one, the train windows were illuminated with reds, pinks, and yellows reflected from the sunlight. The track was mostly deserted except for a few vendors selling steaming bread out of covered baskets and a sleepy conductor; it was surprisingly quiet for such a chaotic, bustling city.

I felt someone's presence behind me. I half-turned and noticed a child huddled in the shadows behind a concrete column ten yards down the train platform, peeking out at me. He was shrouded in darkness so I couldn't make out the details of his form, but he was staring curiously at me while still trying to remain hidden. Since he was my only company on the train tracks and I had time to kill, I figured I'd make him feel welcome, so I turned around to face him and smiled. He jumped further back into the shadows, afraid at first, but then I gave him the thumbs up sign so he knew I was saying hi to him and that it was safe to come out. He hesitantly stepped into the sunlight. My companion looked to be around 8 years old, though it was hard to tell because he was so filthy and malnourished; he might have been 13 for all I knew. He wore layers of dirty rags covered with train soot and black shoes that were falling apart. I looked closer and saw that his skin was dried and diseased, covered in scales that plagued most of his body, including his face. Even on his nose the skin was cracked and permanently marred. His fingers were withered and raw with red sores where they weren't covered with dirt.

At first his appearance shocked me, but then I made sure to smile at him again to make him feel comfortable. He'd probably never seen a foreigner or even a white person before, something I found surprisingly often when I trekked through remote parts of Asia or the Middle East and the jubilant kids would run up and touch the blonde hair on my arms. He stared up at me with big black eyes, taking in every detail. This boy was obviously a street kid with no roof over his head, no one to look out for him, and not enough to eat. The thought occurred to me that maybe he lived somewhere near these tracks and got his food by rummaging through the garbage cans and others' waste at the train station. Of course, I'd seen plenty of street kids over my last year of traveling; in fact, I'd seen much worse — people dying right in front of my eyes — but there was something different about this kid, something warm and alive in his eyes that registered much more than just the pain I expected.

There was an empty soda can on the track near my feet. I nudged it a few times with my sneaker like I was dribbling a soccer ball. He looked up, intrigued. I kicked the can in his direction and a huge smile broke out on his face as he realized I was playing soccer and including him in my game. He stepped closer and kicked it back to me. We kicked the can back and forth a few times, both chuckling at how quickly our new friendship had formed. I said my name in English and then said a few words in Arabic. He tried to respond, but when he opened his mouth only a grunt came out, even as he strained his throat muscles. It seemed like he was also mute. Damn, that's rough.

A chill from the morning air overcame me, so I zipped up my fleece jacket. Was he cold? If so he didn't show it, even though he was only wearing flimsy rags that were falling apart, the remnants of a matching sweat suit that was so yellowed with age I couldn't even tell what color it originally was. I noticed that on his sweatshirt were printed the words "The Best Quality" — now if that ain't irony I don't know what is.

Since he couldn't talk, I held out my hand for him to give me five. He didn't know what I was doing at first, and then his face lit up when he realized that I wanted him to slap my palm. I bet that this kid was used to no one wanting to touch him or go near him because of his skin disease. He probably had no one to hug him, and that thought broke my heart. He had no chance to live a normal life: He would never be safe, never be well-fed, never be able to sleep indoors, never get an education, never know what it feels like to be loved and have family around him, and get married and raise children. No matter what this kid did he was destined for a short life of pain, misery, and suffering. Yet it was by no choice of his own — his only crime was being born at the wrong place in the wrong situation to the wrong people. But even with all of these disabilities and detriments he was a smiling, good-natured soul, expecting absolutely nothing out of life but enjoying any little scrap of mercy it threw at him.

I felt ashamed that I didn't appreciate my own life sometimes. How dare I complain, feel sad, get stressed — I mean, what the hell in the grand scheme of things did I really have to worry about? I sometimes felt that I had it hard, yet in my cakewalk life I had every advantage and opportunity, and very little of it was earned. I suddenly felt guilty about my own hypocrisy; sure, I was traveling and witnessing all of this stuff, but what was I actually *doing* to make it better? I watched him dribble the soccer ball around an invisible defender and then kick it to his new teammate. Why wasn't I the homeless one — mute and eating out of a garbage can? Why was I instead a tourist to his misfortune, on my own grand adventure but able to head back to comfort and luxury after this year? What separated the two of us? Why were we different? Luck. Bad friggin' luck.

It frightened me, and enraged me to my core how unfair life was. And this was just one kid on one train track in one Third World city — imagine how many billions of others were out there who were suffering and needed help. There was so much sadness in the world that you could get lost in it if you weren't careful. How were we ever expected to overcome it? Was there enough light in the dawn to warm such endless and drowning darkness?

I motioned the kid closer and handed him a $1 bill. It didn't seem like enough. I handed him a $10 bill. His face showed disbelief, and his big, ancient eyes registered a gratitude I'd never seen before, nor since. He looked around to make sure no one else was watching so he wouldn't be robbed once we parted, took the money in his small, shriveled hands, and tucked it safely under his sweatshirt. If possible, his smile got even bigger, but he was not focused on the money — he had found something kind in my face and that was most comforting to him. Fuck it — I handed him a $20 bill, the last money I had with me, and closed my wallet. Thirty-one U.S. dollars could probably feed a kid like this for six months. He was now the richest urchin in the slums of Cairo, the king of his train platform.

It still wasn't enough — these small tokens, though greatly appreciated, didn't even come close to what I felt for him. I motioned for him to hold on and went into my bag, rummaging around until I fished my best pair of gray Nike basketball shorts and my favorite T-shirt and handed them to him. He proudly put them on over his rags. They were so big on him that he looked like a child playing dress-up in his dad's clothes. He admired his reflection in the train window, proud of his new wardrobe like he was the luckiest kid alive.

My train pulled up and the conductor whistled for everyone to board. We looked at each other and smiled. There was an understanding that we would never see each other again; our worlds couldn't have been further apart, but in some transcendent way in our kinship we'd fought the darkness together and done well, even for one small, fleeting moment. I walked onto the shiny train that reflected the new sky like the windows were on fire. I found my seat and plopped down and in a few moments the engines whirred to life and we started inching along the track.

I didn't want to go; I didn't want to leave him, and something had changed in me. I'd been all over the world that year, registering about 70,000 miles over six continents; I'd seen ancient wonders of the world and majestic vistas that would steal your breath, witnessed people worshiping at 2,000-year-old temples and walked in the same footsteps as mankind's most famous explorers, but somehow, inexplicably, there on that dirty train platform with a little street kid, I had found what I was looking for: I had found my purpose. It finally clicked what I was supposed to do with all that meaning I had been carrying inside of me: I would be his voice. I would make sure that he was heard, that the world knew that he took breath. I would be the one to fight for his place in eternity because he could not, and I'd be the voice of all the underdogs — the weak, the forgotten, the scarred and stained — who ask for nothing but someone to tally their existence. That's what I wanted to do with the rest of my life.

The train started to pick up speed and I looked back for him one last time and saw that he was looking for me, too. He waved and a huge smile bloomed on his wrinkled, dirty face. As we rolled on I watched him grow smaller, but before it all faded away I could make out a street urchin turn and walk on down the platform back into the ruins of Cairo, kicking a soda can. I stared at the seat in front of me for a long time, just listening to the comforting "gilickety-clack" of the train heading on down the line, and for the first time I started thinking about going back to a place called "home."

For Sunflowers and Survivors

Germany, May 2000

I didn't plan on visiting Germany when I originally mapped out my trip around the world, but it just sort of happened that I ended up there. I was in serious need of some civilization after trekking through remote areas of the Middle East for months, desperate for some good meals and R & R to try to shake a nasty stomach bug that I had picked up in Egypt. I didn't expect much out of my time in my motherland — just a chance to take hot showers and do some laundry before I flew out of Frankfurt back to New York. I enjoyed the care of my beloved Aunt Barbara, who stuffed me with cakes and sausages and beer just to fatten me up so I wouldn't look like a scarecrow and shock my mom upon my return to the States. As I spent quiet afternoons with her, strolling through the main plaza of her village where people sat on the west side of the fountain, faces upturned to soak up the first spring sun, it began to sink in why fate had placed me there.

For a whole year I had been asking questions about other people: how did they live, what was their culture, their history — what were their stories? But I never thought about turning that same lens of discovery on myself, to contemplate my own family and our small place in the world. My sister and I were raised in the United States and were very Americanized so we would fit in, but we did return to Germany many times as kids to visit. She and I joked around that if things had been just slightly different, if my mother or father hadn't immigrated to the United States and met, how our lives would instead look as German citizens. I speculated that I would have buckteeth, wear short shorts with socks and sandals, and have a bad mullet, but who the hell knows. But things turned out the way they did, as they always do in the course of history, and the final days of my journey spent in Germany were a precious gift, allowing me to be the curator of my own existence.

My aunt's charming medieval town of Goslar, close to the East German border in the north, was familiar to me — I had been there a few times as a child twenty years earlier. What stood out the most from those memories was the time we all drove east to the border. I remember being stuck in a little car for what seemed like forever, and it smelled funny in there, but those trivialities were forgotten the second we got out and laid eyes on East Germany.

I remembered what I saw so clearly, and even drew a map and did a report on it back in my elementary school when they asked what we did with our summer vacations. They expected a sunny synopsis of Disney World and little league baseball, but what I gave them was a detailed account of East German border security that was more befitting a CIA dossier.

I explained that we followed a dirt road through a pine forest until it butted into the border and ended abruptly. There was a heavily reinforced dividing line and we were not allowed to go across, and the people who lived over there were not allowed to come over to our side. About a football field away stood a high concrete wall with guard towers and serious-looking men with binoculars and machine guns patrolling the wall. In front of that was a 10-foot-high row of rolled barbed wire, and then closer to us a blank expanse of sand that was about 50 feet wide. This was called the "death strip," left open so anyone trying to run across would be fully visible out in the open and have no cover from sniper fire. That area was packed with sand or crushed gravel so they could track footprints and also slow down would-be runners. On our end of the death strip was another roll of barbed wire, then concrete embankments and a minefield to stop any charging vehicles or tanks, then closest to me a high electric fence with barbed wire on its top. The West Germans had built a smaller chain-link fence on their side to protect people from wandering forward and being electrocuted. The final symbol of security in front of us was a small wooden railing that served as a gentle reminder that if you stepped foot beyond that point you could be shot, so not to do it, please, and to take it very seriously. I had pressed my chest against the wooden railing, and quickly passed one leg beyond its threshold so I was in East German air, like it was a game. On the drive home that day I couldn't stop asking questions. The adults answered matter-of-factly, but it was all mind-blowing news to me.

They explained that as World War II came to a close the country was split into four zones, each occupied by one of the Allied forces: either Russians, French, English, or American soldiers, and regular German citizens were forced to house and feed these soldiers. No one wanted the Russians, for they were as brutal as animals and pillaged and preyed on people at will. The French were pigs, so the women had to be careful, but they didn't have the same taste for violence. The Brits were tolerable, and if your part of the country was occupied by American troops it was like you had hit the jackpot — they were considered the kindest of gentlemen compared to the other options. The Russian troops bunkered down in what was considered East Germany, and when their usefulness had expired they failed to leave.

Russia was being built into a furious war machine by Marxist-Leninist Soviet ideology and over the years, East Germany adopted their military ideology and decentralized form of government that answered to the Kremlin, as did many puppet Eastern Bloc nations. Under Communism, wealth and property were (supposedly) evenly distributed. Any dissension or criticism of the government was met with arrest, torture, and even death. All expressions of creativity or individuality were suppressed. The people were forced to work all day for nominal wages, and they were always cold and hungry and had barely enough to live on. They had no art in their lives, no music, no colors, and no hope, for all products, material goods, and media were issued by the state and therefore were black and white and square, including the cars and their opinions of the outside world. (I was told as a kid, and it stuck with me through all the years, though I have no idea if it's true, that even toilet paper was rationed, so each person was assigned one square per day.) The stores mostly had bare shelves. Each citizen was given an allotment of East German marks every month for them to buy what they wanted. But they would wait in line for hours at the stores, not even knowing what they were waiting for, and at the end had to purchase whatever item was being sold, whether they wanted it or needed it or not. They could have been given a million marks and still there was nothing to buy — except for on the thriving black market, where people could get cigarettes or chocolate, or for a small fortune, women's stockings.

The people in East Germany lived cold, bland, desperate lives under the thumb of a totalitarian Soviet state. So why didn't they just pick up and leave? Well, in the 1950s — the decade after World War II — they did, emigrating over the open border to the west in masses, sometimes up to 300,000 people a year in the 1950s. To respond to this exodus, the government instituted a strict policy of visas and travel restrictions, but to no avail. So their Soviet puppet-masters pressured them to seal their borders to protect against "western aggression and spies," and on August 13, 1961, the Berlin Wall went up.

The dividing line was born at midnight, unannounced and non-negotiable. Neighborhood by neighborhood, along the 840-mile border with the west, East German troops marched in and went to work. At first, it was with temporary measures to restrict movement — they damaged the roads so cars could not pass, and then ran temporary blockades of rolled barbed wire and concrete embankments, and troops guarded the new wall with shoot-to-kill orders for anyone who tried to escape. Citizens who found themselves on the wrong side of the border, or just went to work like any other day, soon realized they could not come back in, and families were split up, forever.

Seeing the wall put up, a razor-wire symbol of their national incarceration, many citizens became desperate. People who lived in houses or apartment buildings along the new border jumped out of third-story windows, trying to clear the wall. Some ran for freedom and were shot or strung up in the wire, and more than a few cars tried to break through at full speed. As time went on the border was fortified, and the Berlin Wall separating West Berlin, an island of West Germany territory completely isolated within East German borders, was erected. Concrete walls were built and rebuilt higher, permanent guard stations and minefields were constructed, and buildings right on the border were either razed or had their windows bricked over so no one could jump. And it worked, because only about 5,000 people ever attempted to defect from East Germany over the decades until it became free, many of them succumbing to a grizzly death in the attempt. They built hot air balloons out of clothing sewn together, or crude ultralights that they launched off of rooftops that they prayed would carry them 300 yards when the wind was right, zip-lined aerial wire systems into the west, or tried digging tunnels under the wall, though few made it.

My father's people were from the East German side. I don't know much about them because we lost contact with them after my father passed away, but I do know that my grandfather owned a factory, which meant he probably owned it before the war until the Communist government took it away, and he still managed it. He was an industrialist with a wife and four children, and was better off than most in East Germany, but still he could not live with the yoke on his freedom. My father's parents were strong and recalcitrant, indomitable spirits who couldn't be contained even by the walls of Communist suppression. The details of their escape are sketchy — they somehow managed to flee to the west, but in doing so they had to leave everything behind: their factory, their house, their clothing, and their friends and relatives. My father's immediate family spent a good amount of time in a refugee camp in West Berlin before being evacuated to West Germany in the historic Berlin Air Bridge. It was on that airplane that my father, as a little boy, was given a colorful piece of fruit by an American GI, and for the first time in his life bit into an orange.

Eventually, my father went to school and became a skilled engineer, hand-building plastics and machine-design molds with genius precision, and was recruited by a company called Polymer to work in the United States. It was there that he met my mother, who had been recruited by the same company as a secretary and translator, as she was perfectly fluent in German, English, and French. They fell in love instantly.

I remember the day when the wall came down. I was sitting in history class out in the dingy portable classrooms at Hamden High, and the teacher wheeled in a mammoth TV from the '70s and played a clip from the news the night before. For some reason I recall it all vividly: I was wearing my best black acid wash jeans that I had rolled tight at the bottom and was already fantasizing about sneaking onto the golf course that night with a few bottles of Mad Dog and some dirt weed and trying to get to second base with this sophomore chick I was sweet for, but when the newscaster started talking about the Berlin Wall, I snapped to attention. Hadn't I been there? Or at least at the East German border? It all came back to me, and I watched on, mesmerized.

The fall of the Berlin Wall was some time in the making. The Soviet war machine was overextended and bogged down in bureaucracy, and over the summer of 1989 that ship began to leak.

The official reunification of the country happened on the chilly night of November 9, 1989, when a shocked newscaster on the state-run East German television station was handed a news brief, written only an hour prior, and read that citizens would now be allowed to visit the west. A press conference ensued, and the government spokesperson assigned to manage it was equally caught off-guard and had no further details. "When will this new policy take hold?" he was asked by a western reporter. He wasn't sure, so he just guessed and said, "Effective immediately." That was the wrong answer, but East German citizens swarmed the border and demanded that the gates to Checkpoint Charlie be opened.

The guards had no knowledge of what was going on, nor official orders that contradicted their "shoot to kill" mandate, but as the hundreds became thousands they were unwilling to start shooting into the crowd and start a massacre, so they simply opened the gates and let people rush forth: free. Soon after, young rowdies from the east and west, ebullient by the opening of the border, climbed atop the Berlin Wall and started chipping away pieces with hammers and sledgehammers.

The wall was ripped apart by the hands of newly freed citizens, until in early 1990 it was taken down altogether with cranes and bulldozers. New Year's Eve 1989 was like no other in the new Berlin, and they even had David Hasselhoff, of German ancestry, sing "Looking for Freedom" live at the event. He stood atop the wall with a leather jacket lined with roving digital lights and belted out an inspirational song that rallied the crowd into a celebratory frenzy, and it became the anthem for the falling of the wall, and that's why "The Hoff" is so huge in Germany.

Aunt Barbara lives in a town called Goslar that's only 10 miles from the border. On that autumn night in 1989 when the border was opened, she received a phone call from an excited friend around midnight. "They're opening up the wall! The wall is coming down!" her friend yelled. My aunt called friends of her own with the same shocked enthusiasm, and the rumor spread like wildfire. No one could sleep, or just wait around, so they all went into the street and jumped in their cars and started driving toward the border, unsure of what they would find. In the middle of the night the roads were filled, people yelling and honking horns, all filing toward the closest border point a few villages over.

At the border there were hundreds of cars, and thousands of people, with wine and flowers, hoping to greet some East Germans. Sure enough, a column of citizens walked out of the night and into freedom, right through a military checkpoint where the soldiers were unwilling to shoot them as their orders dictated. They had very few possessions — just what they could carry — and were dressed in drab gray clothing and masks of disbelief. They were greeted by everyone in the west, who hugged them and offered congratulations and they all danced in the streets. Someone passed the hat and a collection was made, and each East German was given a few Deutsche Marks. The mood was festive, so right there in the early morning hours the shopkeepers in the village turned on their lights and opened their doors so the East Germans could buy things in their stores if they wished. It had been thirty years since they could peruse a store and buy what they wanted with free will.

My aunt was in one store where a man picked up a flute and turned it over in his hands like it was the most beautiful thing on Earth. He used to play when he was a kid, before the war, but hadn't touched an instrument in all that time. With encouragement, he put it to his lips and played a few notes. Another older East German lady joined him in song, and together they managed a rusty rendition of the West German national anthem. She remembered it still after all those years because sometimes in East Germany she would hum it to herself, silently of course, and recall better days that she would surely never see again. The others in the shop, East and West Germans together, watched in stunned silence and cried at the beauty of it all.

The party went on all night until the sun came up, the first sunrise they would witness as free men and women. They had no place to stay, no blankets, and no food, so each person from the west took a family into their homes and made sure they were warm and had enough to eat. The opening of East Germany was an international triumph like no other, enrapturing the zeitgeist of Europe for many months to come. However, it was not all sledgehammers and songs — there were serious social and economic problems with reunification, but freedom is a commodity that cannot be measured with pragmatism.

On the last few weeks of my journey around the world, Aunt Barbara and I took a drive one sunny afternoon toward where the East German border used to be. She was eager to show me the exact spot where I had witnessed guard towers, landmines, and barbed wire as a kid. She drove along the single-lane paved road winding through thick forests of pines, and then we rolled into a clearing and she stopped the car. This was it. I got out of the car and stood there and looked around. What I found took my breath away, and I had to ask her three times to make sure we were in the same place as when I was a kid. There were no signs of the former border, or even that a human being had ever touched this place. We were in an expansive field with a babbling stream running through it, with nothing but yellow sunflowers as far as the eye could see, climbing toward the sun but bent with their own weight.

That week I took a train south to Munich, the charming city nestled in the Bavarian Alps that was originally founded by the Benedictine monks in 1158. Munich is a surprisingly funky, cosmopolitan place, a mix of the best of old and new, and probably most famous for being home to the world-renowned drinking hall, the Hofbräu House, where millions of countrymen and tourists get properly sloshed and soused together every Oktoberfest. I thoroughly enjoyed visiting the Hofbräu House to sip at gigantic steins of beer in the mid afternoon, and took in every detail of the storied wooden hall that made you feel like you were enduring a long voyage within the hull of a great ship.

I had been there before — back when I was just finishing high school and I took a trip through Europe with my buddy Goo and his mom. We had an auspicious introduction to Munich when Goo and I got drunk as sailors at the Hofbräu House and then infiltrated the strip club next door, the Club Casanova. Wolfgang Amadeus Mozart had lived only a few blocks away, though I'm guessing he wasn't into clear heels and brass poles, but Goo and I toasted to his health just the same.

After doing way too many shots of schnapps, we got 86'd from the Club Casanova (which is hard to do) when Goo started falling off his bar stool and I told an adoring stripper that I'd sleep with her if she paid *me* 14 Deutsche Marks ($8.64 in US currency). I thought it was a reasonable offer, and I would usually never go below $9 for my services — a guy's gotta have his standards — but apparently that kind of wise-ass-ism is frowned upon at the Club Casanova. After getting tossed out onto the street by the bouncers, we stumbled into a taxi and both passed out unconscious in the back seat.

Mercifully, the driver just ran us around town a few times to run up the fare and then deposited us on the sidewalk in front of our hotel, instead of the much more likely scenario of loading us up with heroin and selling us to a Turkish sex-slavery ring. Or maybe he did try to pawn us on the black market as still-living organ donors, but no one wanted Americans covered in gold glitter whose internal organs were pickled with schnapps and beer. But either way, Goo and I woke up safely in our cramped and over-heated hotel room two hours later. That morning, we had to endure a 14-hour train ride to Italy, in which he ran out of our compartment to the tiny train bathroom to power-barf every twenty minutes.

This second visit to Munich was thankfully far more mellow, because I had learned how the Hofbräu House can creep up on you and kick your ass, ninja-style.

Through my mom back home, I arranged to meet up with a cousin on my father's side, whom I had only met once when I was a baby. It was a big deal because we had pretty much no contact with that side of the family anymore, some of whom were living in South Africa. This cousin and I were to rendezvous outside a train station in the Marienplatz in central Munich. It was a sunny spring day, and I stood against a stone fountain and watched children running into flocks of pigeons, sending them to flight. My cousin was standing nearby but didn't recognize me because somehow in the language barrier, she understood that I was very tall.

Two German police officers strolled through the plaza, harassing people and pointing their nightsticks at the youths who were skate-boarding, ordering them to relocate. They walked right toward me in a show of testosterone, fully expecting me to move out of their way as they passed. I did not, and one of the police officer's shoulders bumped into me, jolting him a little. They looked back and said something in German, presumably an insult, but they walked away. I laughed out loud at them. These guys were kitty-cats compared to what I had been through. My long-lost cousin saw me laugh openly at the police and instantly knew it was me — only an American would do that, she said.

We had a nice visit for a few days and then I went on further south, almost to the Swiss border, closer to Zurich than Munich. This truly was God's country, in the Bavarian Alps close to Lake Constance and the Black Forest — majestic vistas I could easily recall from when I visited there as a child, for after my father died my mother brought us back to Germany almost every summer to spend time with her mother and father.

I never really appreciated those childhood visits to my mother-land. Like any punk kid, I just wanted to play video games and hang out with my American friends. But traveling through Germany again I cherished every memory of staying with my Oma and Opa in their tidy little apartment over a bakery, in the tiny village of Stockach.

Every morning, my Oma dressed up in her best shoes and grabbed her handbag and she and my sister and I would walk up the impossibly steep cobbled streets toward the church, stopping at the butcher, then the dairy, then the produce store, each proprietor greeting us American grandchildren as if we were movie stars and giving us savory chocolate bars or warm bread with Nutella. We stopped by to see an uncle who owned a lighting store, with chandeliers and crystal fixtures hanging everywhere like a cave with sparkly stalactites, and he gave us each a flashlight, a peculiar gift to a 6- and 8-year-old. We were allowed to feed sugar cubes to the strapped and blinded horses that pulled a buggy through the village, which they eagerly ate out of our palms.

At one in the afternoon, we had the big meal of the day in the formal parlor of my grandparents' apartment, where my Opa tucked a napkin into his collar, still in his three-piece wool suit with a pocket watch, sitting as upright as a Pharaoh on the velvet parlor sofa. Oma, robust and full of rosy kisses, donned an apron and carried soups and platters of spätzle (doughy noodles), sausages, cabbage, potato cakes, and cow tongue with gravy that smelled like a black-and-white photo makes you feel. We all ate, but did not talk much, under the watchful eye of two framed paintings of their American grandkids; it's strange having a portrait of yourself looking at you while you eat.

After lunch we took a walk with Opa, which was always a treat, as he took us up to the public park where we laughed and ran from bees amongst banana leaf plants and beds of yellow roses, but never wandered too far from his knee. My Opa was born in 1890 of a big, poor family of masons, a lineage of stoneworkers who could be traced back to the 1600s. They had no electricity and no indoor plumbing, and for Christmas or his birthday he may have received an egg whipped with a pinch of sugar in it if he was lucky. As he got older, he discarded his ancestors' vocation of freezing fingertips and broken backs for a scholarly life of books, collecting stamps, and opera. Self-taught, he also became fluent in Latin, French, English, and the old form of Middle High German. He was a naturalist who knew all the names of the trees and flowers and loved hiking and mountain climbing. Once, in his younger days, he was mountaineering in the Swiss Alps with a friend when a powerful blizzard moved in and trapped them in the peaks for the night. They huddled for warmth in a cave steep up a cliff, trying not to be blown off the mountain by the wind and ice. They didn't think they were going to survive, and shivered all night, and his friend vowed to God, with Opa as his witness, that if he answered their prayers and allowed them to survive the night, Opa's friend would dedicate his life to the cloth. Opa, who probably would rather face death than even the thought of a chaste life as a priest, made no such promise. They made it to morning, and escaped off the mountain, and the friend did become a priest.

Opa had been lucky, some would say. He wore thick eyeglasses, so he was disqualified from fighting in the first Great War, though he was only 24 at the time, and he was too old to serve in the second, so he settled comfortably into his career as the lone postmaster for the village. His family survived the war because his postal route took him out to the countryside, and oftentimes the farmers would trade him a few eggs or some hard-to-get potatoes or turnips in exchange for good news.

When Oma was pregnant with my mom, the Allied forces strafed and bombed the village, so she had to run into the woods to hide, a bittersweet reminder that the liberators' work was not done yet.

When the war was mercifully over, times were still tough, and their village was in the French-occupied zone. They lived in a little apartment over the post office and had to house a soldier, but he turned out to be a good guy and even brought my grandmother baby shoes for my mom when he returned from leave in France. She also got care packages from the U.S. — aid sent from church groups and school children — with fancy pencils with erasers on the ends, candy, and chewing gum, which she tried for the first time. Many were not so lucky, and the rape of young women was so rampant that the brave priest in town invited all women who didn't feel safe to bring their bedding and sleep in the bell tower of the church. Every night for months, he locked them in there and slept on a chair at the front door, making it known that the French soldiers would have to kill him to get in.

Opa wrote, studied, and admired nature with an unquenchable curiosity and wanderlust, not to publish or for profit. Even my father's family name, Schriever, comes from the German word *schreiben*, meaning "to write," so I guess writing is in my blood. But one of my Opa's books did garner attention: a thorough history of his village that bestowed him a silver medal from the German government, which my mom showed to me one day decades later in America, and then put back in its soft purple-lined box.

They were not Nazis, of course, and not even Party members, but just poor, humble people trying to eat and raise their families, like most Germans were. But one always wonders, especially as I was growing up in the States during a time where to be German or Russian was met with lingering suspicion. But then, one day I heard a story about my Opa that put all my worries to rest, and made me eminently proud like I cannot even verbalize. People who'd been through war and seen horrible things usually didn't talk about it; they preferred to leave it in the past and do their best to move on, so these things weren't the topic of many conversations in my family. But I think I really knew my Opa for the first time (for he was already an old man when I was born) more through this story than I ever did in real life. It was a gift to glimpse what kind of man he was, and I loved him deeply for it — and I hoped that some of his caring heart had been passed on to me.

My Opa had a good friend, a man named Herman Weil, who owned a successful clothing store on the main street in their village, Stockach. Every Thursday night, they met with a few other gentlemen and played cards and drank brandy at a local restaurant, and Herr Weil's wife was also friendly with my Oma. Herr Weil was Jewish, and as the Nazi party overtook Germany, he was arrested by the dreaded SS officers and taken away late one night. My Opa was distraught over his friend's disappearance, and a little digging confirmed his worst fears: He had been taken to Auschwitz, herded into a rail car along with other Jews and prisoners of war and transported to the death camps in Poland where he likely faced starvation or the gas chamber. When Herr Weil arrived in the concentration camp he was assigned a prisoner number that was tattooed on the inside of his left forearm. If you want to read an accurate yet horrific account of Auschwitz, you will find none better than *Night*, by survivor Elie Wiesel, as he describes his first night in that same place:

> *Never shall I forget that night, the first night in camp, which has turned my life into one long night, seven times cursed and seven times sealed. Never shall I forget that smoke. Never shall I forget the little faces of the children, whose bodies I saw turned into wreaths of smoke beneath a silent blue sky.*
>
> *Never shall I forget those flames which consumed my faith forever.*
>
> *Never shall I forget that nocturnal silence which deprived me, for all eternity, of the desire to live. Never shall I forget those moments which murdered my God and my soul and turned*

my dreams to dust. Never shall I forget these things, even if I am condemned to live as long as God Himself. Never.

And that is where Herr Weil found himself, in striped pajamas and tattooed, surrounded by walking skeletons with sunken black eyes who would fight in the dirt over a discarded scrap of rotten bread, awaiting a certain death. My grief-stricken Opa worked every angle, called in every favor, and leveraged every friendship up the governmental chain of command to try and help Herr Weil. Opa was not a Party member nor SS, but a postmaster, but that held some pull in those days, so amazingly his campaign to free his friend was successful.

But of course, Herr Weil didn't know anything about this. One day, his prisoner number was called over the loudspeaker at Auschwitz — which meant for sure that you were headed to your death at the gas chambers, or worse, subject to unspeakable medical experiments. Herr Weil thought he was a dead man, but when he arrived at the guard station they looked at him with disdain as they smoked their cigarettes and told him to "just go." He didn't understand. Just go, get out of here, they said, and they opened the gates and shooed him out of the camp. He walked from the camp on shaky legs, expecting a bullet in the back of his head, and when he was out of sight he ran.

Herr Weil begged some clothes and bread from a farmer and managed to cross the countryside out of Poland, back into Germany in secrecy, and then into neutral Switzerland where he was safe and reunited with his wife. They were granted political asylum as refugees in America and arrived in New York City, where they remained for the rest of their long lives, never to return to Germany. My Opa and Herr Weil kept in correspondence by writing letters back and forth, remaining friends, and Opa even got Herr Weil's German social security benefits reinstated and made sure they were delivered to New York City. But the two men didn't see each other again until the summer of 1968, when my mom moved to America to make a new life for herself, and my grandparents came to visit her. They all went to the Weils' cramped, humble apartment in New York City to be reunited, a connection that was over 25 years in the making. The two good friends, who used to play cards on Thursday nights, were old men by then. Both were haunted by more memories of those war years than they wished to remember, scarred — like numbers tattooed on a forearm — by the things they'd seen. The first time they saw each other since Herr Weil was hauled off to the gates of Auschwitz and certain death, they grabbed each other and embraced, collapsing into each other's arms and weeping like babies for a long time, unable to speak.

Heading Home

The Netherlands and the
United States of America,
May/June 2000

My trip was winding down and I was mentally and emotionally ready to go home, but as a last hurrah I had to end the year-long odyssey with a weekend in Amsterdam, the incredibly cultured city of canals and cathedrals, world-renowned art galleries and street artisans. Amsterdam is in the Netherlands, also called Holland, and the people are referred to as the Dutch, if that's not too confusing. About 20% of the Netherlands lies below sea level and the streets are interrupted with many waterways flecked with boats and dykes to keep the city dry. It also serves as the "Vegas on Steroids" of Europe, where people can easily fly in and party their assess off for a weekend before heading back to their law-abiding, responsible home country.

To witness the craziness, all you need to do is just spend an hour in the *airport* in Amsterdam. It was a surreal scene, with red-eyed and whacked-out travelers walking into walls and mumbling incoherently to themselves. So *that's* what I looked like in college, I said to myself. Nine out of 10 people were coming off a bad coke binge or tripping balls on space cakes, so they had a hard time just reading gate numbers and staying in a line without getting paranoid and freaking out. The airport staff and security guards were there more to baby-sit those having bad trips and to remind people to empty their pockets and discard party favors in the bathrooms *before* they went through security checkpoints, than they were to screen for bombs and hijackers.

Most of the hotels were booked, so I found a four-story walk-up Victorian on the outskirts of town where I got a cheap room in the attic. I went to Amsterdam alone, but within fifteen minutes I found myself in a coffee shop drinking Stella and smoking the "pure" with a bunch of girls from Minnesota.

Most people went to Amsterdam to party like rock stars, and indeed the Dutch made it easy, hawking heroin, cocaine, hashish, and hookers right on the street corners of the red light district, but I was more reserved. I smoked a little reefer and strolled around town marveling at the pre-Renaissance architecture, watching people in scarves and thick wool coats bicycle along the Prinsengracht Canal, and meandering through the Museumplein section of the city, home to some of the most amazing museums and art galleries in the world that housed first-rate Van Goghs, Picassos, Rembrandts, Monets, and Basquiats.

The city was gorgeous, but I strongly believe they should issue rulebooks to every visitor. For instance, I didn't realize that you could only smoke weed at designated coffee shops and bars, so while I was waiting in the lobby of a cinema for my movie to start, I pulled out a huge bumbaclot fatty and started burning it down casually right there. The manager and ushers ran over to me in a panic like I had just set fire to the place, but they were cool and corrected me on my rookie mistake and didn't call the cops. The movie, by the way, was *killer* and the popcorn was the *best* I've ever had!

Another thing that definitely should be in Amsterdam's "Don't Be *that* Guy" rulebook is that you are strongly discouraged from taking pictures in the red light district. Prostitution is legal in the Netherlands, so the red light district is the world-renowned central neighborhood in Amsterdam where working girls from Africa, Turkey, and poor Eastern European countries set up shop — literally. They rent space in the ground floor of buildings, booths with glass windows facing the street. They are usually back-lit with red neon, and the girl dances in the window or shows off what her momma gave her to attract a client — who just walks into the building, and then she closes a curtain over the window and they get busy like a Burger King bathroom. Romantic, huh? Its sort of like eHarmony on crack, only without the computer, and there's only one level of compatibility. Every tourist walks through there, but I was the one who pulled out my camera and wanted photo documentation of this landmark system. Instantly, chicks rushed out of their windows and fell upon me like we were in a bad zombie movie, berating me in seven languages that I wasn't allowed to take pictures. OK, OK, already — calm down. Jesus, did they think I was going to jeopardize their future political careers or something?

After the weekend was over I spent two more days in Germany, trying unsuccessfully to fatten up and booking the very last leg of my round-the-world ticket without fanfare. I don't even remember getting on the plane from Frankfurt to New York. Seriously — I have absolutely no recollection of it. The first thing that shook me to consciousness from my surreal fog was meeting my sister in Danbury, Connecticut, where my shuttle dropped me off. She hugged me and put her 20-month-old baby, my nephew Colin, in my arms. I cradled him closely and looked into his beautiful, peaceful face and felt blessed to have this precious gift … and then he puked all over me. Welcome home.

When I saw my mom, she cried and hugged me and then cried some more. I didn't know what the big deal was, but I get it now.

We drove home and I unpacked my lone bag, mostly filled with gifts for my family: a handspun Turkish rug, pottery figurines from Peru, jade statues from Thailand, and a beautiful gold-leafed Koran with Mohammad's interpretations of Allah in both Arabic and English. My family was amazed to see how few possessions I had — I was down to one pair of jeans, which I wore every single day, one pair of black knock-off Reebok sneakers that I picked up somewhere along the way, two T-shirts, a short-sleeve shirt, and a black fleece jacket to keep me warm when the sun went down. I don't think I even owned underwear at that point.

My family told me I looked great, but a closer inspection would have revealed the trials that my body had endured. I was used to sleeping on infested mattresses and bus seats and dirty floors. My hair was falling out from using cheap hotel soap. My skin had been subjected to every bug bite, rash, and infection known to man. I was so dark from sun and dirt that the locals were sometimes confused as to my origins.

More often than not, my stomach was sick, sometimes so bad that I should have been hospitalized. I started the trip at about 185 pounds, but I went down to a sickly 162 pounds at the lowest point, though by the end of the trip I was insanely shredded because I walked or ran about 10 miles and did 300 pushups on dirty hotel floors every day.

But I understood that my body was just a temporary physical shell — I would be gone from Earth before I could blink, no matter how hard I fought it and how much I struggled to control it. Over that year I had witnessed such a survey of human existence — people struggling, starving, and praying in the streets right in front of me — yet I had a newfound love for humanity, a new hope for the future, and that was pure. So the important thing was what I was going to do with that brief spark of consciousness that we call "life." I carried around that newfound light inside of me, but that discovery also frightened me because, as they say, knowledge bears responsibility.

Re-acclimating to modern American life was like diving the ruins of a shipwreck and then getting the bends from coming up too fast. Everything seemed so sterile, so orderly and slow-paced, like it was a grand play choreographed with perfect precision but none of it was real. Going into the supermarket for the first time, I jumped in fright as the automatic doors opened for me, and spent a half-hour in the cereal aisle staring at the 500 colorful boxes, unable to choose. Red, yellow, red, yellow, orange, blue, they just stared back at me under laboratory lights in a perfect temperature and humidity, with a vanilla instrumental version of Hootie and the Blowfish playing overhead. People came and went, but no one said hello or even looked up for fear of upsetting the façade of their perfectly sterile lives. The opulence of "normal" existence in the United States stunned me.

It's funny what you miss. My first month back in the States, I went to IHOP twice a day and ate exactly the same thing every time: a big salad with blue cheese dressing and pancakes with strawberry syrup. I thought I was in heaven, but the waitresses looked at me like I had just crawled out of a homeless shelter. I went into Sears to buy a TV remote for my mom, and ended up trying to haggle for half an hour with the confused salesperson. I got together with my friends, and when we talked about what we had been up to I noticed how they looked at me a little differently, as if I were wearing my clothes backward and inside out but they didn't want to say anything.

A newspaper from my hometown sent out a reporter to my mom's house to interview me, and they did a front-page story about the local kid who took an epic journey and trekked around the world. I read the article when it came out and it was nice, and even had color pictures of me catching a fish and hang-gliding and in front of the pyramids in Egypt, but I didn't recognize the person they were talking about. I still have that article, folded up neatly in a box in my mom's basement next to thousands of photographs and seven notebooks from my travels.

I went into my mom's garage and there was the Whip, jet-black and dusty, waiting for me like no time had passed at all. I slipped into the fake sheepskin driver's seat, and quickly cranked open the window because it smelled like a family of squirrels had been living rent-free in there. I checked the rear-view mirror and smiled; I felt encouraged — maybe I could restart my new life and things would be easier than they always had been. I could just be "normal" and get a boring job that paid well, and meet a nice girl and get married and settle down and add forty years to that equation, and stop always doing things the hard way. Maybe I could forget everything I had seen and experienced, unburden my conscience for the world like I was mailing it away on the back of a postcard, and just live a life of simple self-possession and comfort like everyone else. Yup, my future was looking like smooth sailing. I slipped the key into the ignition and turned it, but it just clicked and sputtered before shutting down completely. I tried several more times with the same result. I let out a deep breath, and unhooked the miniature disco ball off the mirror before climbing out. The Whip was dead.

Fuegos Artificiales

Tamarindo, Costa Rica,
January 1, 2011

I woke up feeling like the world was inside out. I couldn't breathe — my lungs were screaming for air in the choking darkness. I shot up and looked around. I was drenched with sweat, lying on the floor on a dirty mattress. In the strands of moonlight I could see ants crawling about and a tiny iguana scampering up the color-washed concrete wall. Outside, a stray dog barked at a drunk who had fallen asleep in the bushes, but then it was so quiet again that you could almost hear the night crawling through town. I felt like I'd been asleep for a hundred years.

I'd just had a dream of the kid — the street kid on the train tracks in Cairo. A long-forgotten feeling of falling vertigo overtook me. It was painful just to be in existence, like something deep in my psyche was screaming to be heard. I tried to re-create the last few days. Where was I? Was I in my house in California? No — that was two weeks ago. It was the night of January 1, 2011, and I was in Costa Rica, taking a much-needed vacation before I returned to the United States. I'd partied all night with my gringo friends Pistol Pete and Uri in Tamarindo, a sleepy little surf community on the Pacific Ocean. All of the hotels were booked because of the raucous New Year's Eve crowd, so I had to rent part of a private house on the outskirts of town and sleep on the floor.

I sat up and tried to clear my head; I hadn't had that feeling of vertigo, or even thought of that mute street kid, in a long time. Maybe being on foreign soil, reunited with the elegant entropy of the Third World, had triggered these recollections from my past life on the road.

Had it really been 10 years since I traveled around the world and met him? What had I been doing with all that time? I had been busy, for sure, but after a while just being busy starts to feel like running in quicksand. I was living in Sacramento and had a big house and nice cars and all of that material bullshit that we're told are the tokens of responsible adulthood, but day by day it seemed like I was working more and smiling less, my life slipping by without me even noticing.

I rubbed my eyes and looked toward the window at silhouettes of palm trees shifting and blowing. Man, 10 years ago I was so full of fire, ready to take on the world and try to make it a better place, and now it seemed like I was just getting by. Had I forgotten about him — that poor, diseased kid who ate out of trash cans and couldn't speak but who was still so illuminated with gratitude? I could still envision clearly that day on the train platform and the connection we had and knew I had not forgotten. A shiver ran up my neck even though it was stifling hot in the room. It still shook me that he would never be able to talk or scream in anger against the pain life inflicted upon him. That urchin, who didn't even have a name, would never be able to tell his mother he loved her nor pray out loud for a better future, but somehow he had passed part of his soul on to me to carry forth, and in doing so charged me to tell his story ... but for 10 years I had not.

And then the fireworks started going off. The pack of sun-kissed, barefoot children in town must have fished the abandoned ones out of the garbage, or combed the beach for those that had misfired and were still good, and they were shooting them off from the alley behind Voodoo Bar not far away. They called them *fuegos artificiales* down there — brilliant greens and purples and starlight reds, and gold and clouds of smoke lingered with the laughter long after they had fallen from the sky. I jumped up and walked to the window to watch and instantly thought of Pablo Neruda with the same view, the poet exuberant like a child on his privileged balcony over the seaport of

Valparaiso every last night of December. It must have been a moment like this which made him write:

Someday, somewhere — anywhere, unfailingly, you'll find yourself, and that, and only that, can be the happiest or bitterest hour of your life.

The colors of the fireworks danced into my room. I passed my hand through them like slivers of fire, and looked at it all as if for the first time, and it finally hit me why I was there, why my life had come full circle 10 years later, and for the first time it really made sense what I was supposed to do. I think I'd heard a little voice for a long time, a whisper that was telling me I wasn't on the right path, that I wasn't living the life of purpose that I had dreamed and so I needed to make a grand change. But I had always drowned it out with thoughts of work, the trappings of social achievement, and stressing more and more over money. When the nagging voice grew louder and more urgent I would just raise my level of distraction so I could ignore it. But there in the tropics, in a *tranquilo* beach town where my soul had space to listen, that whisper had grown as loud as the roar of the ocean, trying to shake me awake so I could follow my destiny. It all just clicked, and I resolved to make it the happiest hour of my life.

My breathing slowed and I felt better, though I knew I had a long, difficult road ahead. There was a lot of work for me to do; once I got back to the States I would get rid of all my possessions, my fancy cars and my big house that looked good but didn't make me happy, and instead live a life of truth. I would move to Costa Rica to honor my dream of being a writer, and by doing so become *his* voice. It had come late, like discarded *fuegos artificiales* on the day after the new year, and I'd most likely be poor and suffer in obscurity, but none of that mattered to me now. There was still time for me to do what I had promised. For him I would write a book and tell the world what I'd seen.

So I got started.

Epilogue

Exactly one year later, I'm writing you from my desk in Costa Rica, which means, as you can assume, I did it. It was a giant leap of faith to uproot my whole life and start over with nothing but an ambition to honor my dream and a blank computer screen, but I was more scared of *not* trying. So I sold or donated all of my possessions and moved down to Tamarindo to write this book. Every morning I wake up at dawn to the sounds of birds and monkeys, who gather in the palm trees outside my small apartment a short walk from the beach. I stumble downstairs and open up the doors and windows to let the ocean breeze in and pour myself a big cup of *café* with a splash of Baileys in it. I sit at my hand-carved wooden desk, crank up some good music on my giant headphones, and get down to the business of creating my art. At first it all felt strange and the idea of writing a book rattled my confidence to no end. But during the rainy season, when life is lived in between preternatural squalls and the town becomes a river of mud, time slows down like Dali's melting clocks and there is nothing else to do but settle into your own thoughts — and either go crazy, turn to booze and ganja, or achieve great things. So I stumbled forward and began with one little word, and then one little story, and soon I was filling up pages like a mad scientist. Once I got started, the words came faster than I ever expected (I wrote about 600 pages this year) and this is the result. My prediction of my circumstances was correct; I am poor, and have sacrificed all, and so far I am suffering in obscurity (I only own a few T-shirts and flip flops, an Apple laptop, and a surfboard) but I am at peace nonetheless. I can slow down and thoroughly enjoy the little things in my life.

I hope you, too, enjoyed this book. You've now traveled with me and had the chance to walk a mile in many other people's shoes. My only wish is that it has changed you, even in some small, subtle way; maybe you will laugh a little more, feel blessed just to witness another sunrise, or appreciate having food on the table with your family. Perhaps now you, too, will feel more connected to your human brothers and even reach out to someone who desperately needs your help.

My words fall short of the proper way to thank all of you who have supported me or are brave enough to part with a dollar and spend the time reading my reflections — that truly amazes me. Seriously, thank you. The journey to writing this book has been a huge unexpected blessing in my life and immensely humbling at the same time. Of course, my naïve goal was to honor everyone and everything I'd seen, to ultimately write a book that would change the world. I know I have failed in that lofty aspiration, but that's OK; I gave it a hell of a try, and for that, I am happy.

The Richest Urchin in Cairo, Egypt 2000

About the Author

Norm Schriever grew up in Connecticut and graduated from the University of Connecticut, where he was never accused of over-studying. He went on to live in North Carolina, San Francisco, California, Boston, and Fort Collins, Colorado, with a brief stint in the Larimer County Department of Corrections, which was nice enough to provide him accommodations. He's traveled the world and written extensively about those adventures.

Most recently, Norm lived in Sacramento, California, where he was a successful businessman but grew dissatisfied with a "responsible" existence. So, in 2011, after experiencing an epiphany while traveling in Central America, he sold or donated all of his possessions, his cars, and his house, and moved to Costa Rica to pursue his passion of writing. He now resides in the little beachside town of Tamarindo with only flip-flops, a surfboard, and a laptop to his name. His first book, *Pushups in the Prayer Room*, about a year he spent backpacking around the world, was written within six months in Tamarindo, where fresh ocean air and Baileys in his morning coffee are his secret weapons. His writing is a way to touch people, to illuminate the commonalities of human experience while still "keeping it real," thereby uniting people to leave this planet a little better than how we found it.

Norm would love to say what's up to you, so feel free to email him at: hi@normschriever.com, or go to www.NormSchriever.com

A portion of the proceeds from this book will be donated to the following charities. They do great work to make our world a better place, so contact them if you would like more information or want to help out directly.

Farm Haiti
Improving agricultural sustainability in Haiti
www.farmhaiti.org
Contact info@farmhaiti.org

Trafigura Work and Learn Business Center
Doing amazing work to teach at-risk youth job and business skills
www.domuskids.org/Trafigura
Contact mdepino@domuskids.org

Fiji Aid International
Aid and programs for Fiji, Haiti, and anywhere natural disasters hit
www.fijiaidinternational.com
Contact damyenti@aol.com

Village of Dampose
Improving education and resources in Ghana
www.villageofdompoase.org
Contact jokofi@gmail.com

Kiva
International microloans for deserving business owners
www.kiva.org
Contact Karen@kiva.org